IMAGES
*of America*

# Hartford Radio

I0807085

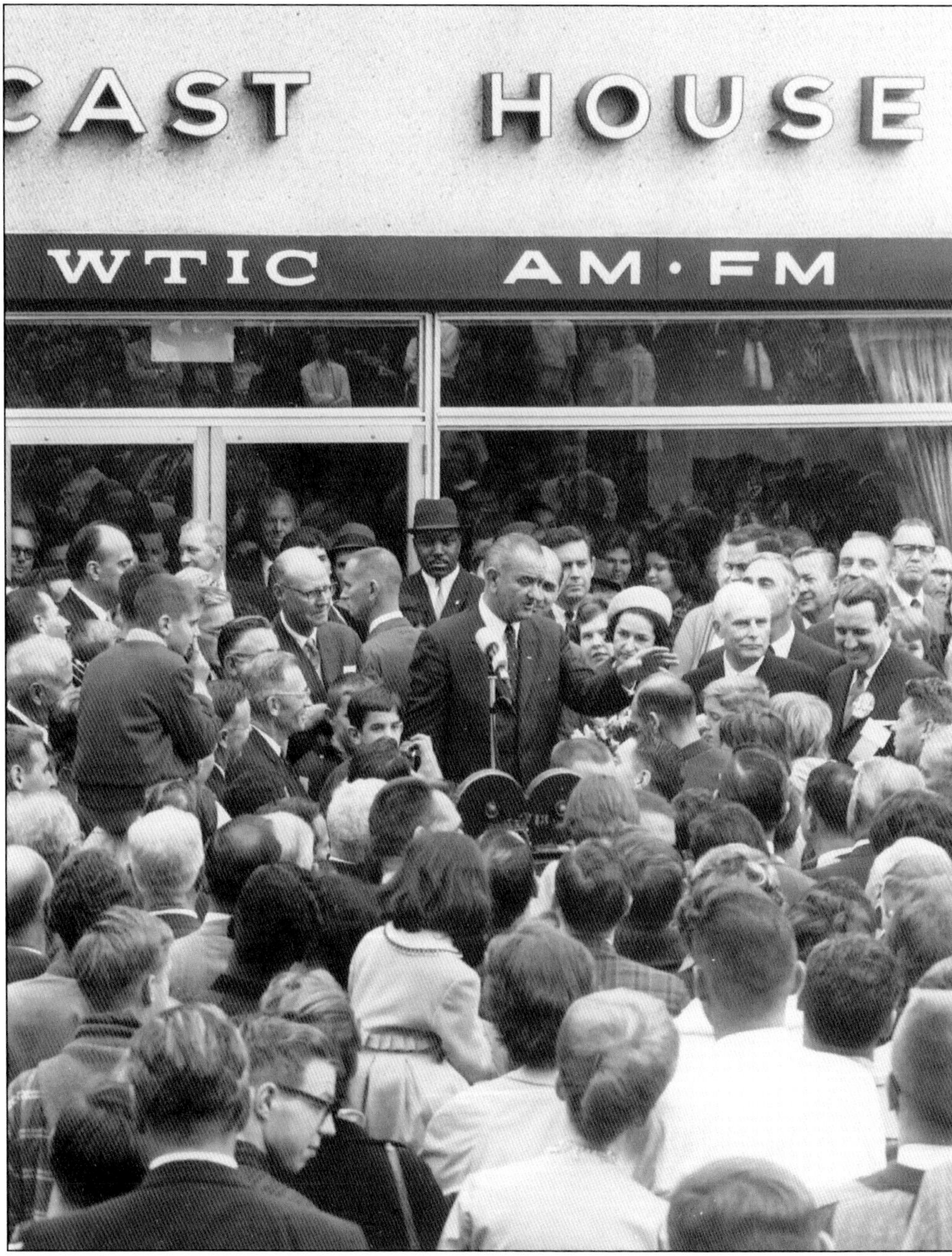


Pres. Lyndon Baines Johnson addresses a crowd in front of WTIC's Broadcast House at Constitution Plaza in Hartford on September 24, 1964. The president's remarks were carried live on WTIC radio and television. (Courtesy of CBS Radio Inc.)

**On the Cover:** Bob Steele was on Hartford's WTIC for over six decades, and during that time, he had some of the highest ratings of any announcer anywhere in the country. His "Word for the Day" segment was very popular. He is seen here with his favorite dictionary doing *The Bob Steele Show* on January 21, 1958. (Courtesy of Phil Steele.)

IMAGES
*of America*

# HARTFORD RADIO

John Ramsey

ARCADIA
PUBLISHING

ISBN 978-0-7385-7666-4

Published by Arcadia Publishing
Charleston, South Carolina

Printed in the United States of America

Library of Congress Control Number: 2011932661

For all general information, please contact Arcadia Publishing:
Telephone 843-853-2070
Fax 843-853-0044
E-mail sales@arcadiapublishing.com
For customer service and orders:
Toll-Free 1-888-313-2665

Visit us on the Internet at www.arcadiapublishing.com

*Dedicated to my wife, Jacki, and my sons, Daniel and Ryan.*

# Contents

# ACKNOWLEDGMENTS

Special thanks to the following individuals and organizations—without their help, this book would not have been possible: Annette Agnos, Marion Anderson, Ben Andrews, Boyd Arnold, Scott Baron, Daniel Blume, Ed Brouder, Arnold Chase, Al Cohen, CBS Radio Inc., Connecticut Historical Society, Prof. Henry DePhillips, Bill Dillane, Mike Drechsler, Rex Emrick, John Eppler, Gene Faltus, Eric Fahnoe, Eugene R. Faltus, Jacki Gilligan, Bob Grip, Dan Hayden, Chris Heerema, Gary Lee Horn, Jeff Hugabonne, Nat Johnson, Brandon Kampe, Bruce Kampe, Dave Kaplan, Peter Kemp, Ryan Krupa, Chris Larsen, Dave Lounder, Chris Marti, Bart Mazzarella, Suzanne McDonald, Peter Miller, Bob Molloy, Victor Nejfelt, Glenn O'Brien, Michael Picozzi, Bob Radil, Dick Robinson, Missy Robinson, John Schwenk, Phil Steele, Vic Vincze, Vintage Radio and Communications Museum of Connecticut, Rick Walsh, WCCC, WDRC, Larry Wells, Graham Winters, Chion Wolf, WTIC, WTIC Alumni, and WWUH. The inspiration for this book came from the late Harold Dorschug, former WTIC director of engineering.

# INTRODUCTION

Radio listeners in the Hartford area during 1922 had very few stations to listen to. Most local radio signals heard in the Hartford region in the early 1920s emanated from amateur and experimental stations, many of which were set up to explore the new technology of radio and/or to facilitate communication between hobbyists. Both WABL in Storrs and the *Hartford Courant*'s WDAK were operating for a few hours during a day with general interest programs that often consisted of impromptu musical performances and discussions of goings on about town. In 1922, New Haven's WPAJ, which would later become Hartford's WDRC, was the first station in Connecticut to receive a broadcasting license from the federal government. The station was owned by broadcast pioneer Franklin Doolittle, who operated it out of the back of his radio and appliance store at 817 Chapel Street in New Haven in the hopes of selling more radio receiving sets.

Hartford did not get its own broadcast station until 1925 when the Travelers Indemnity Company started WTIC. Visionary Walter G. Cowles, vice president of Travelers, is credited with convincing the conservative insurance firm to venture into the broadcasting business. By 1925, Doolittle's New Haven station had become WDRC, which stood for "Doolittle Radio Corporation," and in 1930, he moved the station to Hartford, ultimately setting up studios in the Corning Building at 11 Asylum Street and constructing a sophisticated transmission facility on Blue Hills Avenue in Bloomfield. In 1929, WTIC built a state-of-the-art transmitter on Talcott Mountain in Avon to provide a 50,000-watt signal, the highest allowable.

The great majority of the music heard on the radio in the 1920s and 1930s was performed live by musicians, and Hartford's WTIC and WDRC had sizable studios to accommodate large ensembles. Both stations had a number of musicians on staff, and WTIC even had its own symphony orchestra. But some of Hartford's early broadcasters did not survive. The *Hartford Courant* newspaper launched its station, WDAK, in 1922, but it was silent by 1926. And the *Hartford Times* station, WTHT, which took to the air in 1936, was lost to a merger in 1954.

Radio broadcasting played a vital role in keeping the public informed during disasters and international conflicts. WTIC, WDRC, and WTHT were three of the local stations that interrupted their programming during the afternoon of July 6, 1944, to broadcast news of the terrible Hartford circus fire that ultimately claimed 168 lives. Later that afternoon, area listeners heard Gov. Raymond Baldwin's solemn attempt to calm people who had not heard from family members who had been at the circus that day. The recording of the governor's description of how the State Armory in downtown Hartford had been turned into a makeshift morgue is chilling. During the disastrous flood of 1936 that knocked out power over a large area, Hartford stations WDRC and WTIC operated their equipment on battery power while announcers read news scripts by candlelight. Radio network correspondent reports from overseas during World War II commanded large audiences. In the days before television, radio was the only medium able to deliver news in real time. Later, radio would play an important role in keeping the public informed during the assassination of John F. Kennedy and the 1965 Northeast blackout.

Maj. Edwin Armstrong's invention of what he referred to as "static-free radio" is today's FM, and Hartford station WDRC played a key role in its development. When WDRC's Franklin Doolittle launched W1XPW from West Peak in Meriden, it was the state's first commercial FM station. It was also one of the first licensed commercial FM stations in the country. W1XPW is still on the air today as WHCN. Meriden's West Peak would later become home to many FM stations and was known at one point as "Radio Mountain." Today, it is the site of seven FM station towers: WNPR, WWYZ, WZMX, WKSS, WMRQ, WDRC, and WHCN. Travelers Insurance Company launched W1XSO (which later became WTIC-FM) on WTIC-AM's 15th anniversary. Two of Hartford's earliest FM stations—WTHT, owned by the *Hartford Times*, and WKNB, owned by Newington-based WKNB (now WRYM)—failed to be successful and were silent by 1960.

In 1943, Ben Hawthorne, the host of WTIC's popular G. *Fox Morning Watch* program, left the station to go into the military. His replacement, Bob Steele, a native of Kansas City who had done some occasional sportscasting and had been turned down by another Hartford station, would stay in the morning drive slot for six decades, seeing some of the highest ratings of any show in the entire nation during a good part of that time. After the war ended, radio stations started springing up everywhere. Several Hartford suburbs got their own stations during this time, including West Hartford (WEXT), Bristol (WBIS), Windsor (WSOR), and Manchester (WINF). Later, stations would be put on in Southington (WNTY) and Vernon (WRTT).

In 1960, WDRC shocked the conservative Hartford radio market when it switched formats and started playing rock and roll. WPOP followed suit a few years later, and the competition between these two stations during the 1960s was fierce. While both were major players in the state's rock-and-roll broadcasting scene, thanks to legendary employees such as program director Charlie Parker and announcer Dick Robinson, Hartford's WDRC will go down in history as one of the most influential Top 40 stations in the country.

College radio in Connecticut can trace its roots back to WABL in Storrs (now WHUS), which went on the air in 1922. As the British music invasion started to hit America's shore in the 1960s, the state's college radio stations began picking up on the new sounds. In 1968, the University of Hartford launched WWUH, which had the first daily progressive music program in the state, the *Gothic Blimp Works*, which can still be heard every night at midnight. Some of the students who helped start WWUH were responsible for WHCN's switch from a classical format to rock in 1969.

In the 1960s and early 1970s, FM had yet to prove itself as a commercially successful medium, in part because of the expense of FM sets. Most FM stations simply rebroadcast the programming of their AM counterparts. Some stations tried unique programming in an effort to generate revenue. WFMQ in Hartford (later WZMX) adopted a "store cast" format, supplying background music to specially leased receivers in stores, which would go silent when the commercials were played. In 1963, Hartford's 93.7 was sold to the First Congregational Church on Main Street, which operated the station commercial-free as a public service for two years.

In the early 1970s, Hartford's WCCC-FM adopted an "all-request" format—the first in the state; and WPOP switched to all-news programming in 1975—also a first in Connecticut. Howard Stern got his start at WCCC in 1978 and would return to the station in 1997 via syndication. By the 1980s, AM's dominance had given way to FM, with many FM stations in the Hartford market getting top ratings. This paved the way for talk radio to take hold on the AM dial. Ethnic programming came into its own as well, and by the end of the 1990s, four Hartford-area AM stations would broadcast in languages other than English.

Over the years, there had been several attempts to improve radio broadcasting with new technology. Dolby FM, quad FM, AM stereo, and FMX were tried unsuccessfully in the 1970s and 1980s. In the early 2000s, the Federal Communications Commission (FCC) approved a new technology known as HD radio, and many Hartford stations adopted the technology, but thus far, listeners have been slow to accept it.

Despite competition from technology such as MP3s and webcasting, broadcasting continues to do well, with several dozen stations licensed in the Greater Hartford area.

# *One*

# The Beginning

During 1922, radio listeners in Hartford did not have had much to listen to. The few stations that were on the air were considered experimental, operated only a few hours each day, and were often owned by amateur radio operators more interested in the technology and two-way communications with other amateurs than in programming for the general public. Two of the first stations with regular broadcasts aimed at the public were WAPL, the Connecticut Agricultural College (now University of Connecticut) station on the Storrs campus, and the *Hartford Courant*'s WDAK. Both of these stations were operating for a few hours a day during the early 1920s with general interest programs that often consisted of live musical performances and discussions of local topics. WPAJ in New Haven, which would later become Hartford's WDRC, was the first station in the state to receive a government license to broadcast to the public. Broadcast pioneer Franklin Doolittle owned the station, which was operated out of the back of his radio and appliance store in New Haven. The station helped Doolittle sell radios by giving buyers something to listen to. In 1925, visionary Walter G. Cowles, vice president of the Travelers Indemnity Company, convinced the traditional insurance organization to venture into the broadcasting business. Hartford's WTIC was started the same year.

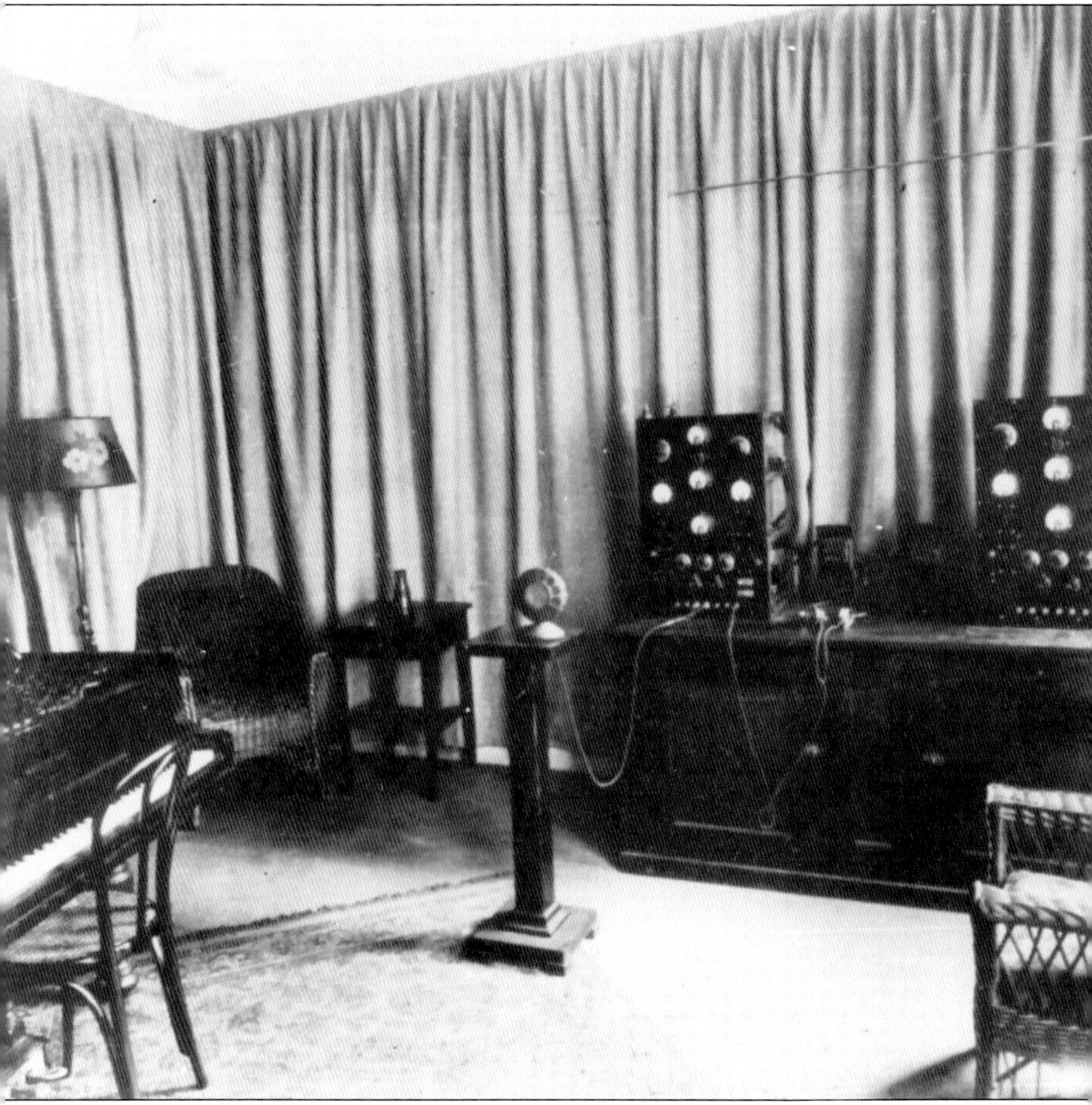

While there were a few other stations broadcasting in Connecticut in 1922, such as the *Hartford Courant*'s WDAK and WAPL on the Connecticut Agricultural College campus in Storrs, those stations were considered experimental. In New Haven, Franklin S. Doolittle established WPAJ, the first station in Connecticut to receive a broadcast license from the federal government. This 1922 photograph shows WPAJ's original studio in cramped quarters above a radio shop at 817 Chapel Street in New Haven. WPAJ would later become WDRC in 1926 and move to Hartford in 1930. (Courtesy of WDRC.)

WPAJ's original tower on New Haven's Beacon Hill is seen in this photograph. Eighty-five feet tall, it was connected to a homebuilt transmitter that produced 30 watts of power on a frequency of 833 kilocycles (kc). The station operated for a few hours a day. (Courtesy of WDRC.)

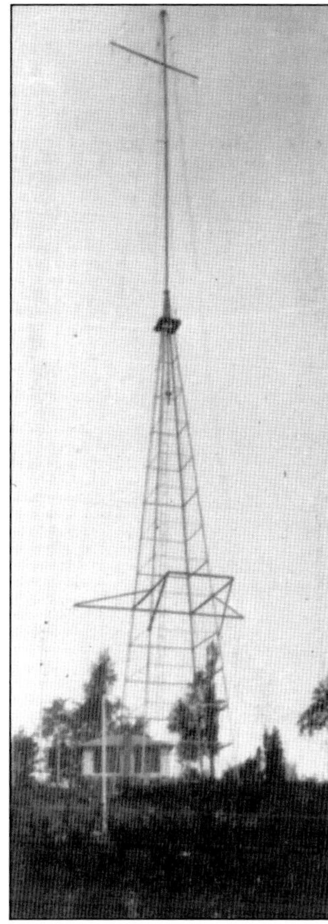

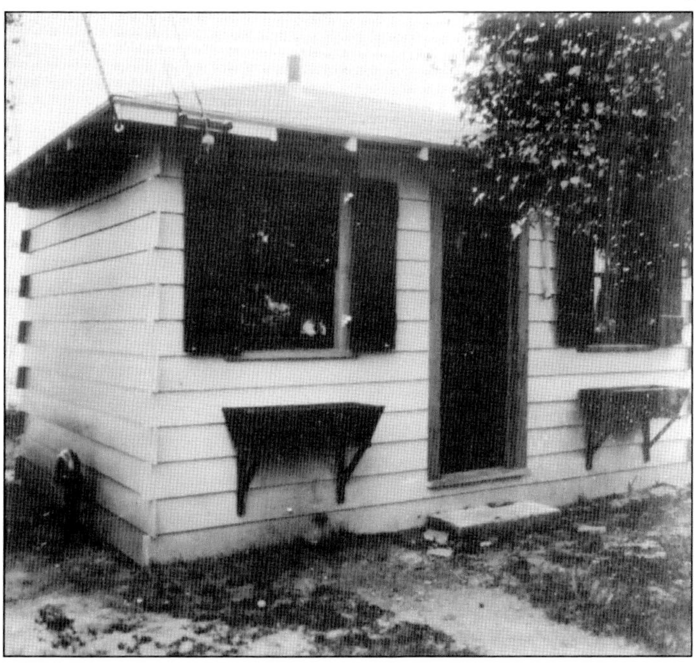

WPAJ's transmitter building was located adjacent to the station's tower on New Haven's Beacon Hill when this picture was taken around 1922 to 1925. It was designed to blend in with the rural New England surroundings. During this time, the station changed frequency to 1120 kc. (Courtesy of WDRC.)

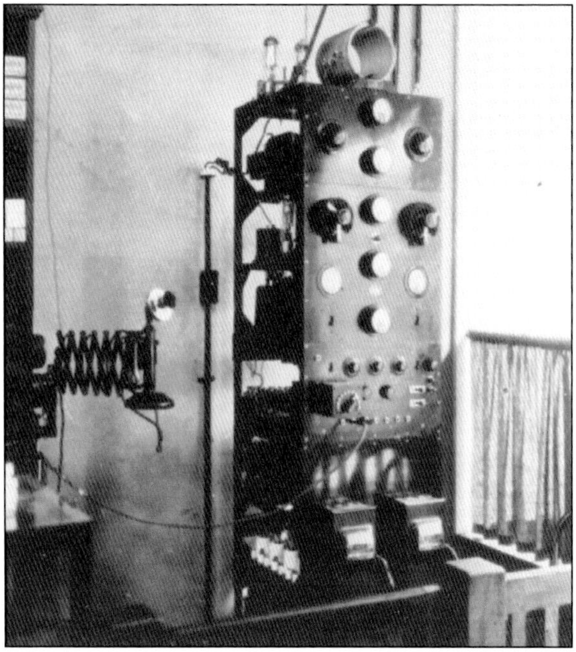

In 1923, very few commercially manufactured transmitters available were appropriate for broadcasting. In this image is the first WPAJ transmitter that owner Franklin Doolittle had modified for broadcast service. It was installed on Beacon Hill in New Haven and operated on 1120 kc with 30 watts of power. (Courtesy of WDRC.)

A waiting room at Franklin Doolittle's New Haven studio is pictured around 1924. During this period, WPAJ was authorized to conduct duplex (binaural) broadcasts on two frequencies. The same program was broadcast over both, with two microphones feeding the two transmitters, creating some of the first stereo transmissions in the country. (Courtesy of WDRC.)

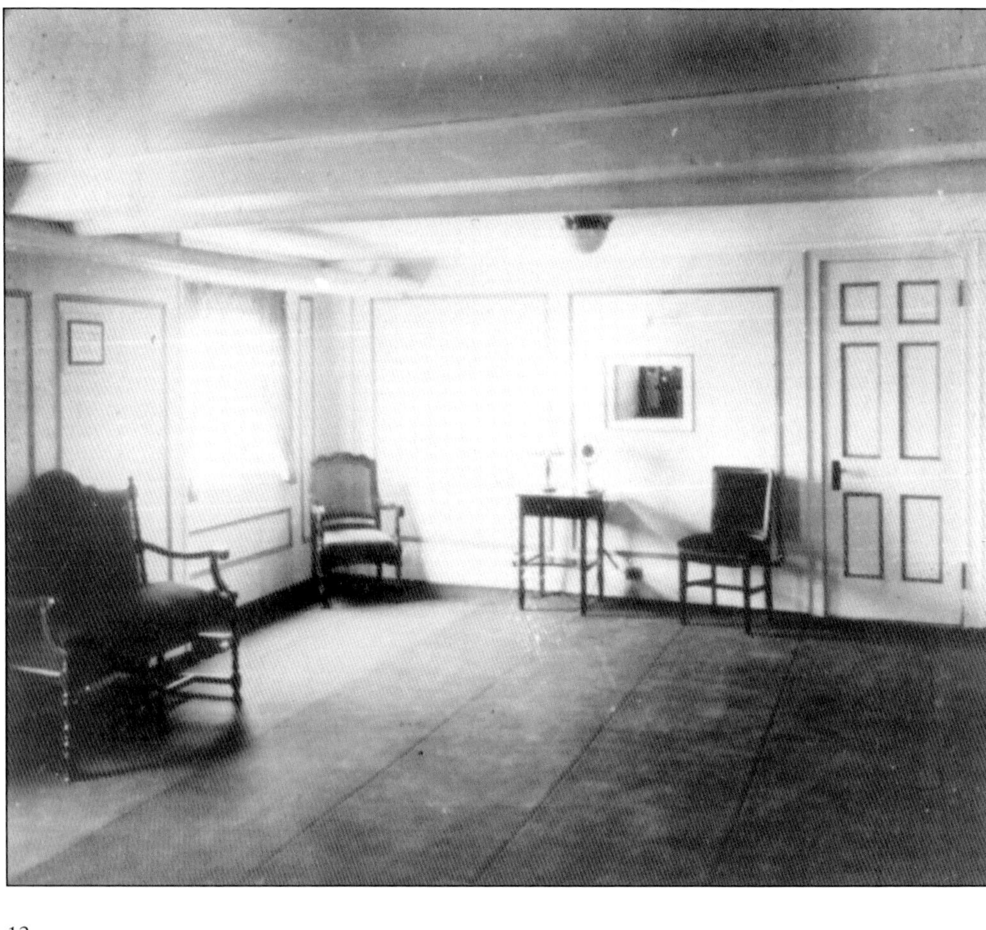

Doolittle's performance studio, shown here, also included a player piano, which is not pictured. Since photograph records were considered to lack the fidelity needed for broadcasting, nearly all musical performances were live. At WPAJ, the use of a player piano allowed music to be broadcast without a musician being present. (Courtesy of WDRC.)

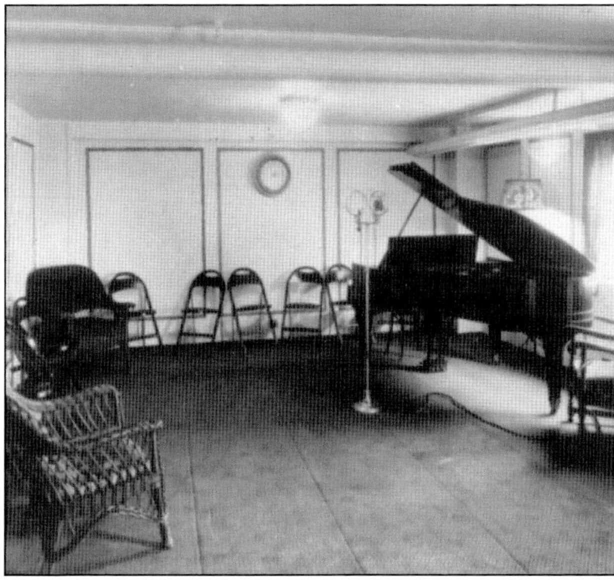

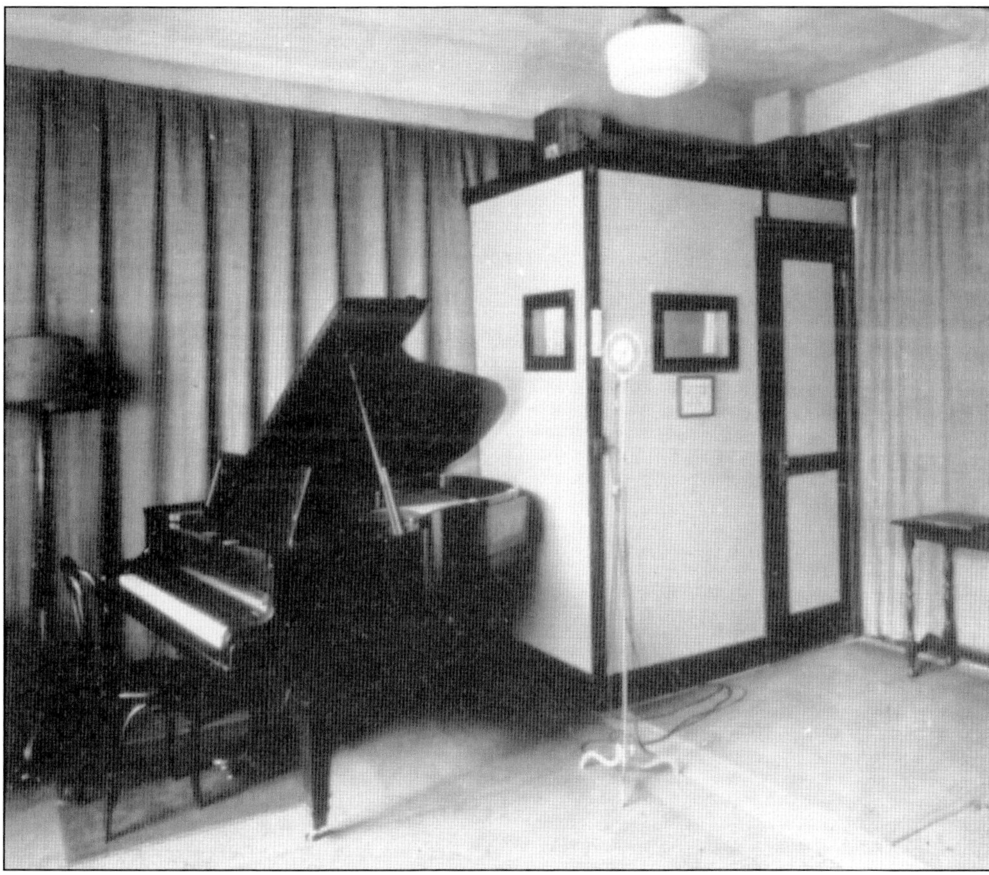

In addition to a piano, this WDRC studio in New Haven featured a soundproof control room with windows from which an engineer could monitor and control the broadcast. The windows also allowed the engineer to signal the person on the air. (Courtesy of WDRC.)

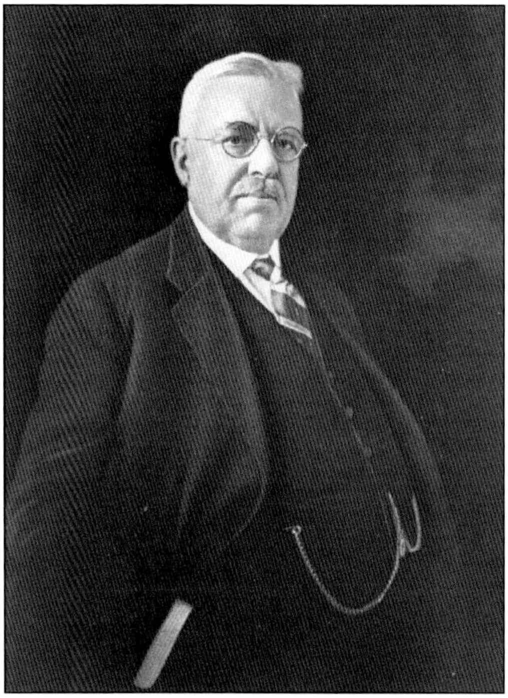

Innovator and visionary Walter G. Cowles, vice president of the Travelers Insurance Company, first proposed that the company add broadcasting to its other functions. In addition to introducing WTIC in 1925, he also wrote and issued the world's first automobile and aviation insurance policies. (Courtesy of CBS Radio Inc.)

An unidentified band plays live in the WDRC New Haven studio. Phonograph records were rarely used in early broadcasting because of their poor fidelity, so live performances were the norm. As radio broadcasting grew in popularity, radio stations started retaining the services of musical performers and groups on a regular basis. (Courtesy of WDRC.)

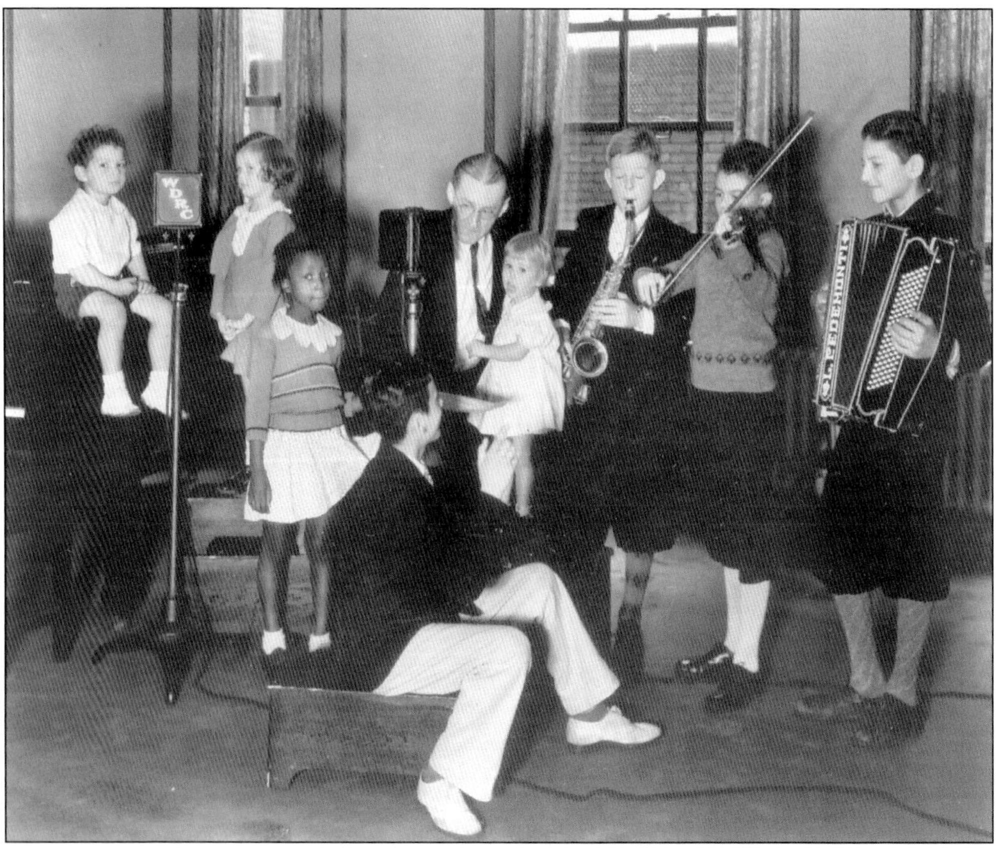

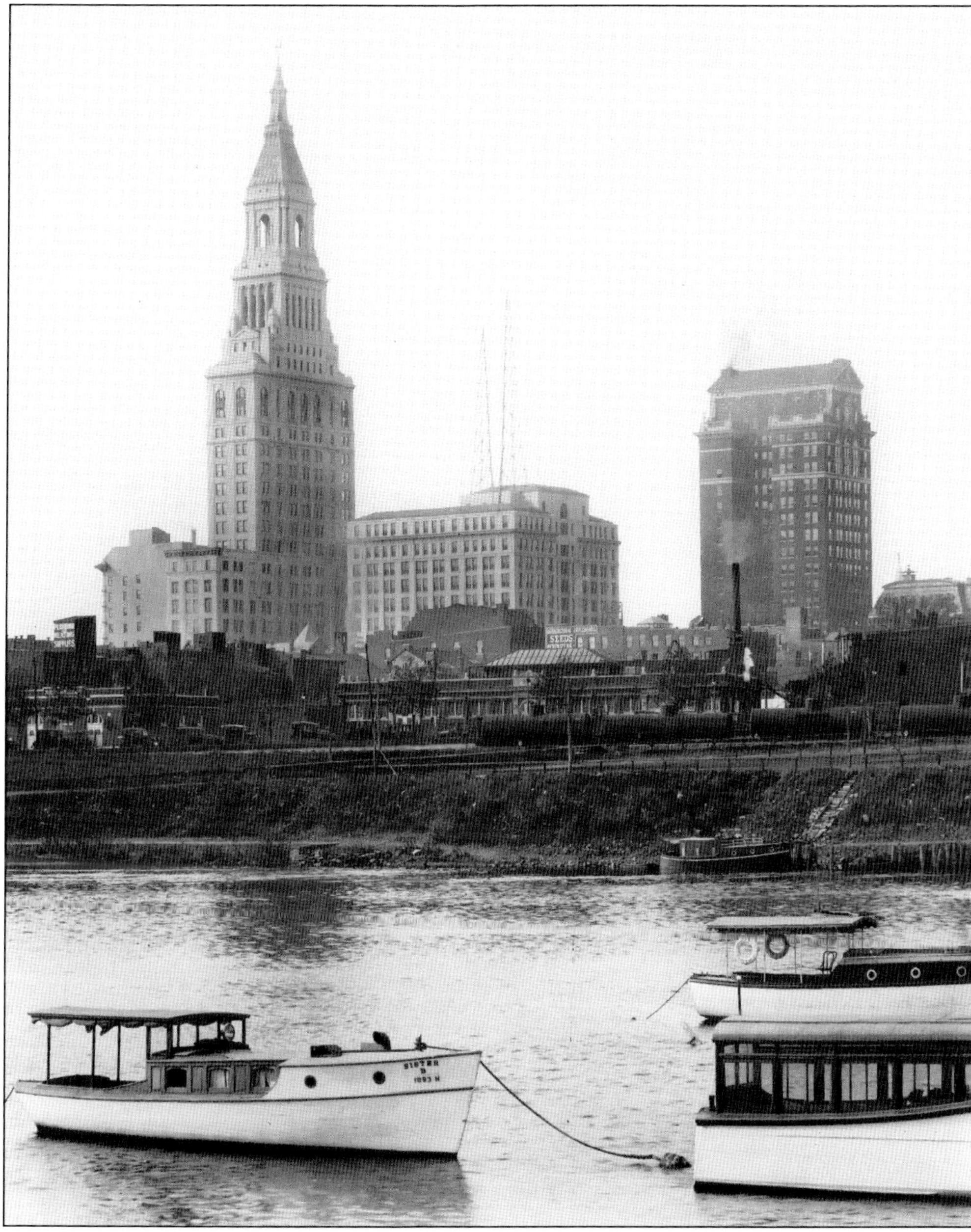

WTIC went on the air for the first time in 1925 from studios located at 26 Grove Street in downtown Hartford. On top of the building's roof were WTIC's two 150-foot-tall steel towers that made up the station's antenna system. This system broadcast the first WTIC programs in 1925 and was in use until 1929 when the WTIC transmitter was moved to Talcott Mountain in Avon, Connecticut. In this photograph, taken from the East Hartford side of the Connecticut River, one can see the two radio towers dwarfed by the landmark Travelers Tower. (Courtesy of CBS Radio Inc.)

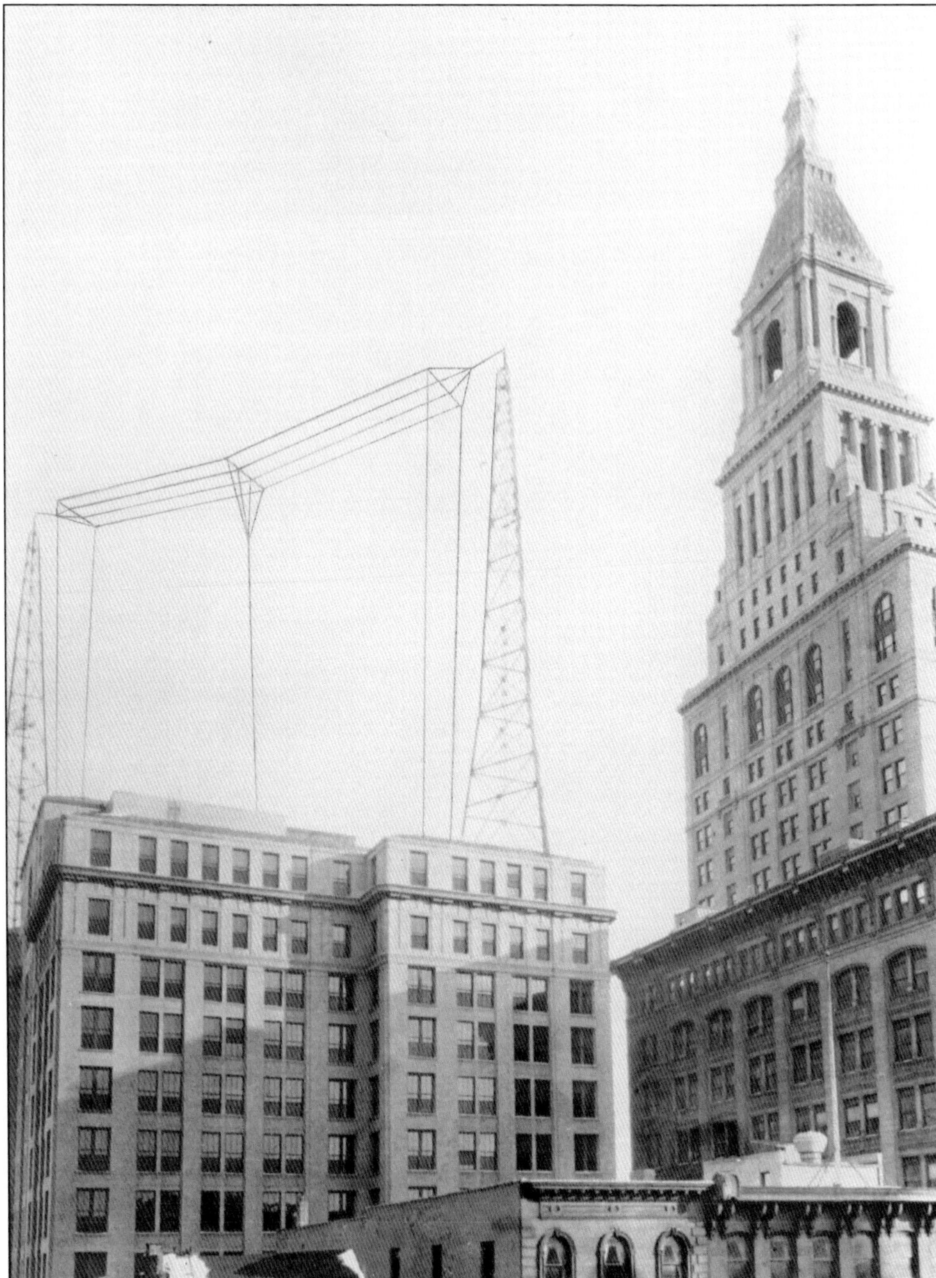

This is a close-up view of the two WTIC antenna towers at 26 Grove Street in downtown Hartford as they looked in 1925 when the station first went on the air. The two 150-foot-tall steel towers supported what was known as a T-cage antenna system. Constructed in 1919, the Travelers Tower, seen to the right of the radio towers, serves as a Hartford landmark even today. When it was completed, it towered above all of the other Hartford buildings, the highest of which was less than 10 stories at that time. It was the seventh tallest building in the world when it was built and the tallest structure between New York City and Boston for several decades. (Courtesy of CBS Radio Inc.)

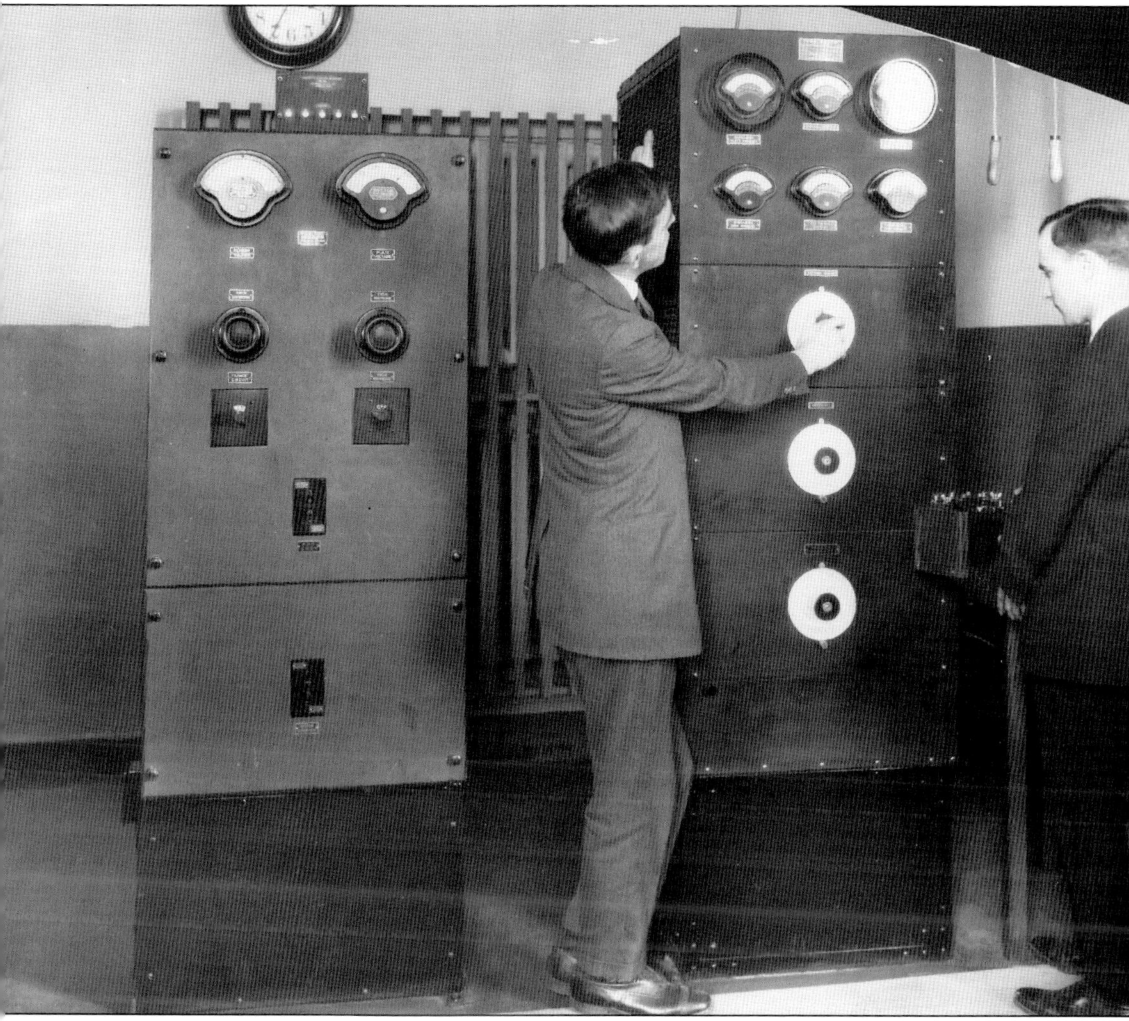

WTIC's first transmitter was located in a specially designed penthouse at the Travelers Indemnity Company's 26 Grove Street headquarters building in Hartford. Manufactured by Westinghouse, the transmitter had an output power of 500 watts and could be operated on batteries during power failures. The cabinet on the left houses the frequency control and modulation section, while the section on the right is the power amplifier. In this photograph, an unidentified man adjusts the transmitter while chief operator Herman Taylor looks on. (Courtesy of CBS Radio Inc.)

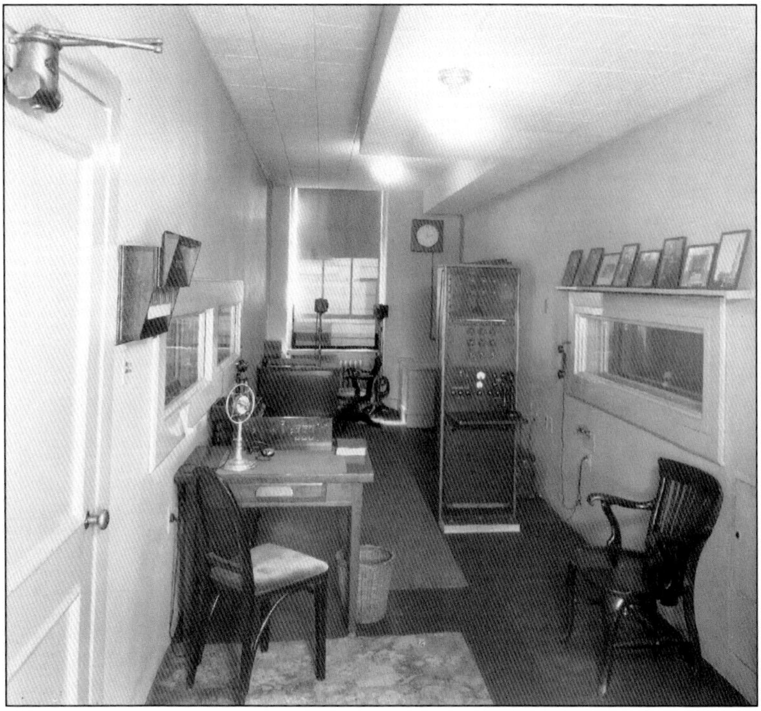

The original WTIC control room in Hartford is pictured in 1925. From this room, the engineer could monitor and control the sound coming from either of the two live performance studios located on either side. The large windows allowed him to view and cue the performers. (Courtesy of CBS Radio Inc.)

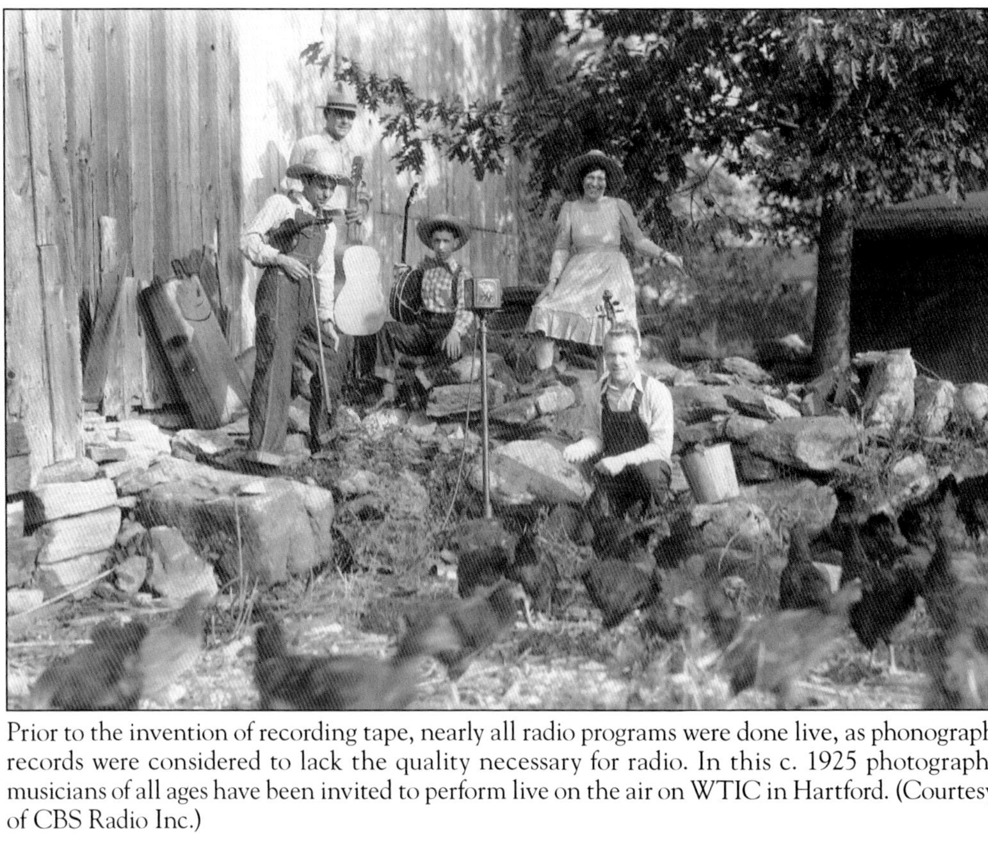

Prior to the invention of recording tape, nearly all radio programs were done live, as phonograph records were considered to lack the quality necessary for radio. In this c. 1925 photograph, musicians of all ages have been invited to perform live on the air on WTIC in Hartford. (Courtesy of CBS Radio Inc.)

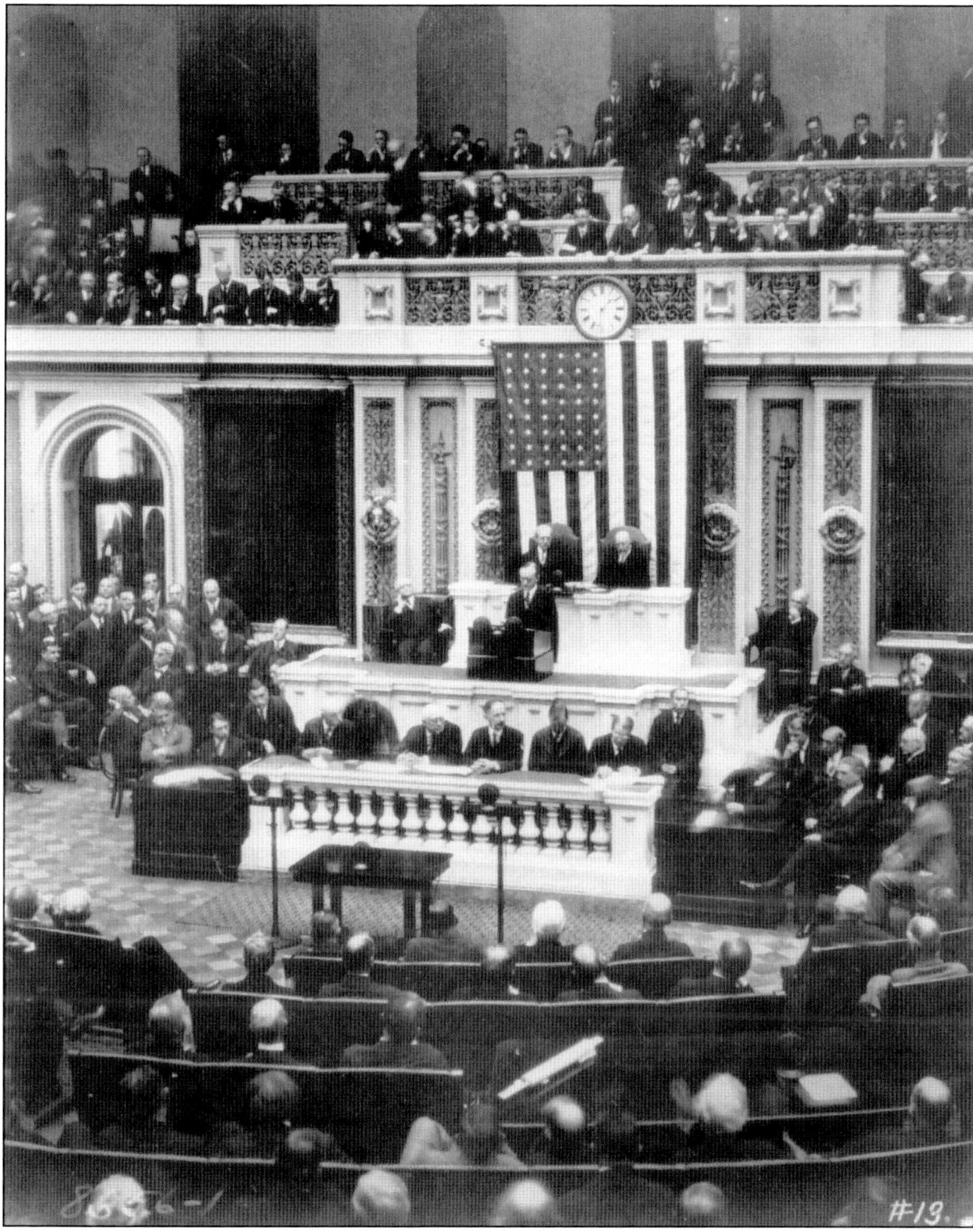

Being located in Hartford, the capital of Connecticut, provided WTIC the upper hand in covering important news stories. In this photograph, Calvin Coolidge, US president from 1923 to 1929, speaks to the Connecticut State Legislature in the state capitol. Coolidge was elected as the 29th vice president in 1920 and succeeded to the presidency upon the sudden death of Warren G. Harding. He was elected in his own right in 1924. (Courtesy of CBS Radio Inc.)

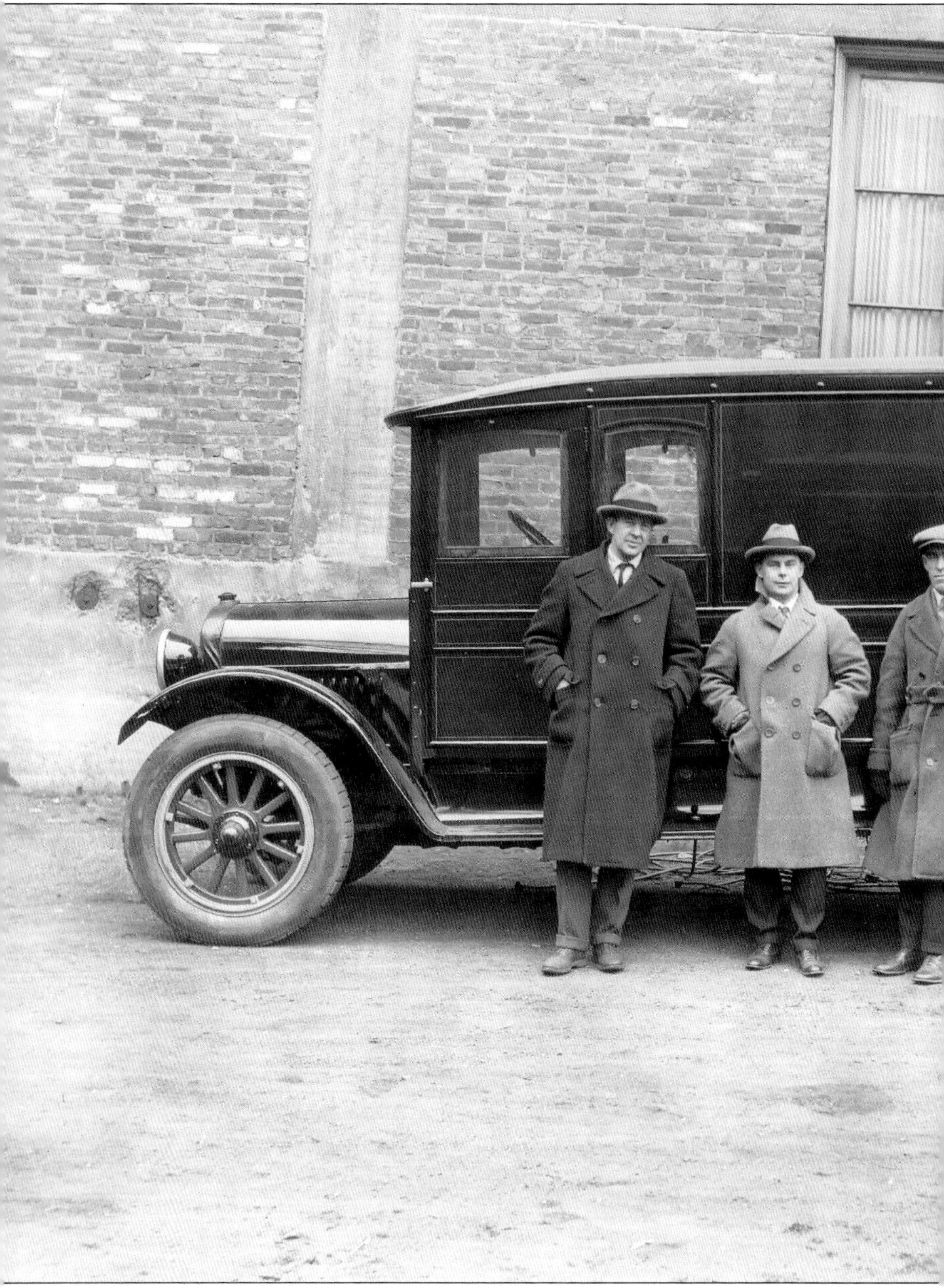

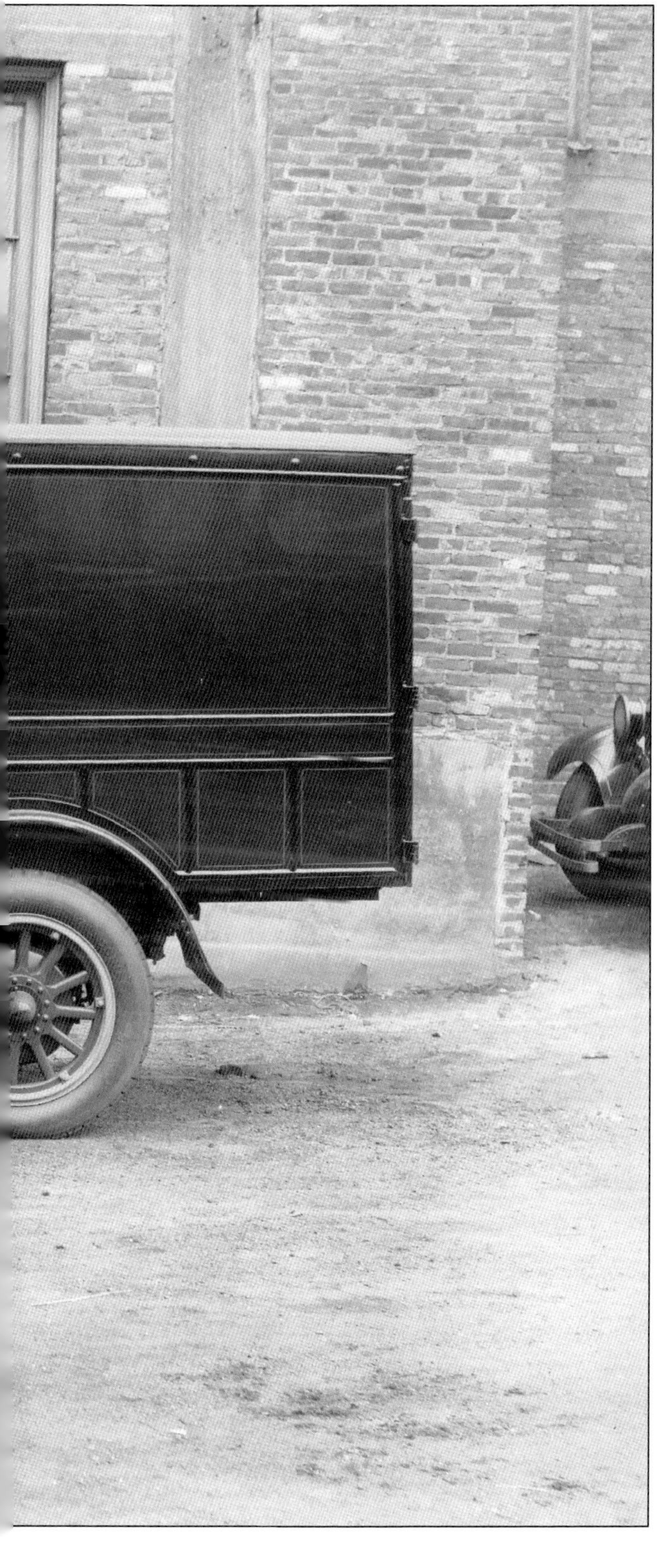

Tuesday, February 10, 1925, was the date of WTIC's first broadcast, which included studio musical presentations and featured a live remote broadcast of Emile Heimberger's trio as it played in the Bond Hotel on Asylum Street in Hartford. Pictured here is WTIC's first special events transmission vehicle with the three engineers it took to manage the broadcast. Today, WTIC would use transmission equipment that would fit in the palm of one hand. The engineer on the right is J. Clayton Randall. (Courtesy of CBS Radio Inc.)

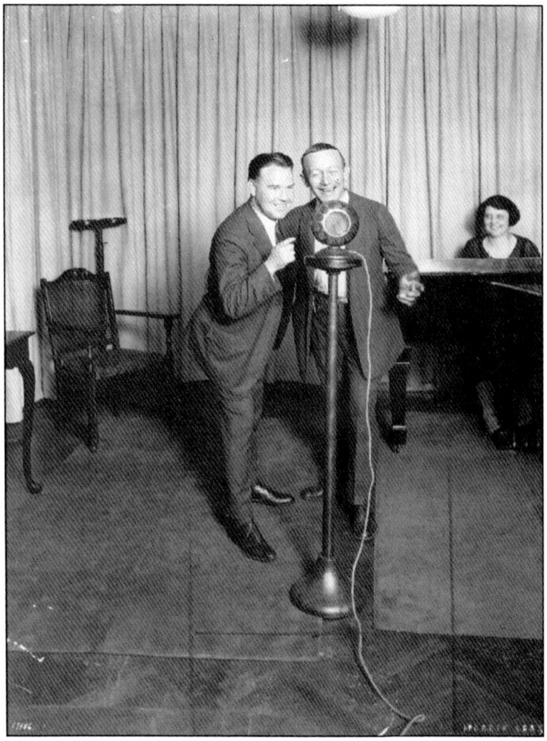

Billy Jones (left) and Ernie Hare were the famous Happiness Boys. The duo sang popular tunes, mostly light fare and comic songs, and engaged in humorous repartee between numbers. Known for their theme song "How Do You Do?", the boys are seen here at the microphone in 1925. Most of their programs on WTIC included a live studio audience. (Courtesy of CBS Radio Inc.)

Producing original radio broadcasts was a major undertaking, and most early stations relied on a significant amount of programming originating from one of several newly formed networks. In this photograph, engineers scramble to ensure that WTIC's first National Broadcasting Company (NBC) transmission gets on the air without a glitch. In 1926, WTIC was the fourth station in the country to join the fledgling network. (Courtesy of CBS Radio Inc.)

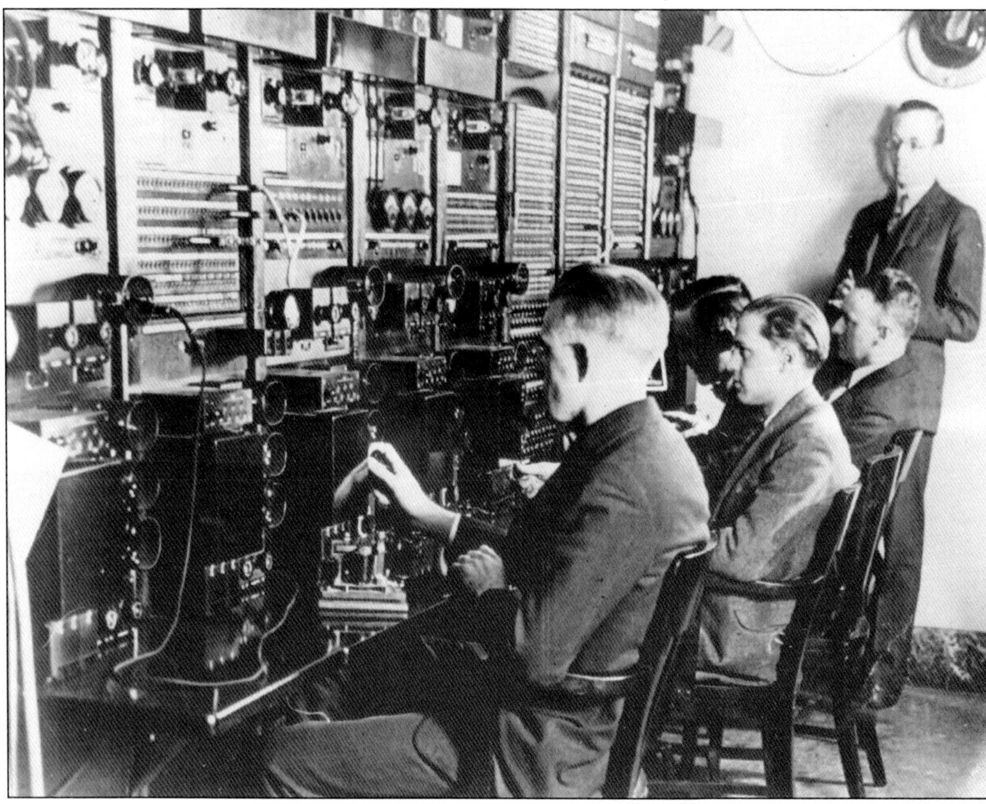

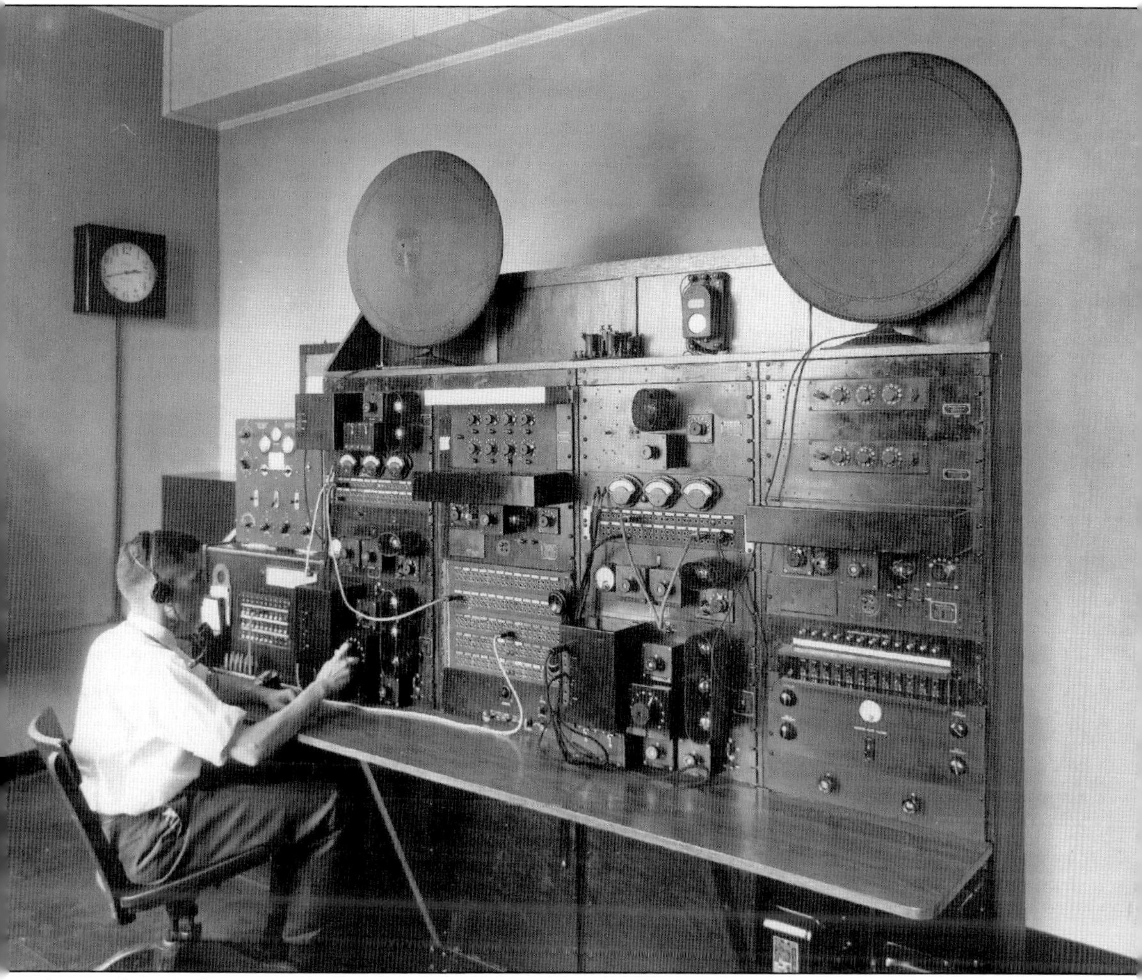

An unidentified engineer sits in front of the equipment in WTIC's Grove Street master control area in 1925. This apparatus was used to control the sound from the various studios and remote broadcast sites and to route it to the station's transmitter. The large round objects at the top are speakers. (Courtesy of CBS Radio Inc.)

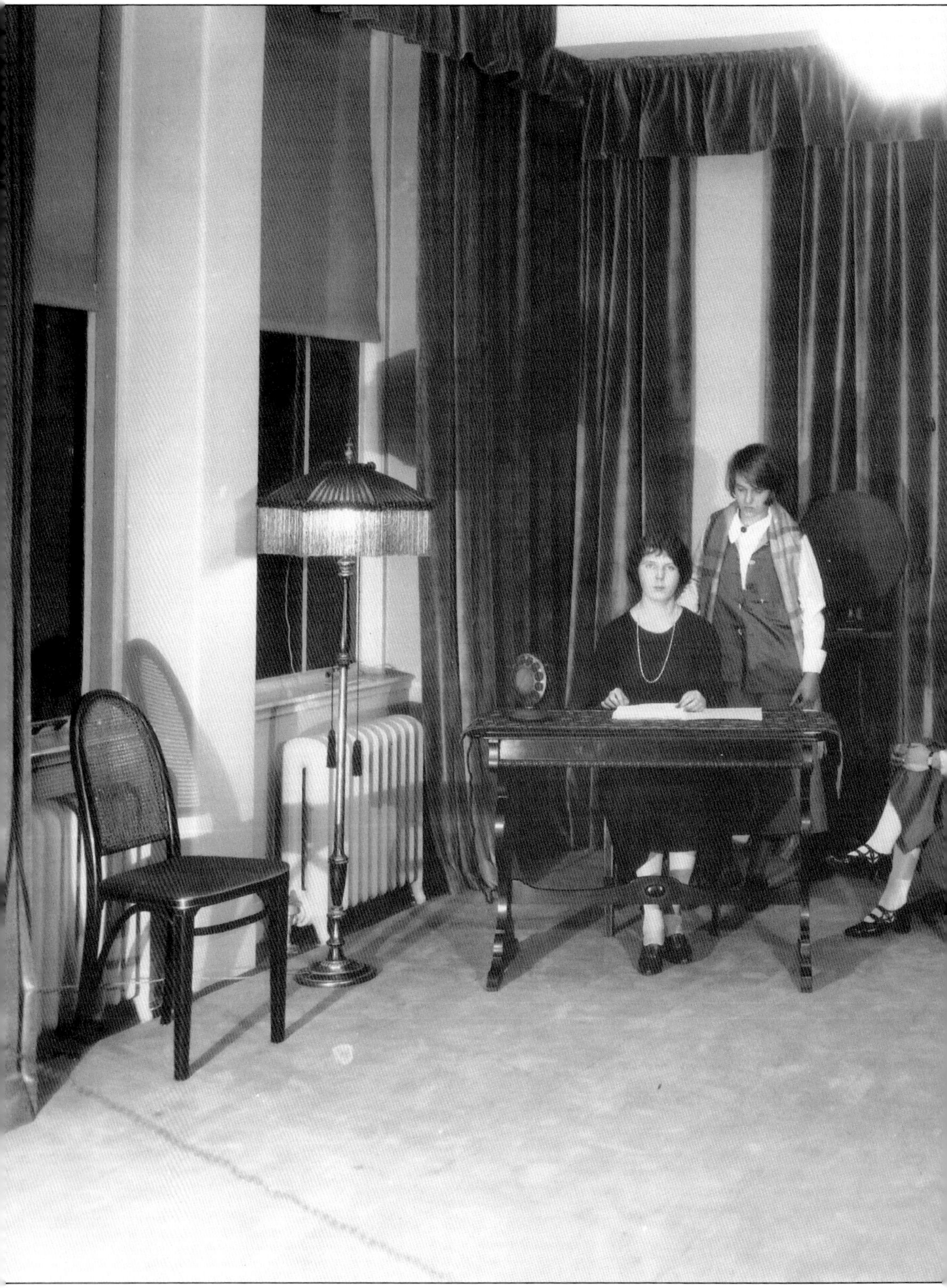

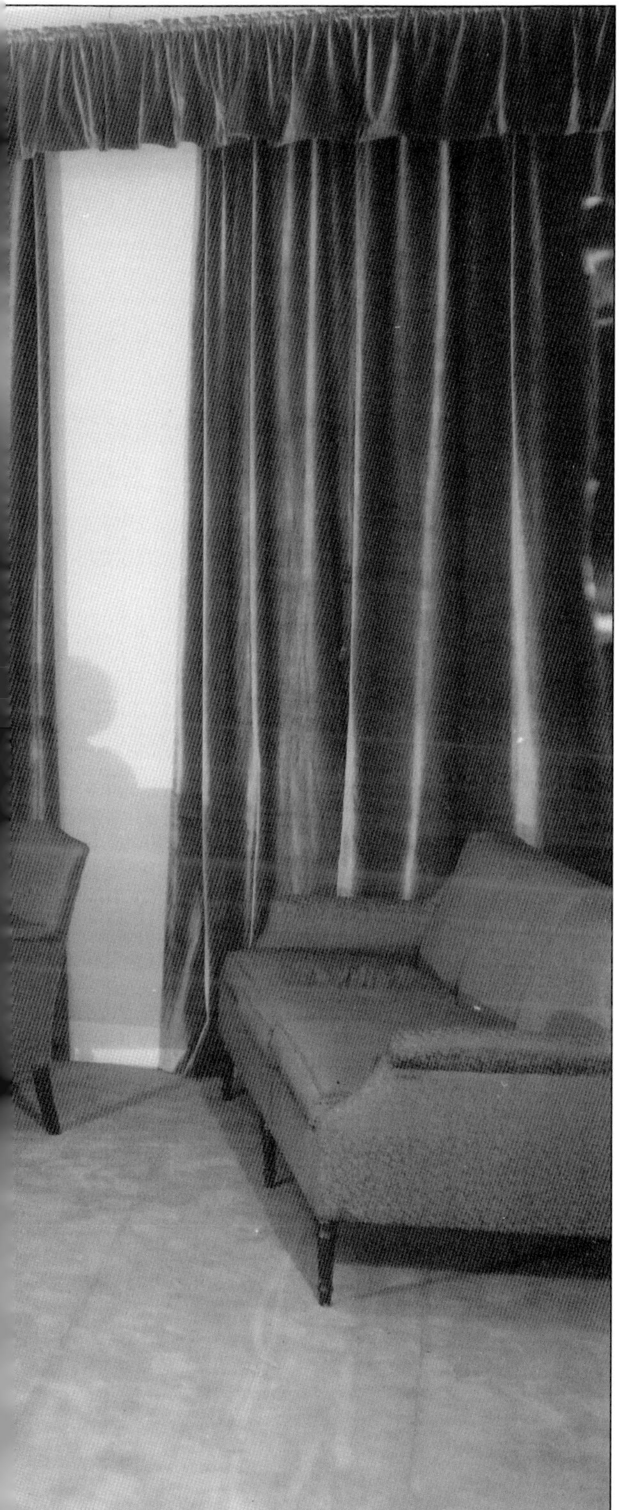

Musicians wait their turns at the microphone in one of the soundproof recording rooms at WTIC. In 1925, nearly all the music heard on the radio was performed live due to the poor quality of phonograph recordings. Tape recording had yet to be invented. (Courtesy of CBS Radio Inc.)

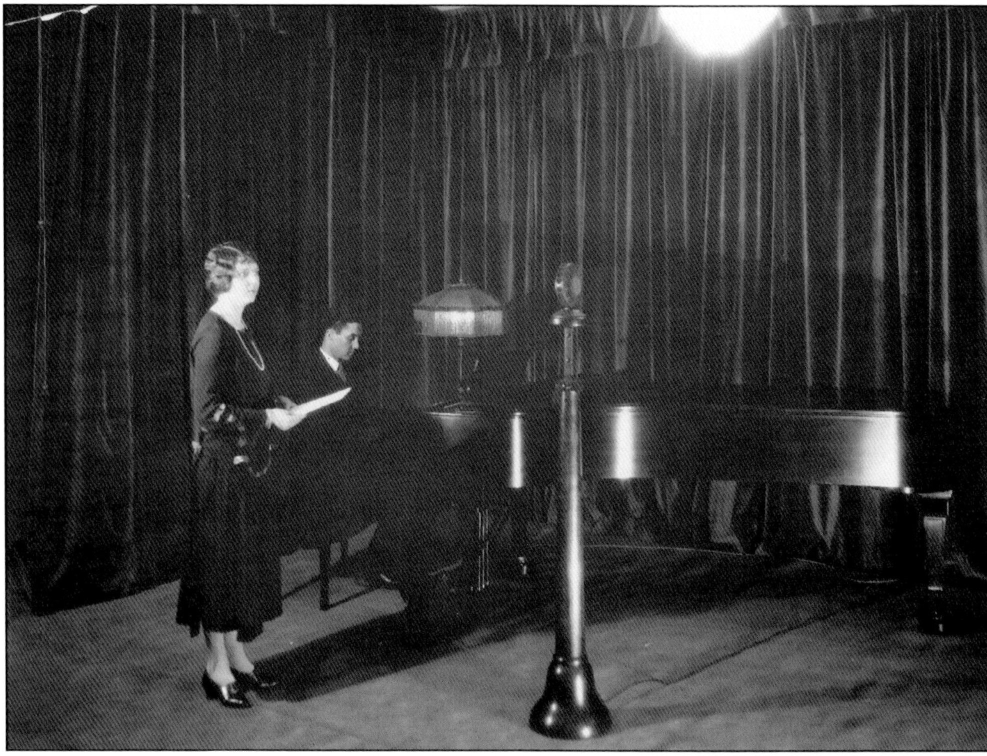

In 1925, the WTIC operations area measured 2,000 square feet and included two studios. The larger studio, pictured here, was decorated with deep-blue velvet drapes and plush carpeting of a lighter blue. The smaller studio was draped in rose-colored velvet. The heavy drapery and carpeting dampened the sound so there would be no echo or vibrations. The carbon microphone is installed on an adjustable wooden stand made out of hand-turned mahogany. (Courtesy of CBS Radio Inc.)

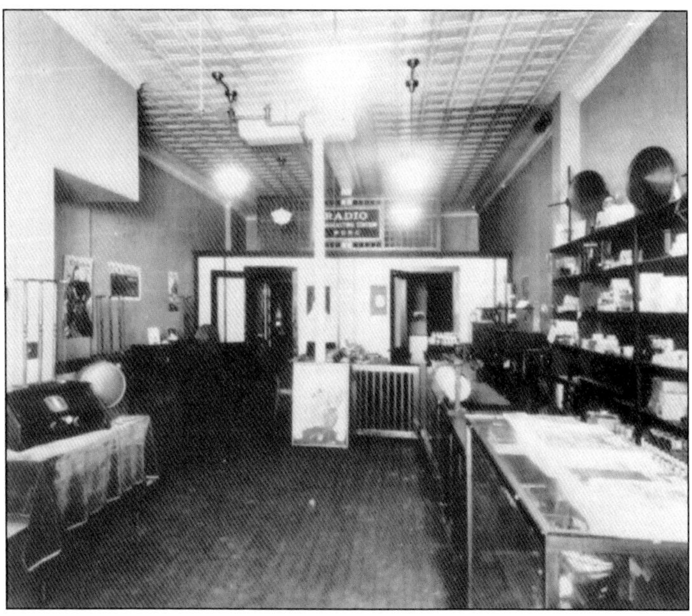


In the 1920s and 1930s, the owners of retail radio stores were often forced to build their own radio stations to help them sell receivers; otherwise, there would have been nothing to listen to. Pictured is radio station WDRC (formerly WPAJ), situated in the back of Franklin M. Doolittle's retail radio store in New Haven. (Courtesy of WDRC.)

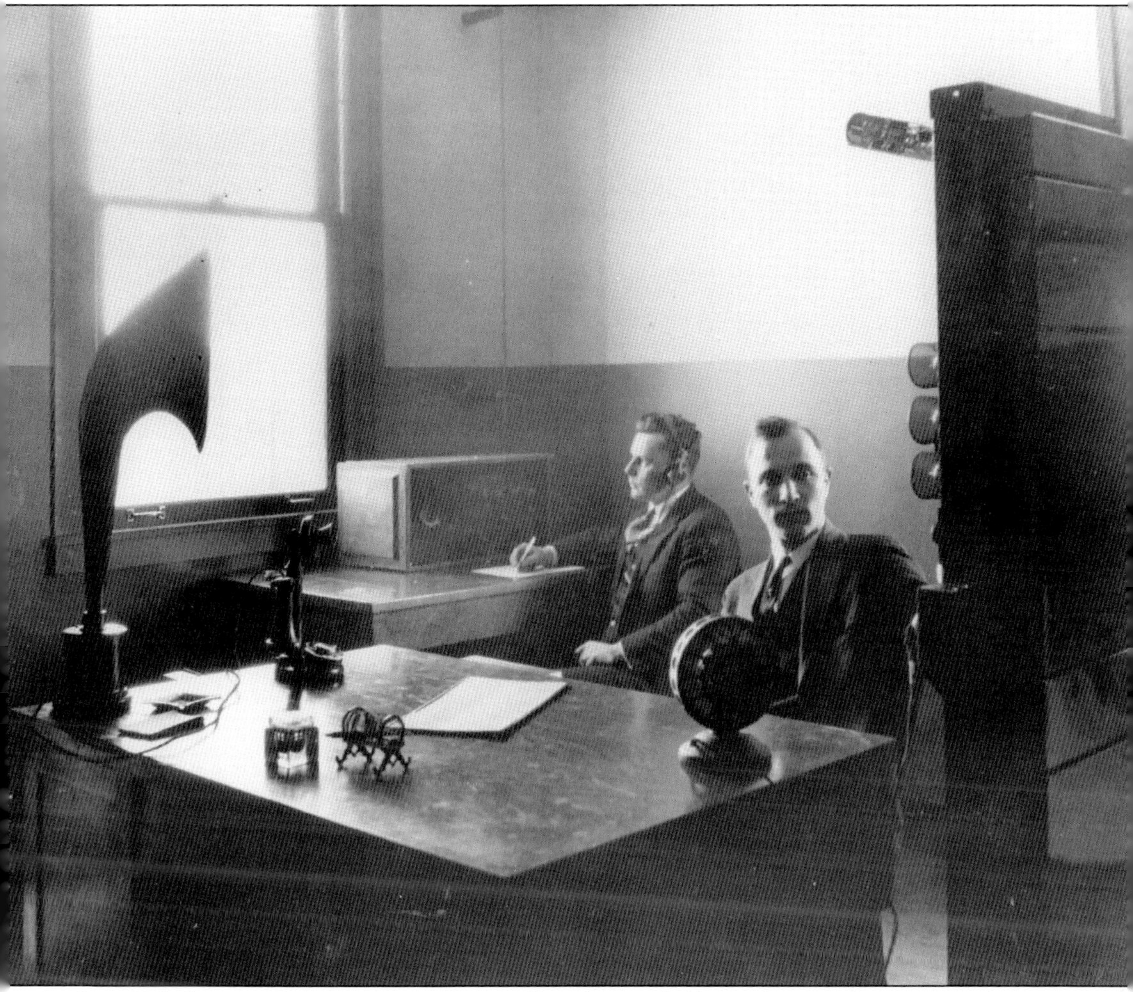

In this 1925 photograph, assistant operator Bill Coleman (left) can be seen listening to ship traffic in the WTIC transmitting room in downtown Hartford. The government required that every broadcast station listen for SOS signals and shut off transmitting if any ship in distress were trying to make itself heard. Chief operator Herman Taylor is seen adjusting the speech amplifier. (Courtesy of CBS Radio Inc.)

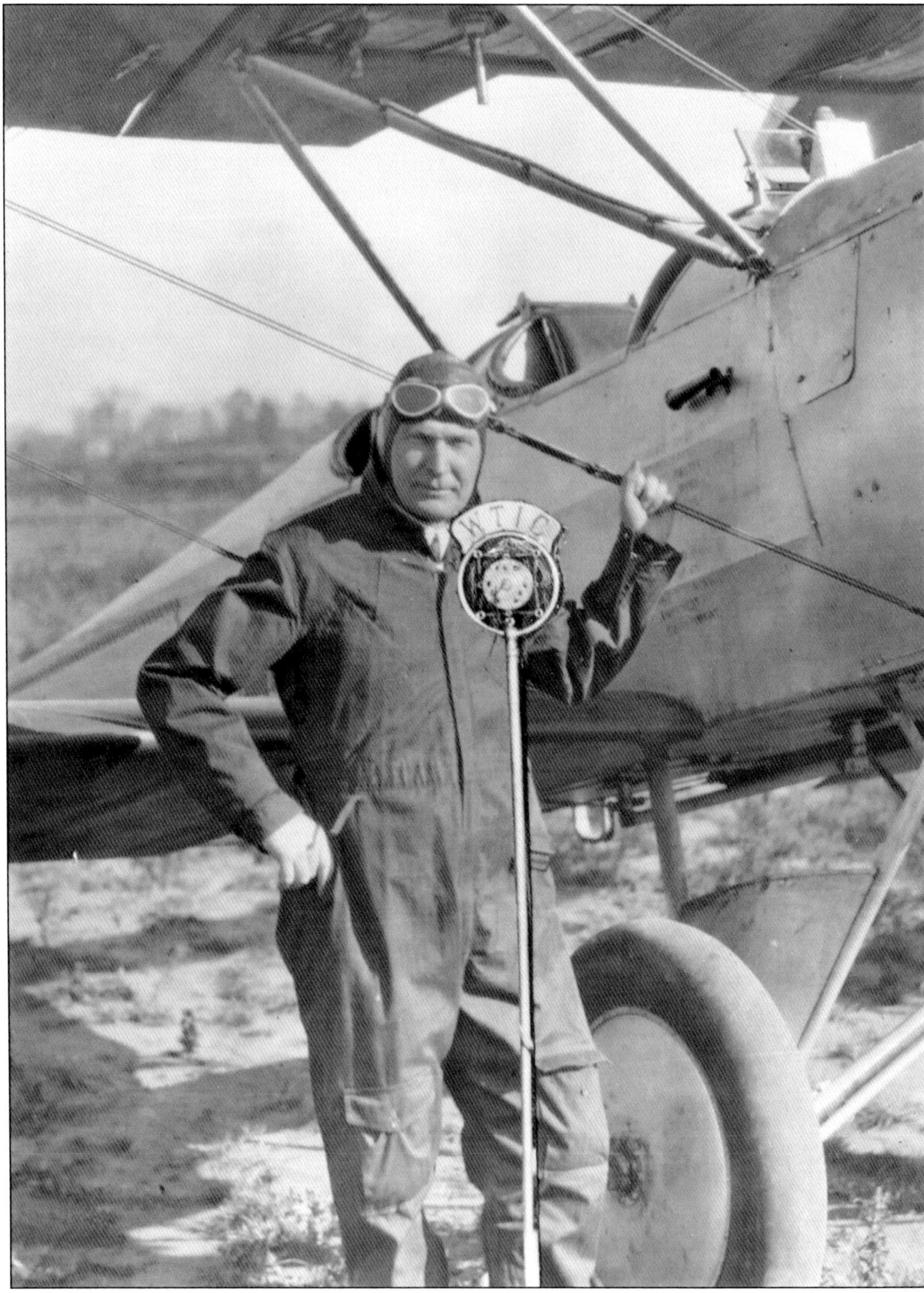


Connecticut's "Flying Governor" John H. Trumbull is pictured here with his favorite National Guard airplane. Governor from 1925 to 1931, he was responsible for one of WTIC's famous firsts. Trumbull made the world's first public broadcast from a moving aircraft. His voice and that of aircraft builder Igor Sikorsky were transmitted by shortwave and relayed by WTIC while the two men were flying over Hartford in late 1926. (Courtesy of CBS Radio Inc.)

In this 1927 image, WTIC's secretarial staff is checking the fan mail received from every state in the union and points all over the compass outside the United States. WTIC's 50,000-watt signal has reportedly been picked up worldwide over the years, and the station has letters from every country in the world in its archives.(Courtesy of CBS Radio Inc.)

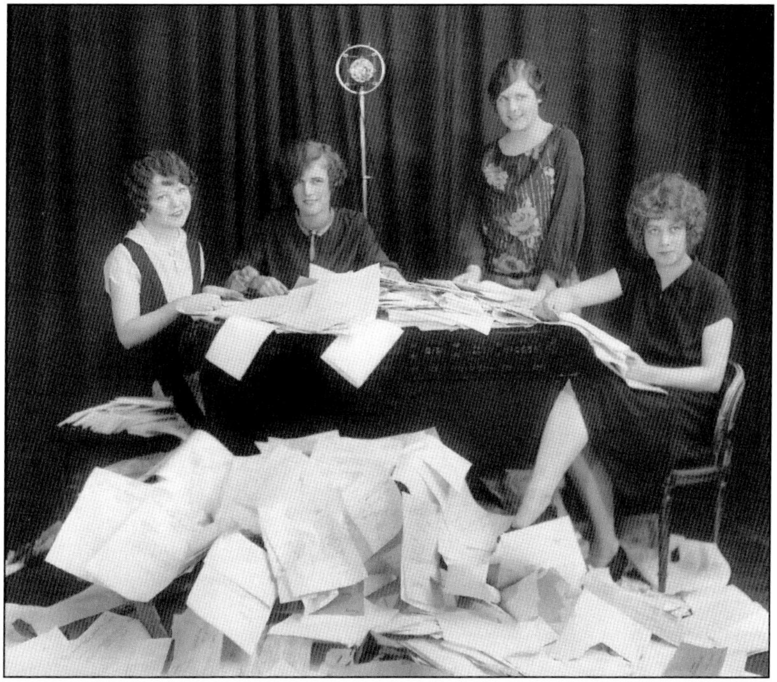

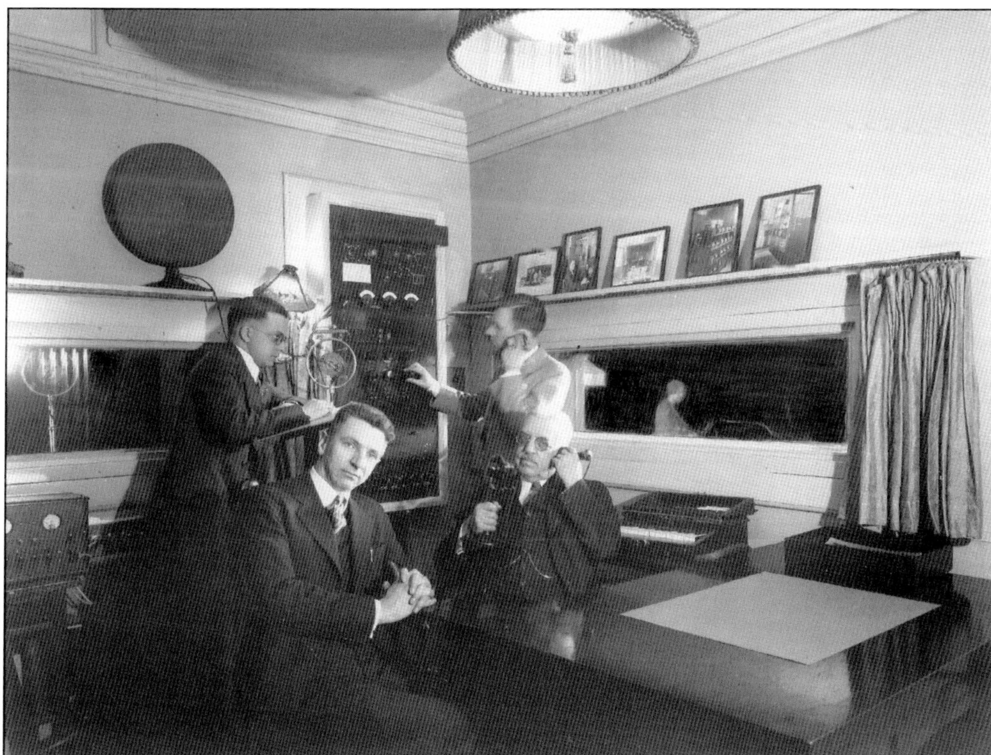

From left to right, Travelers' Walter Cowles, musical director Dana Merriman, first manager H. Billings, and studio engineer H. Wood preside over a live musical performance. They are working in a control room overlooking the studio. (Courtesy of CBS Radio Inc.)

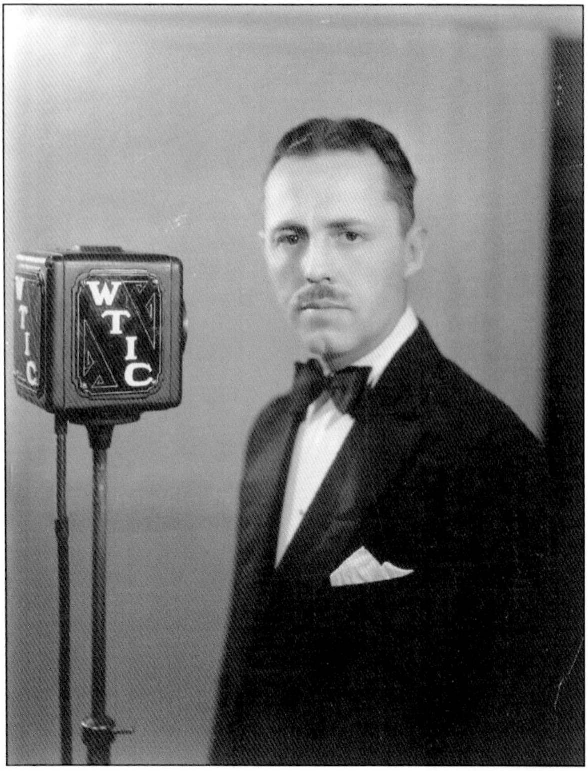


Charles Beach, president of the Connecticut Agricultural College in Storrs from 1908 to 1928, was in Hartford often and was a frequent guest on WTIC. His interest in radio was not surprising considering that WABL, the college's own station, predated WTIC by at least three years. (Courtesy of CBS Radio Inc.)

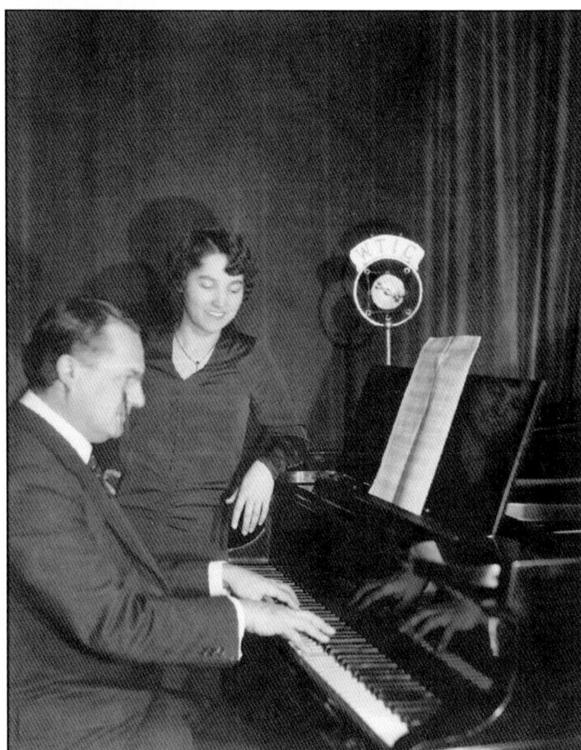


Early recorded music was considered of such poor quality, it was not considered worthy of being broadcast. In 1925, WTIC began hiring musicians, and Laura Gaudet was brought on board as staff pianist in 1925. It was not long before WTIC had built a large reserve of musicians and announcers. In this photograph, Gaudet watches as an unidentified musician performs live on WTIC in 1928. (Courtesy of CBS Radio Inc.)

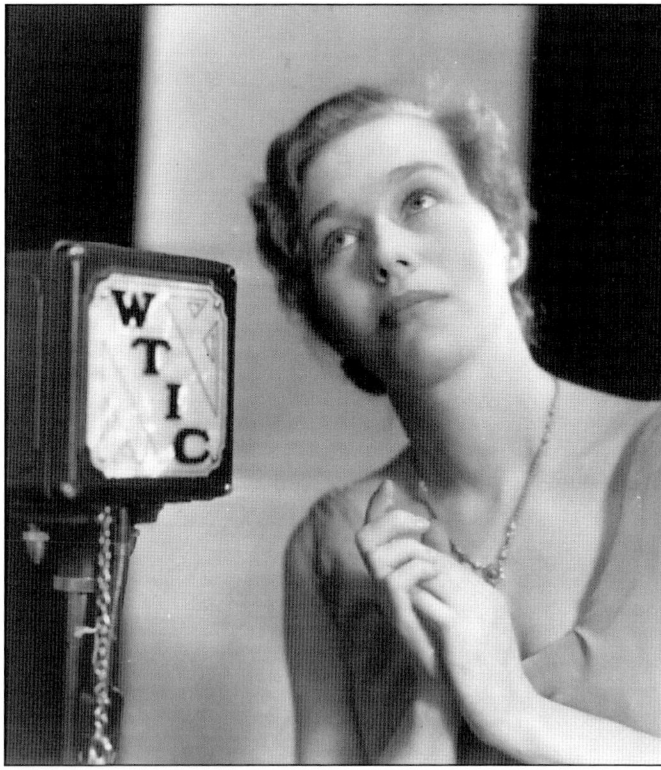


Live music was the mainstay of early radio programming. Guest appearances by regional and national musicians were common. Hartford's central location, approximately halfway between Boston and New York City, resulted in many musicians performing in the city at such locations as the Bushnell Memorial Hall and the ballroom at the Hotel Bond on Asylum Street. In these photographs, musicians perform on WTIC. (Both, courtesy of CBS Radio Inc.)

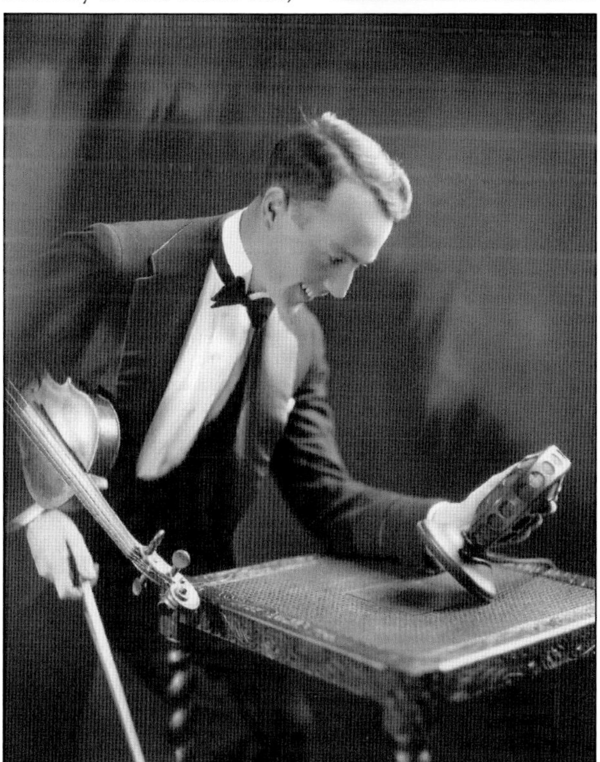

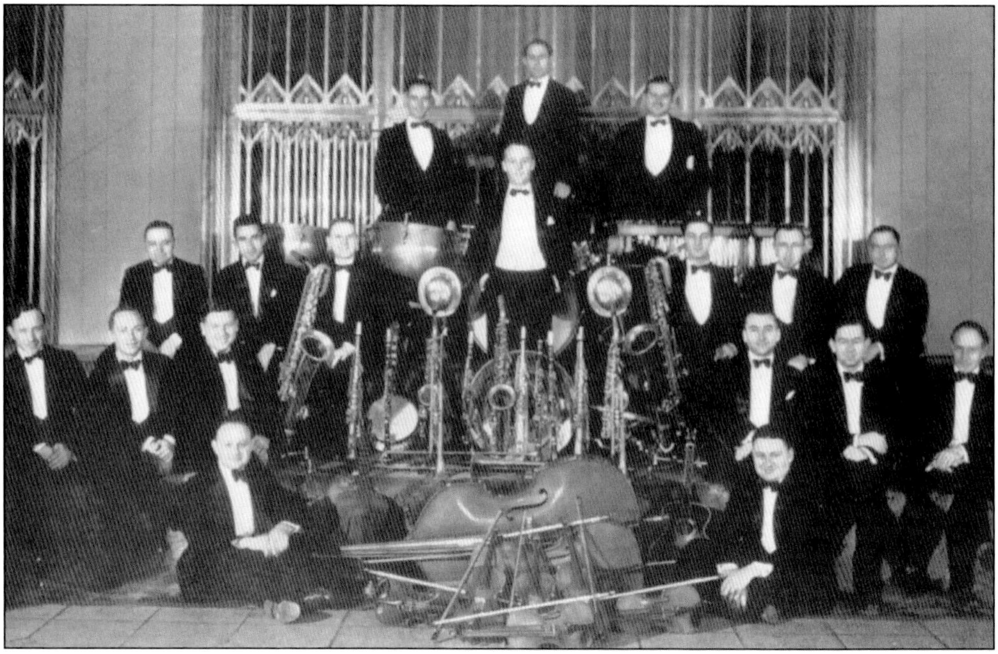

Just prior to a live broadcast, the Merry Madcaps pose for a photograph. They were known for their snappy syncopation and special musical arrangements, which won them a loyal following throughout Connecticut thanks to their appearances on WTIC. (Courtesy of CBS Radio Inc.)

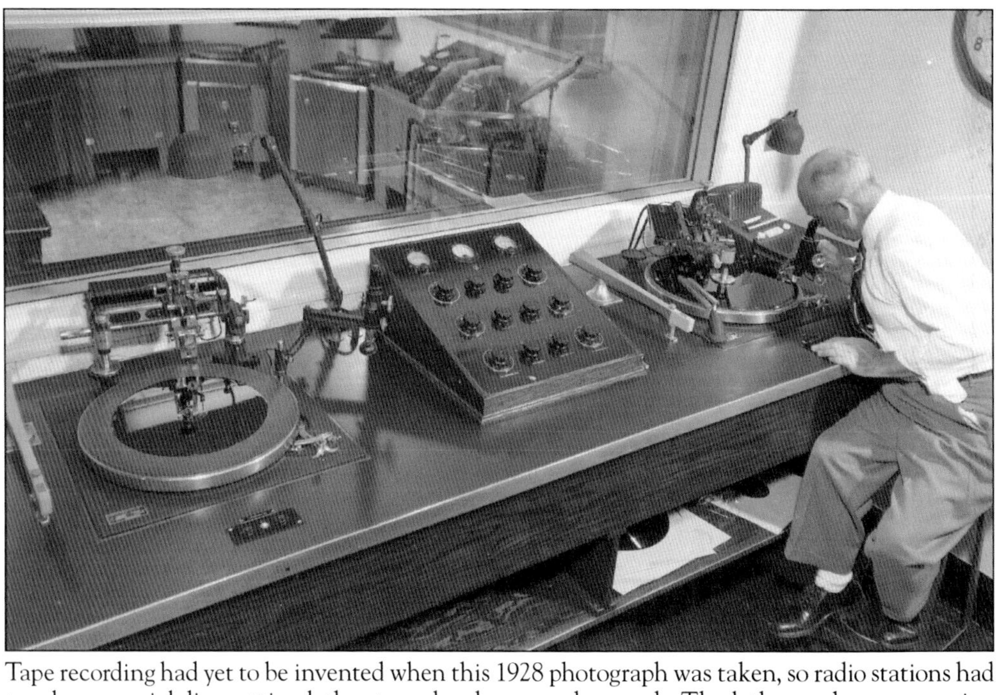

Tape recording had yet to be invented when this 1928 photograph was taken, so radio stations had to rely on special disc-cutting lathes to make phonograph records. The lathes and accompanying equipment required a skilled operator. Several of these lathes are seen at WTIC. (Courtesy of CBS Radio Inc.)

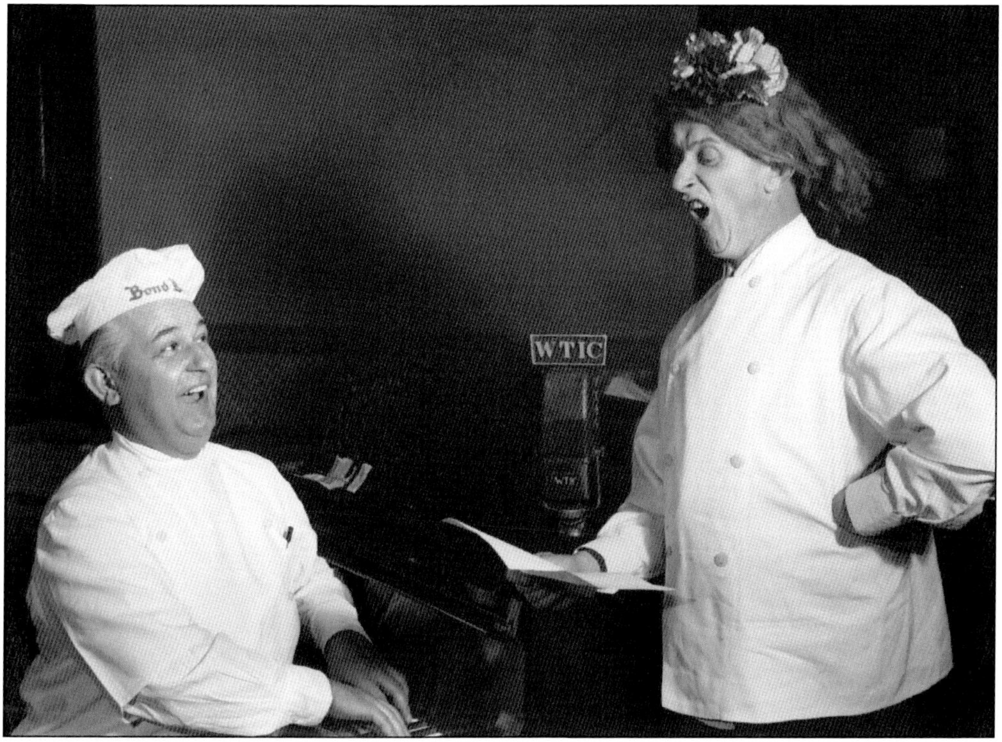


Live comedy by professional actors and comedians augmented the live musical programs heard on WTIC and other Hartford stations in the 1930s. Usually, these performances were conducted in front of a studio audience that provided a live laugh track. (Courtesy of CBS Radio Inc.)

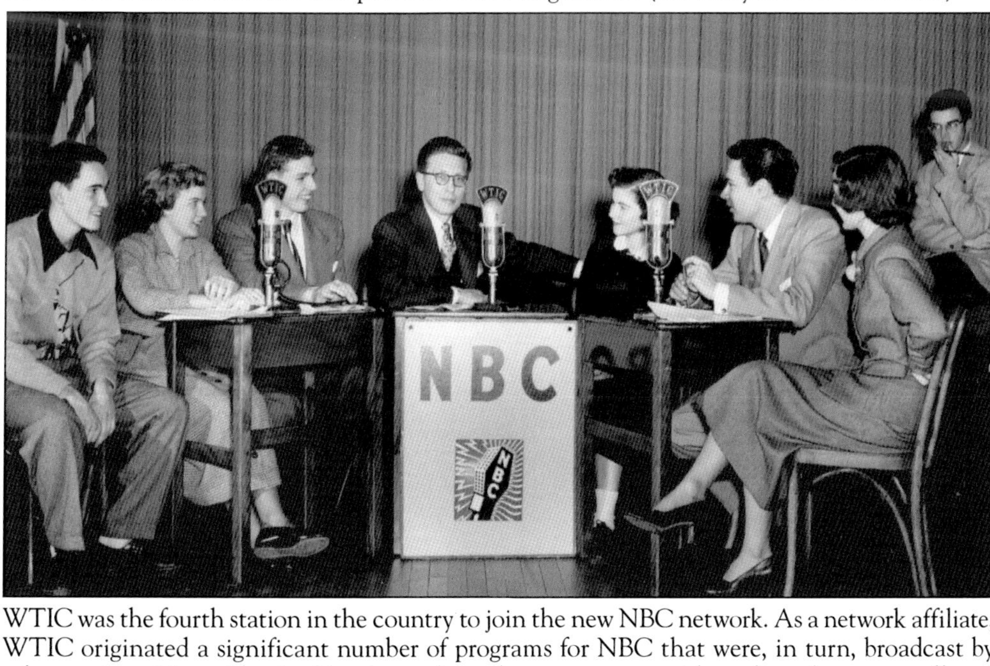


WTIC was the fourth station in the country to join the new NBC network. As a network affiliate, WTIC originated a significant number of programs for NBC that were, in turn, broadcast by other stations. Here, Alan Ludden (center) conducts a program with students from area colleges. (Courtesy of CBS Radio Inc.)

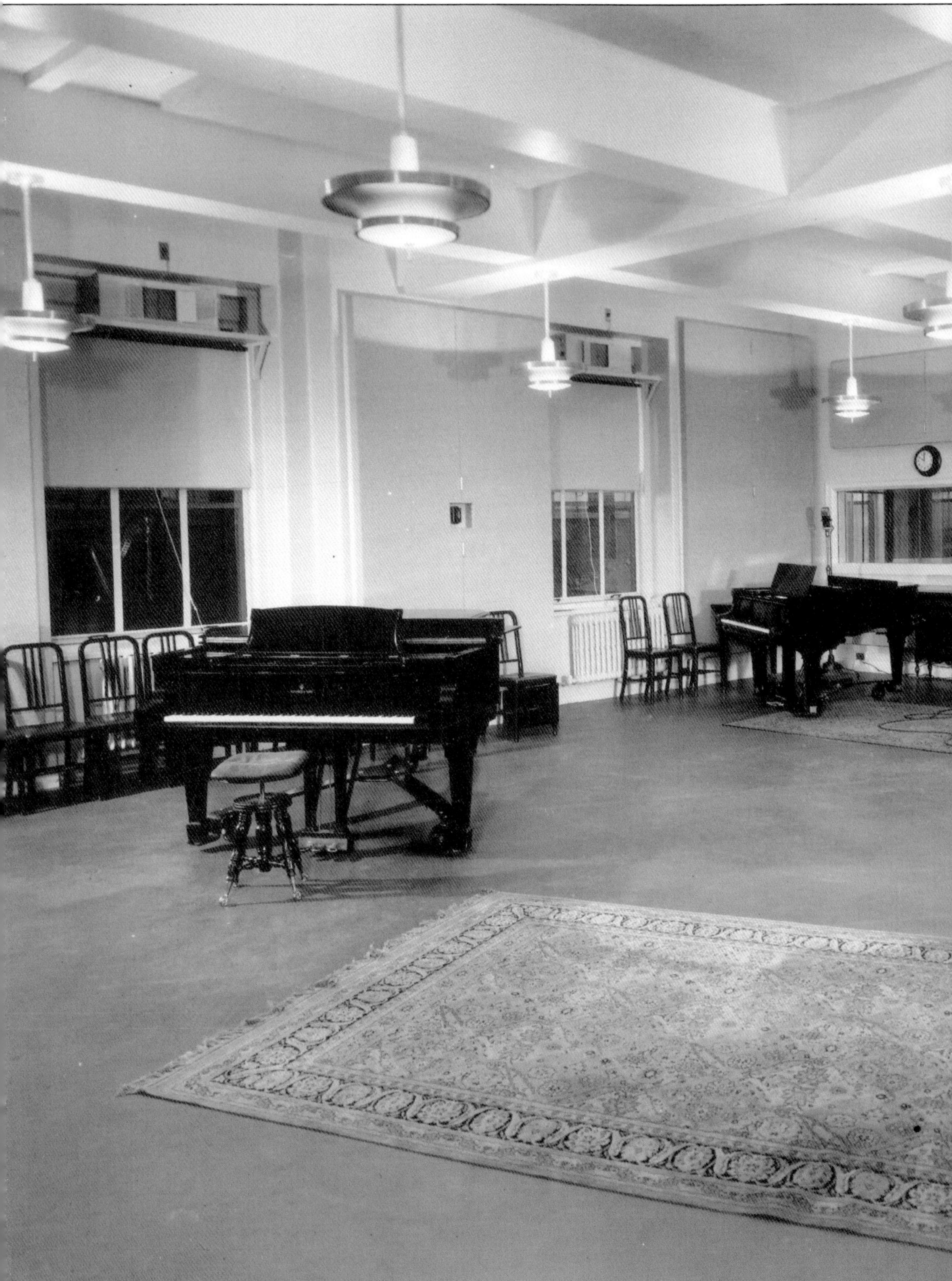

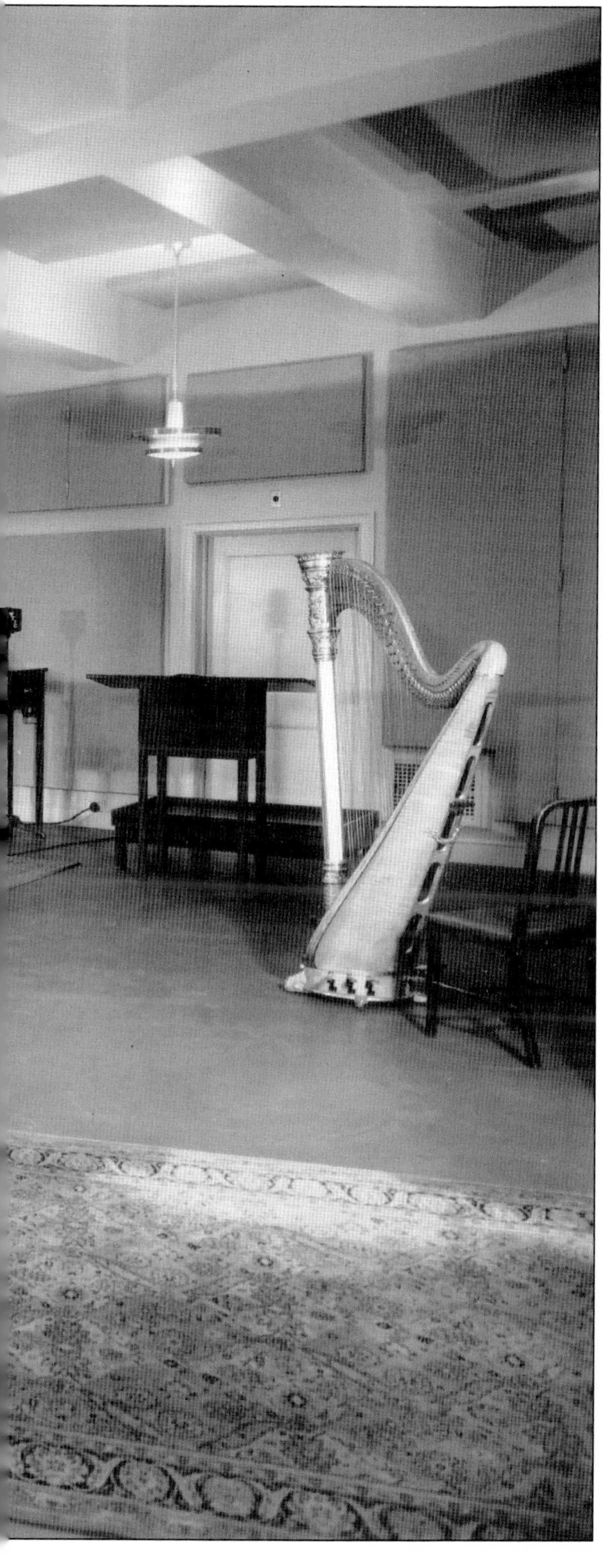

One of WTIC's recently expanded state-of-the-art broadcast studios is seen in this 1928 photograph. The studio had been enlarged to provide more room for the ensembles and performance groups that made regular appearances on the station. Additional space for a live studio audience was also created during the expansion. Radio station studios often had a selection of musical instruments such as grand pianos and harps, as shown in his photograph. (Courtesy of CBS Radio Inc.)

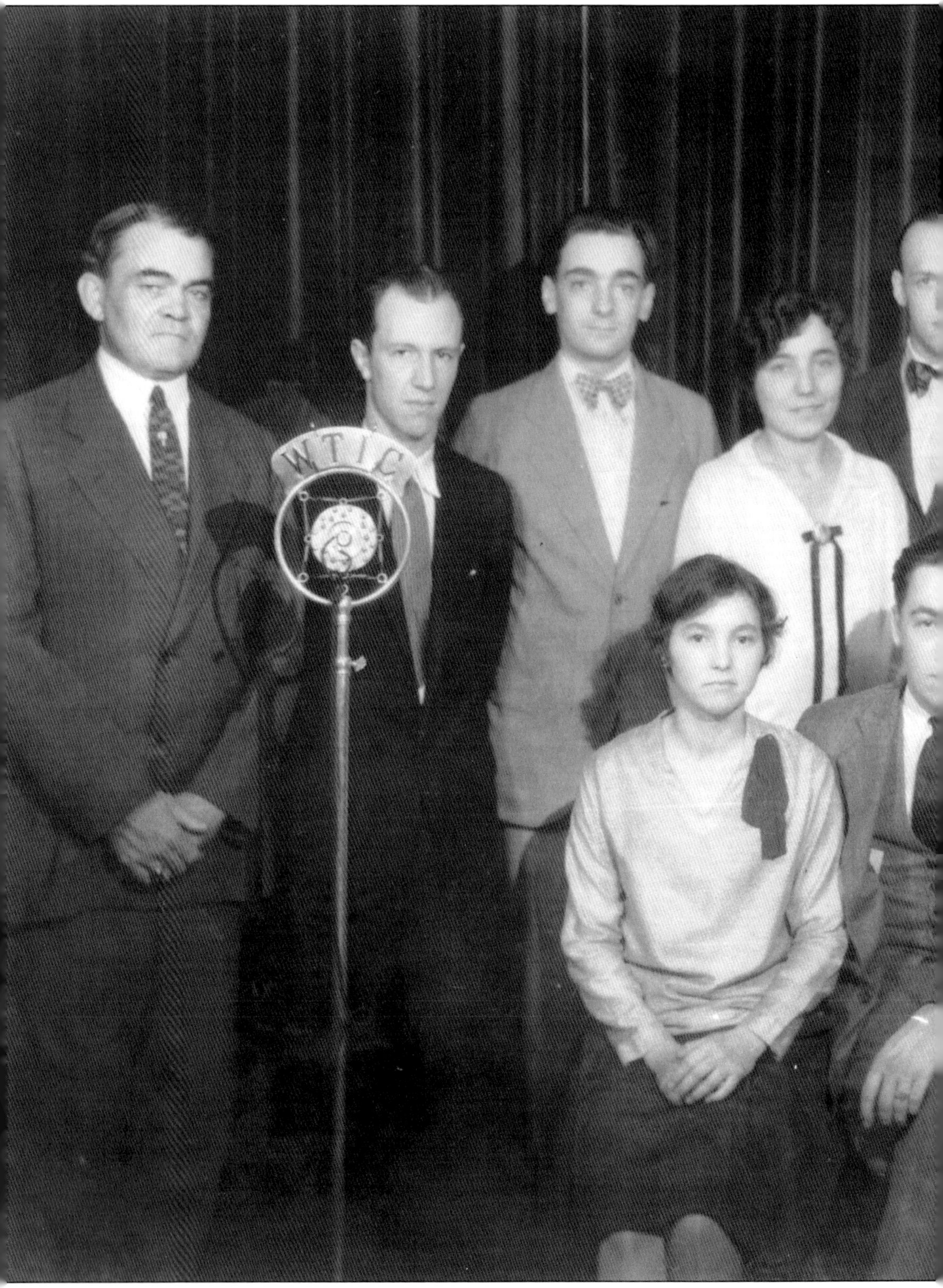
WTIC

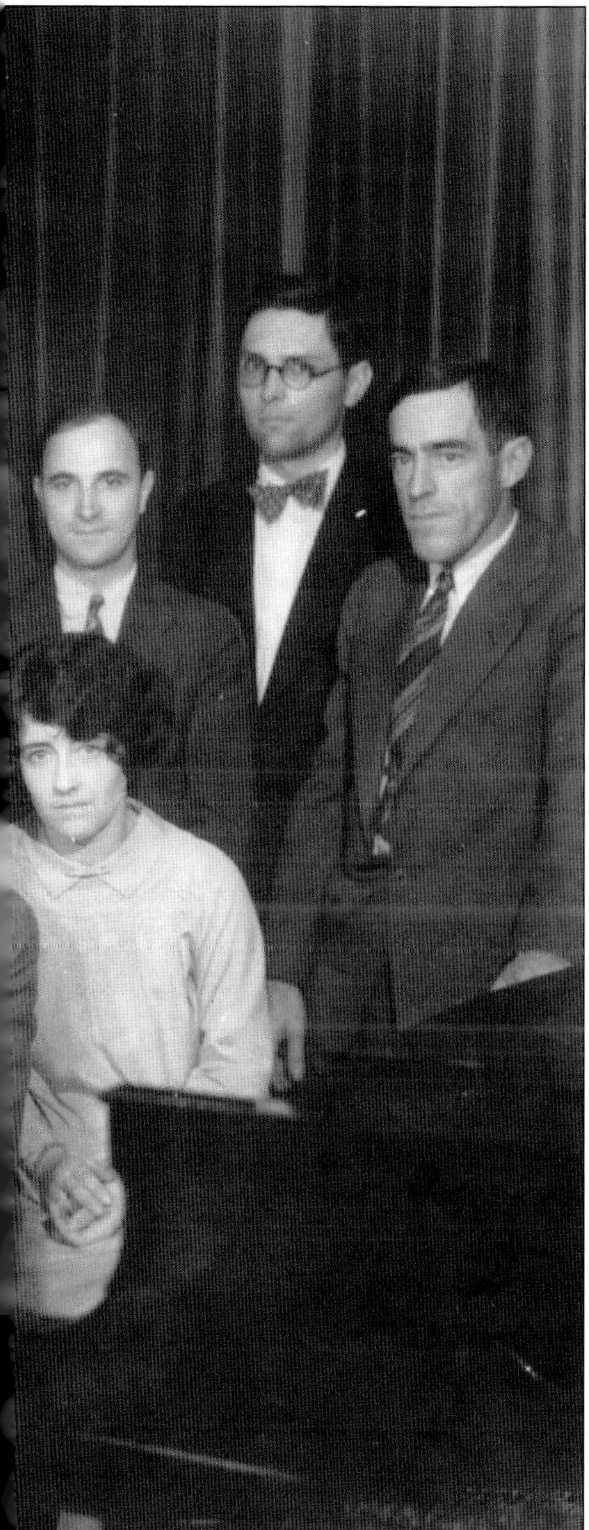

The WTIC staff pose for this group photograph around 1928. Pictured from left to right are (seated) Laura Gaudet, staff pianist; Albert Jackson, operator; and Beatrice Bangs, daytime announcer; (standing) James Clancy, manager; Herbert Wood, studio operator; Paul Lucas, announcer; Mollie Samolis, studio hostess; Thomas McCray, program manager; Herman Taylor, chief operator; Milton Mix, operator; and J. Clayton Randall, chief engineer. Operator William J. Coleman is the only missing staff member. (Courtesy of CBS Radio Inc.)

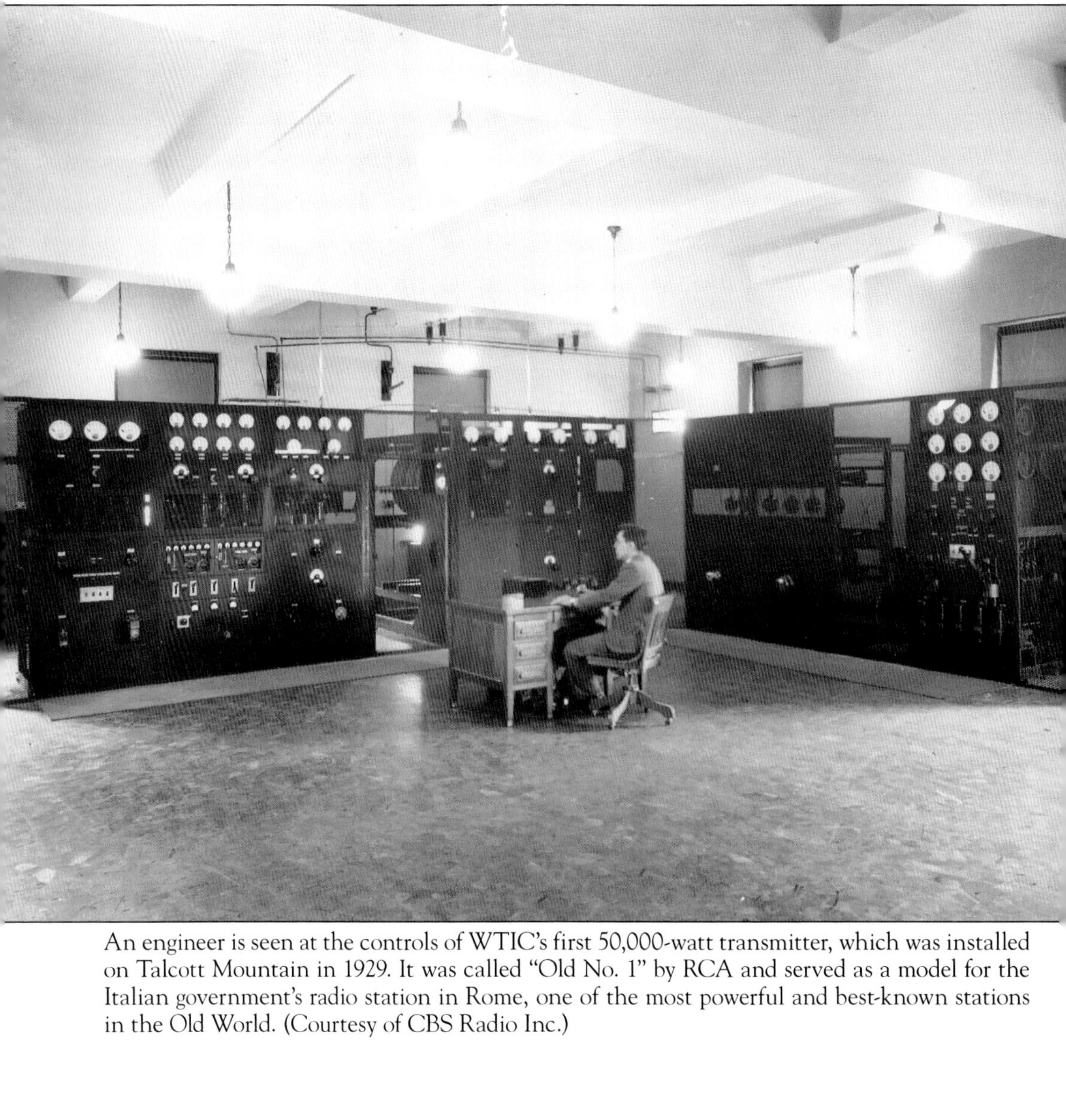

An engineer is seen at the controls of WTIC's first 50,000-watt transmitter, which was installed on Talcott Mountain in 1929. It was called "Old No. 1" by RCA and served as a model for the Italian government's radio station in Rome, one of the most powerful and best-known stations in the Old World. (Courtesy of CBS Radio Inc.)

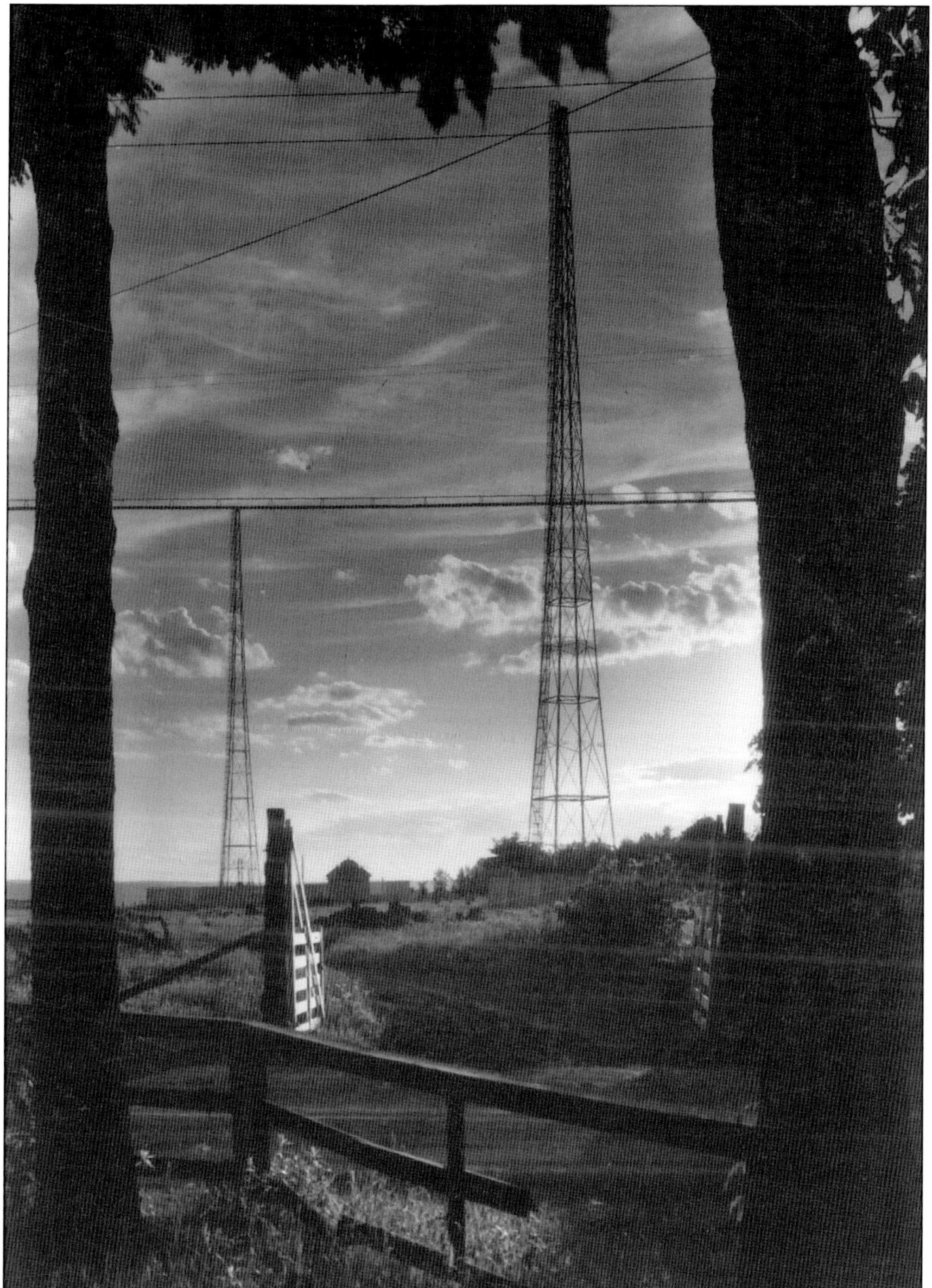

In order to increase the range of its signal, WTIC built a new transmitter facility on Deercliff Road in Avon with a 50,000-watt transmitter in 1929. In this photograph are the original Avon towers, which supported a T-cage antenna. The foundations of these towers are still visible at the site today. (Courtesy of CBS Radio Inc.)

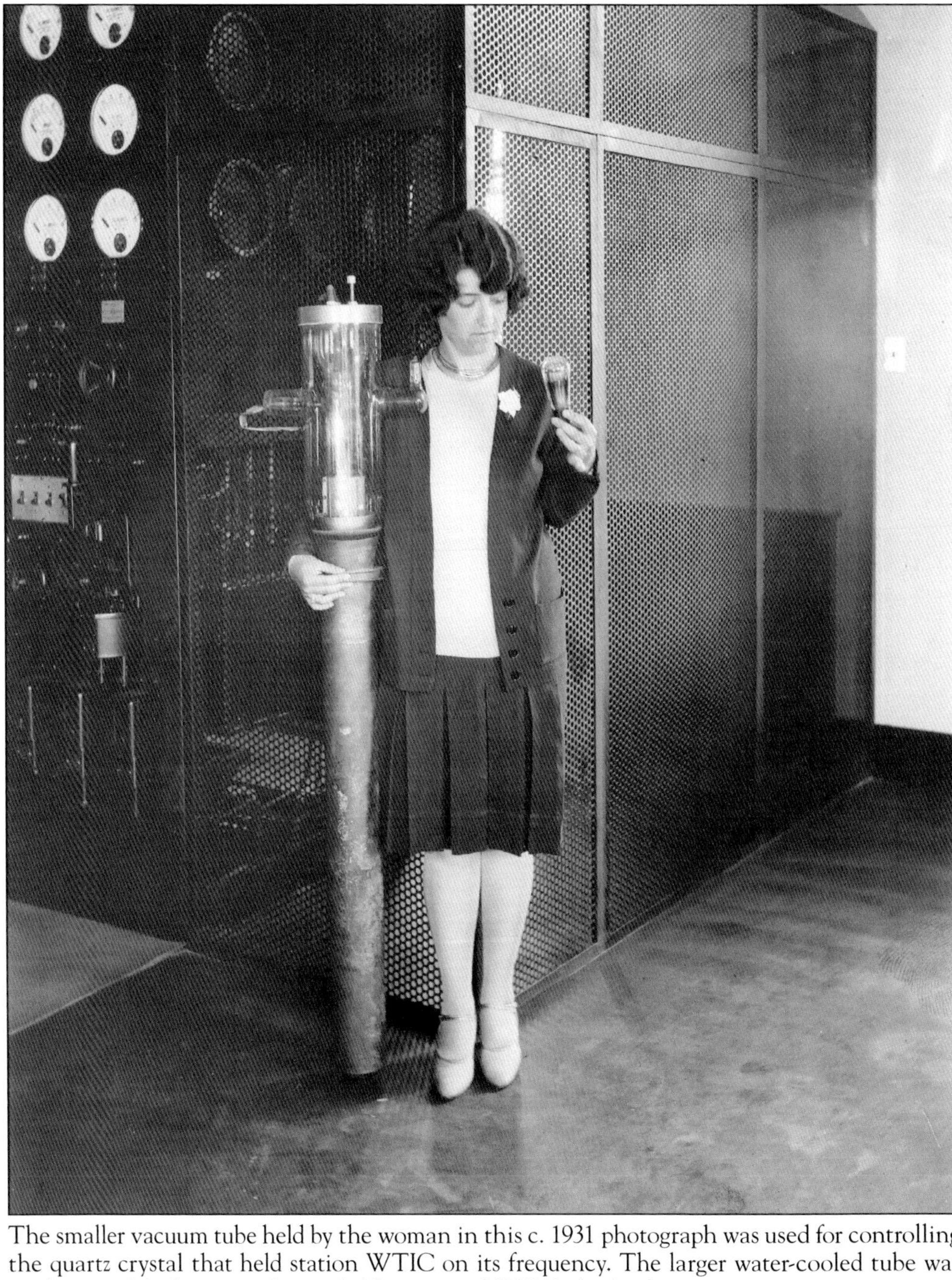

The smaller vacuum tube held by the woman in this c. 1931 photograph was used for controlling the quartz crystal that held station WTIC on its frequency. The larger water-cooled tube was used to amplify the station's signal. (Courtesy of CBS Radio Inc.)

*Two*

# THE 1930S

The 1930s was an exciting decade in radio. The technology of both the transmitters at the station end and the receiving sets at the listeners end was getting better, and the decreasing price of receivers allowed more people to own them. Headphone-only sets were being replaced by those with loudspeakers, allowing entire families to listen at the same time, which helped specific programs generate loyal followings.

During the Depression, listenership increased as people began to depend on radio to uplift them during the major economic crisis. President Roosevelt's "fireside chats," the first presidential use of radio on a regular basis, helped bolster the public's confidence during trying times.

Numerous radio networks provided an endless stream of high-quality programming to Hartford stations. Programs offered variety, comedy, drama, soap operas, quiz shows, and live music and included big-name actors and performers. Advertisers had a significant amount of control over broadcast content, often determining who got hired and fired, even at the national network level. An ever-increasing number of stations drew a growing number of listeners. Radio broadcasting became big business.

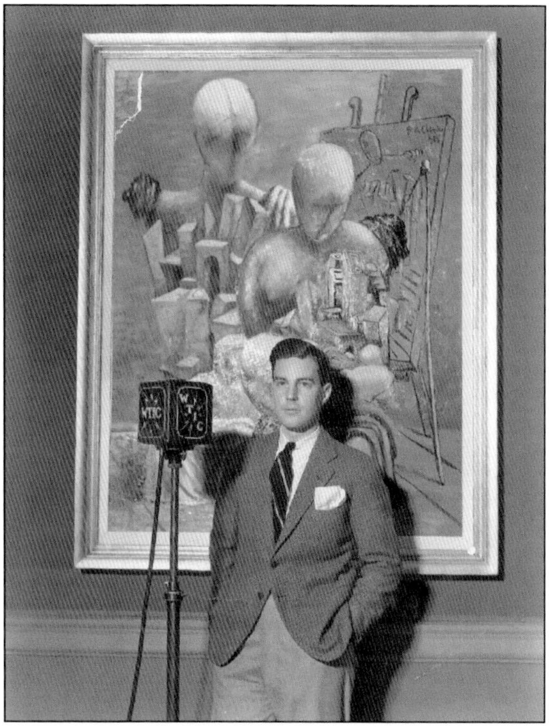

In this photograph, Wadsworth Atheneum director Chick Austin is standing in front of a famous painting by Giorgio de Chirico called *La Famille du peintre* (*The Painter's Family*). The event was a live WTIC broadcast on November 15, 1931, from the Gallery of the Athenaeum to celebrate the opening of the exhibition *Newer Super-Realism*, which was the first surrealist exhibition in any museum. (Courtesy of CBS Radio Inc.)

The Ilima Islanders with Mike Hanapi (seated left) began a series of programs in September 1930 that featured the music of their native land, Hawaii. Prior to joining the staff of WTIC, they were featured in many talkies and were members of Vincent Lopez's St. Regis Orchestra. (Courtesy of CBS Radio Inc.)

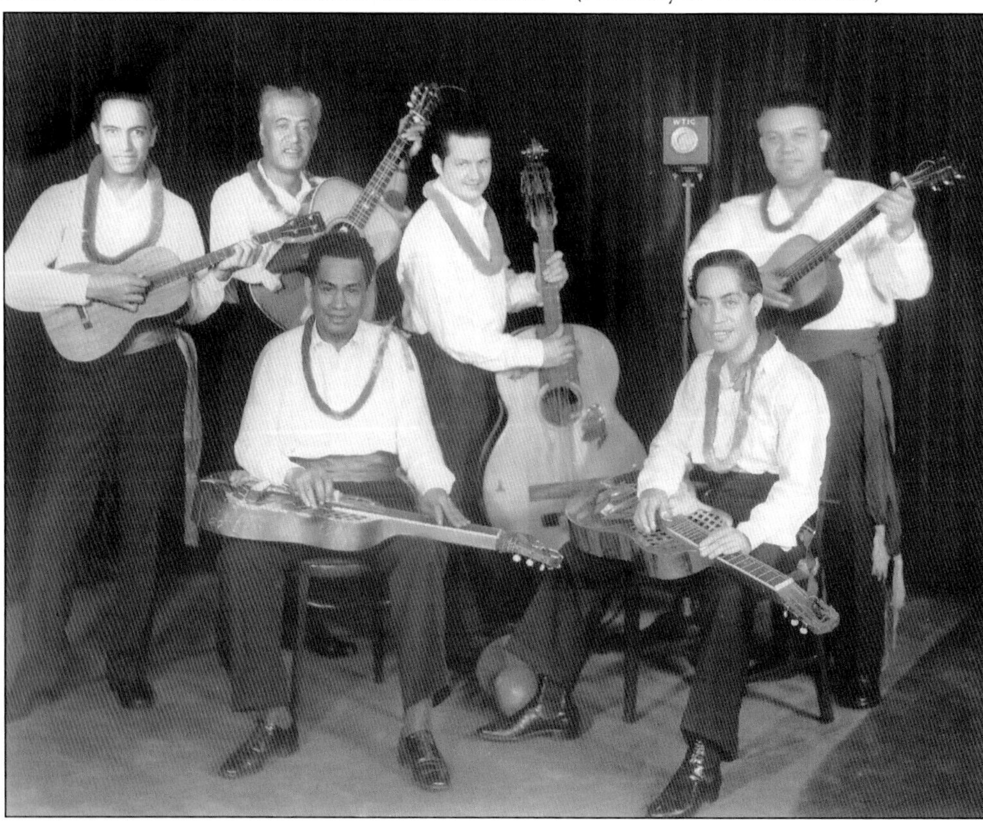

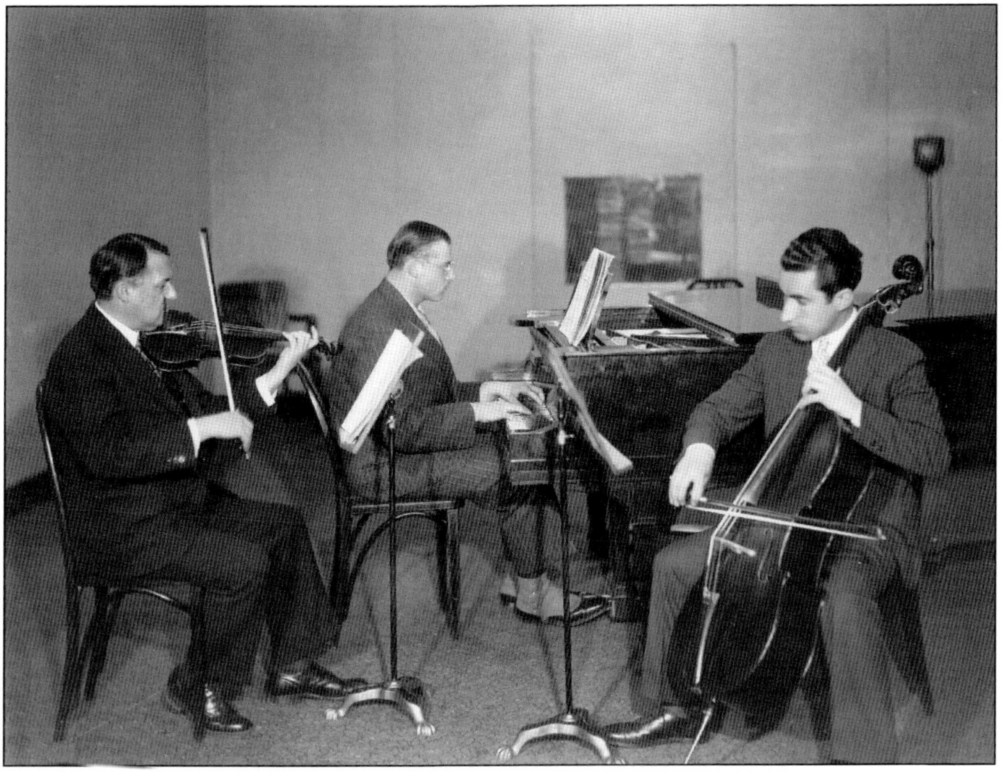

Joseph Blume (right) performs in the WTIC staff trio in this undated photograph. Early stations had musicians on staff full-time, and large stations, such as WTIC, had complete symphony orchestras along with a number of smaller musical ensembles, such as this one. (Courtesy of Daniel Blume.)

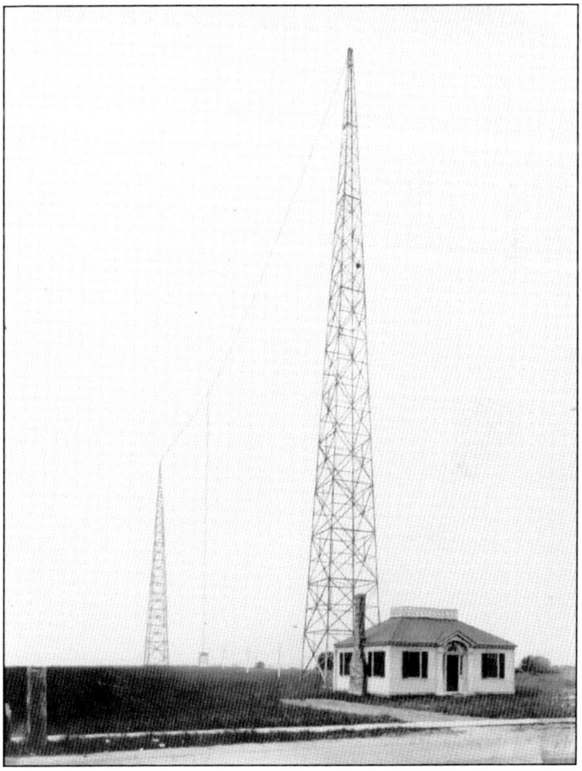

WDRC's new Bloomfield transmitter site is pictured in the early 1930s. WDRC moved to Hartford in 1930, acquiring several acres of land at 783 Blue Hills Avenue from G.J. Maher for the site. The cost to build the new facilities reportedly exceeded $50,000. The station still occupies the site, which was renumbered by the town as 869 Blue Hills Avenue. (Courtesy of WDRC.)

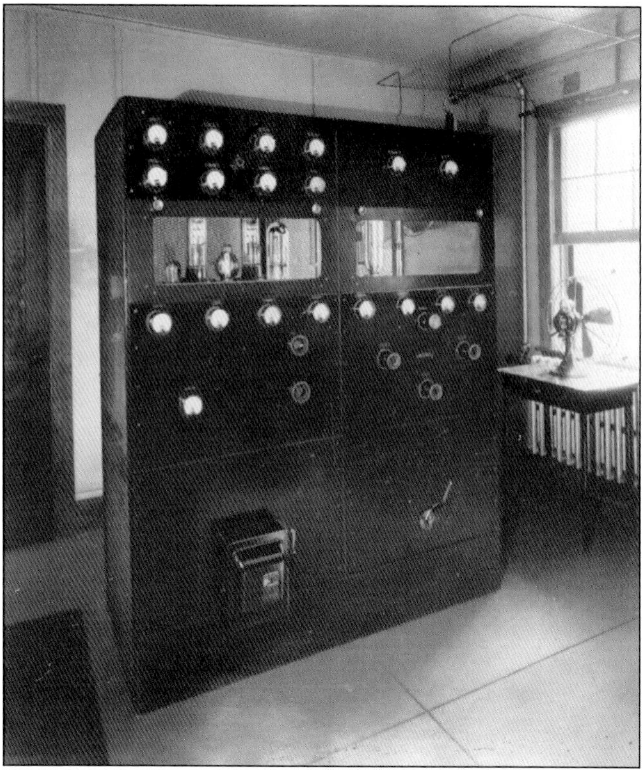

WDRC's first Hartford transmitter is seen in this 1930 photograph. It operated with 500 watts of power from the station's Bloomfield transmitter site. During this period, the studios were located on the third floor of the Corning Building at 11 Asylum Street downtown. (Courtesy of WDRC.)

One of the two large studios for WTIC was at 26 Grove Street in Hartford. A skilled operator was located in a room behind the soundproof window on the left and able to control the broadcasts. This 1929 picture shows a studio that had recently been enlarged. (Courtesy of CBS Radio Inc.)

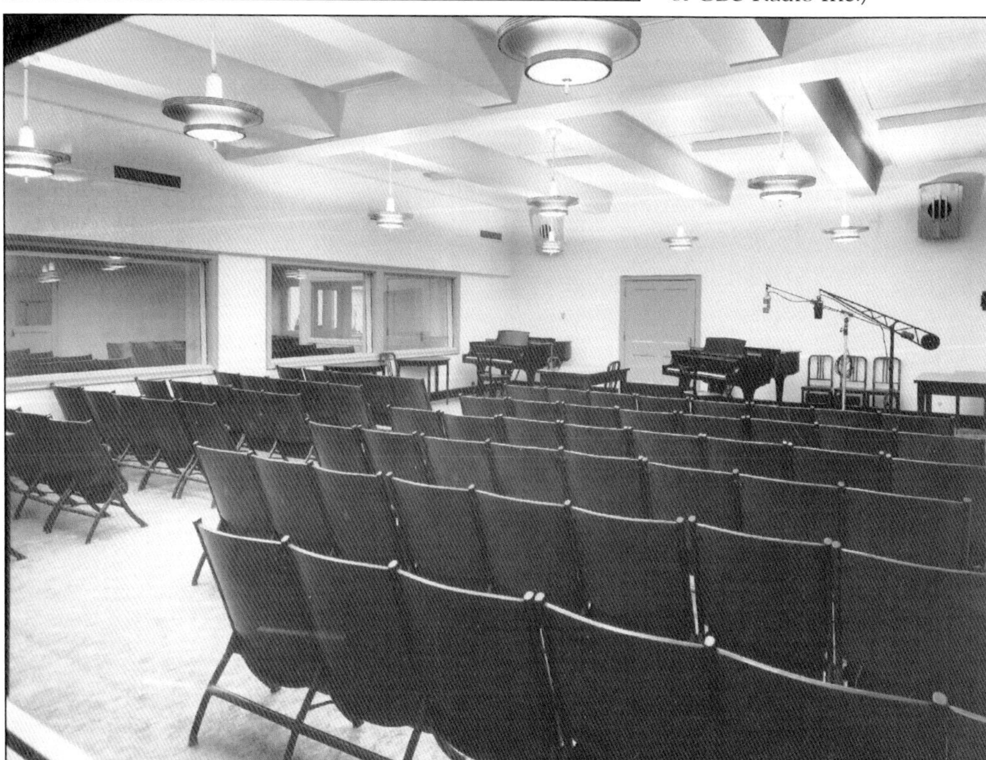

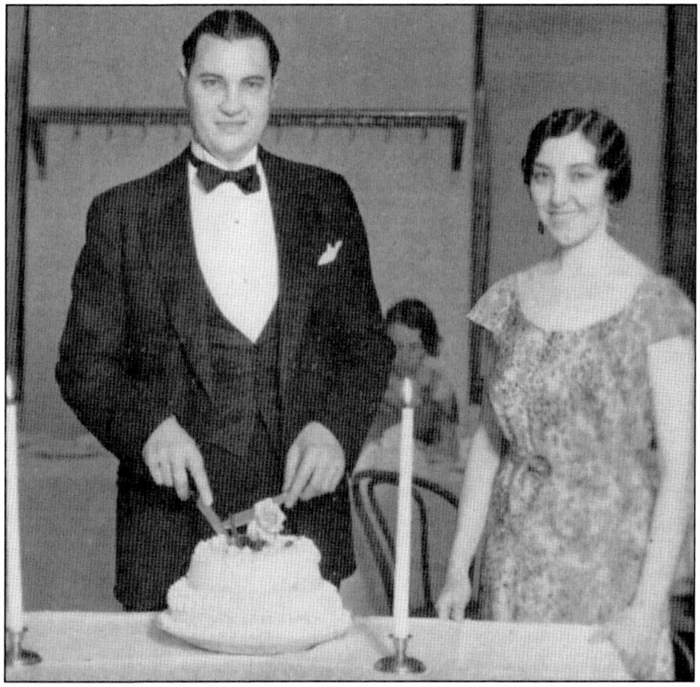

Paul W. Morency, general manager of WTIC, cuts the first slice from the WTIC birthday cake in 1931. Florrine Bishop Bowering, director of *The Mixing Bowl* and maker of the cake, presides over the ceremony. (Courtesy of CBS Radio Inc.)

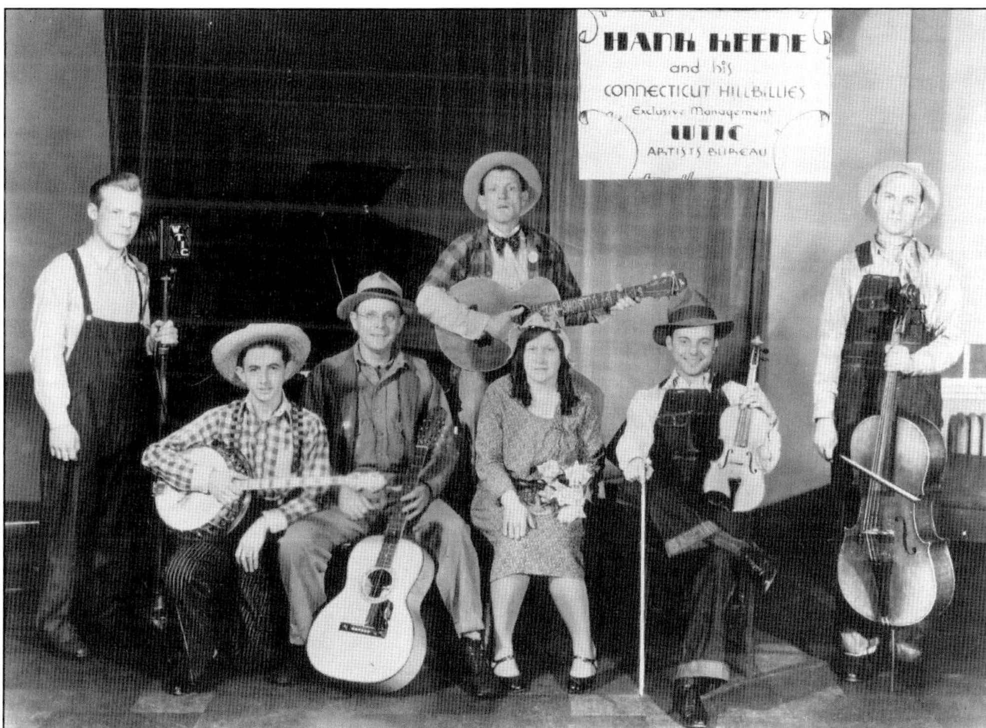


Hank Keene (at the microphone on the left) and his Connecticut Hillbillies were featured in over 125 WTIC radio broadcasts in the early 1930s. Their program was so popular that 6,000 fan letters were reportedly received in the first year from listeners throughout New England. (Courtesy of CBS Radio Inc.)

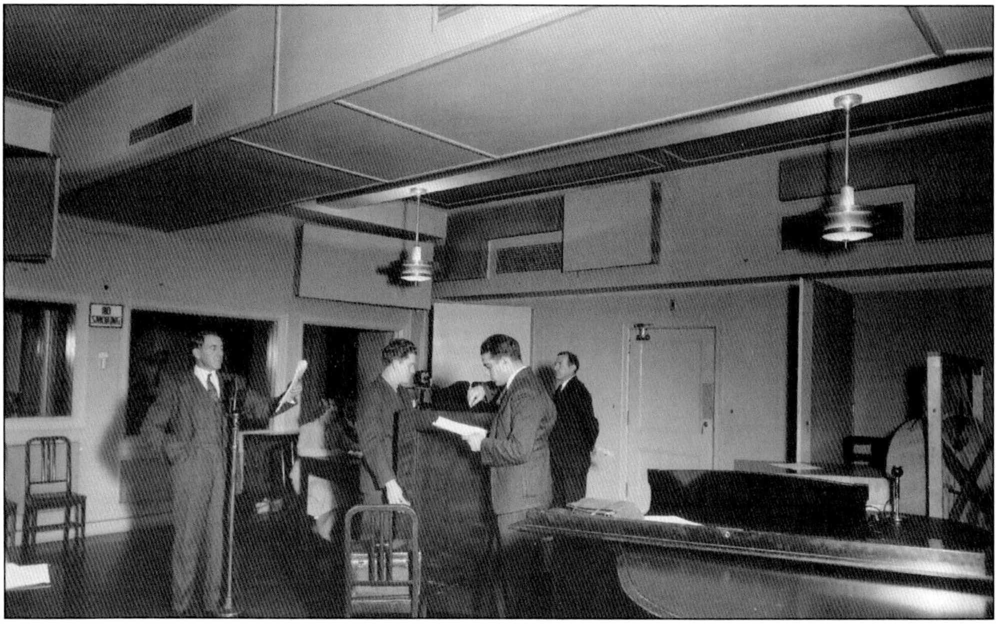

Pictured is the *WTIC Playhouse* program, which was on the air from WTIC's old Studio C at 26 Grove Street in Hartford. Shown from left to right are Guy Hedlund (at microphone), Gertrude Warner, Michael "Eddie" O'Shea, Ralph Klein (handling live sound effects), and Ed Begley. (Courtesy of CBS Radio Inc.)

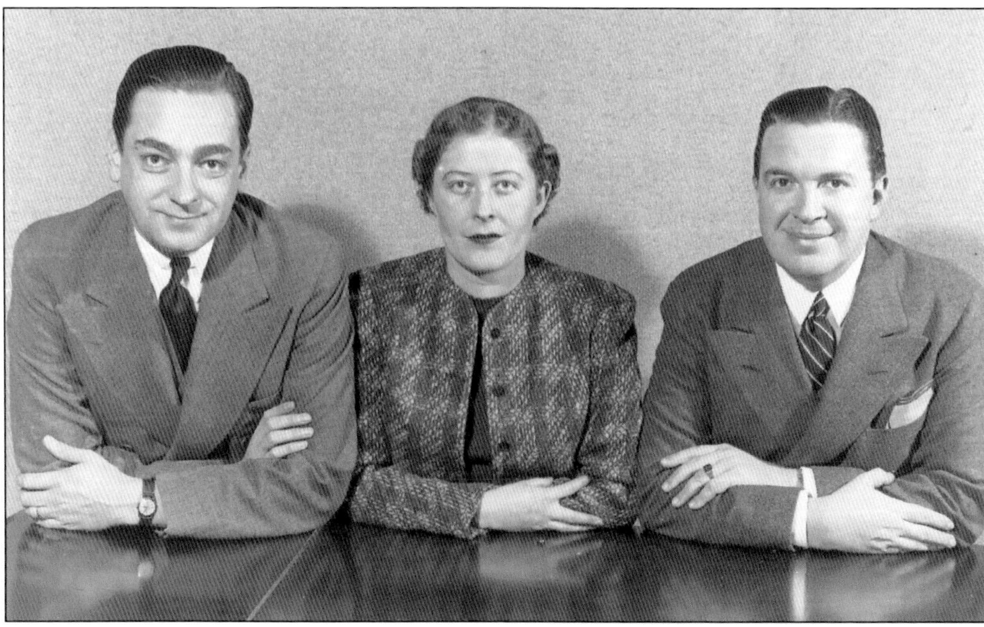

On May 29, 1933, *The Wrightville Daily Clarion*, which would become one of WTIC's most popular dramatic programs, took to the air for the first time. Broadcast nightly at 6:00 p.m., the rural program featured country characters who got themselves in and out of folksy situations. The editor of the *Wrightville Clarion* was played by Paul Lucas (left). Sister Janey, who reconciled many a humorous difference between characters, was played by Eunice Greenwood (center). The man on the right is Fred Wade. (Courtesy of CBS Radio Inc.)

On December 6, 1935, WDRC celebrated its anniversary by announcing the leasing of the entire 16th floor of the Hartford-Connecticut Trust Building at 750 Main Street downtown. The station would call this building home twice, once in the 1930s and again in the 1960s. (Courtesy of WDRC.)

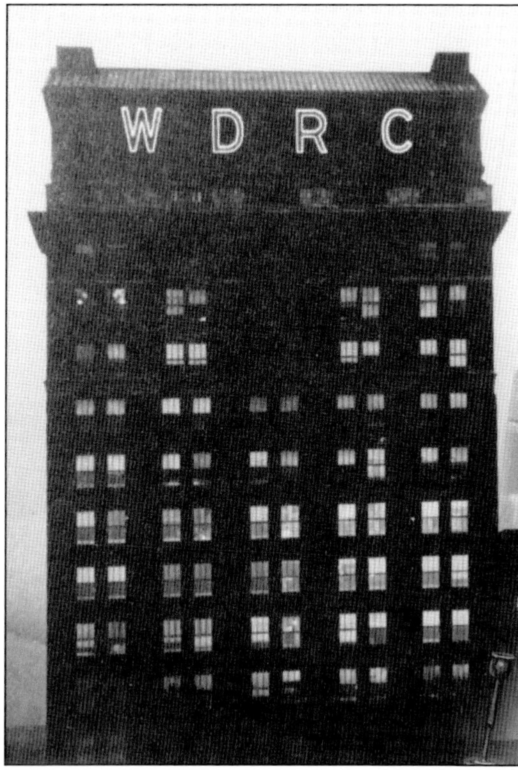


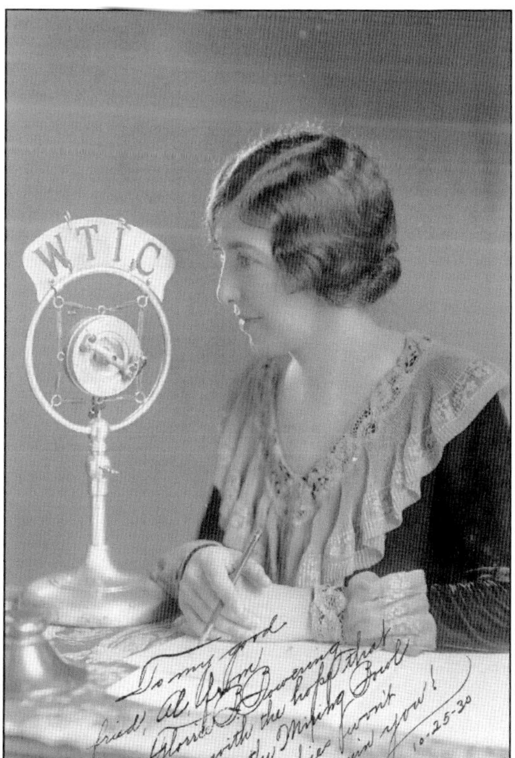


Florrine Bishop Bowering directed WTIC's cooking school of the air, *The Mixing Bowl*. Beginning in the fall of 1930, she broadcast three half-hour programs weekly. Bowering would reportedly test her recipes on the staff in a specially constructed kitchen on the floor above the studios in the Travelers Grove Street building. (Courtesy of CBS Radio Inc.)

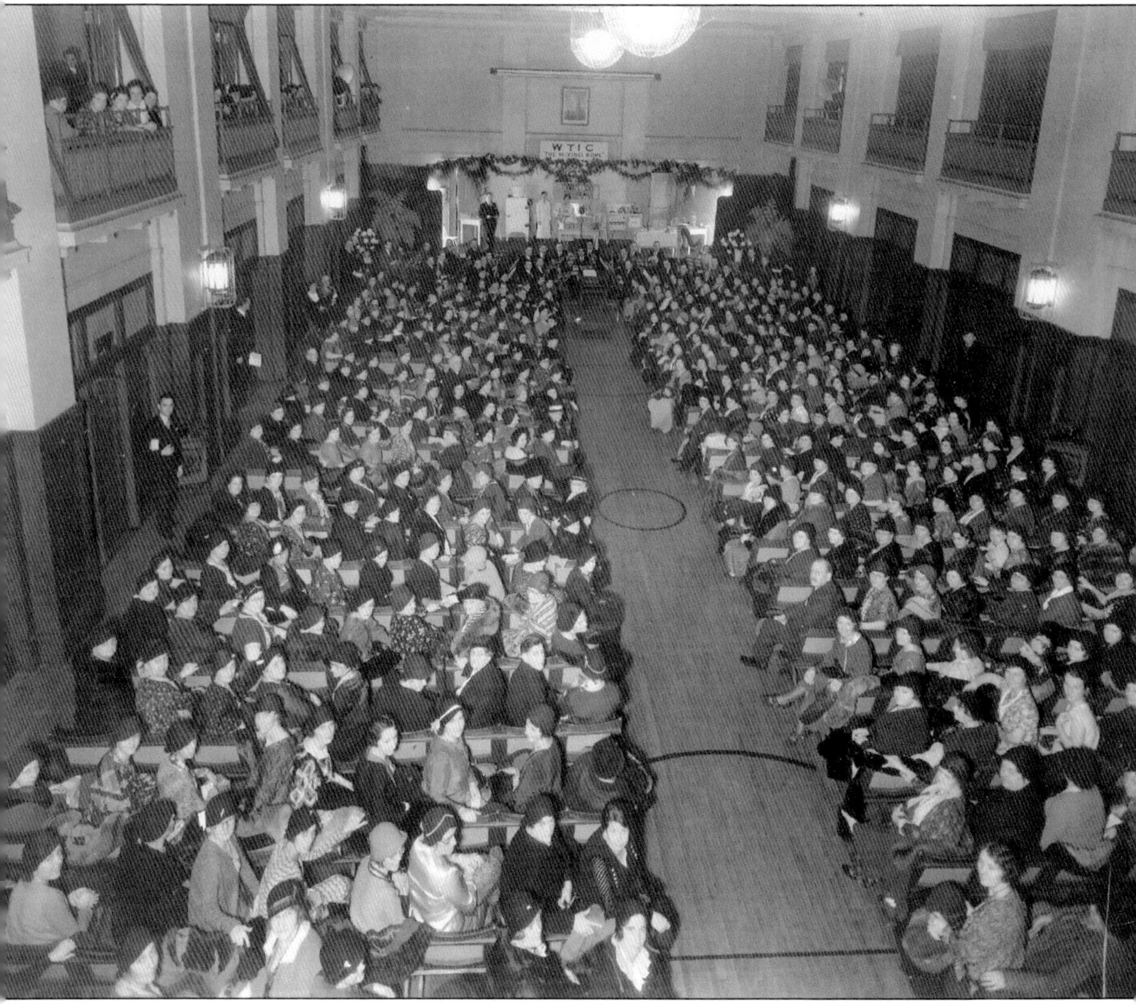


The popularity of Florrine Bishop Bowering's *Mixing Bowl* cooking program on WTIC is apparent by the large turnout for this remote broadcast. She directed and starred in the program, which aired three times a week on the Hartford station. (Courtesy of CBS Radio Inc.)

This is a 1935 photograph of the WDRC control room on the third floor of the Corning Building at 11 Asylum Street in Hartford. Decades later, the same building would become home to WCCC, which occupied the fifth floor from about 1966 to 1980. (Courtesy of WDRC.)

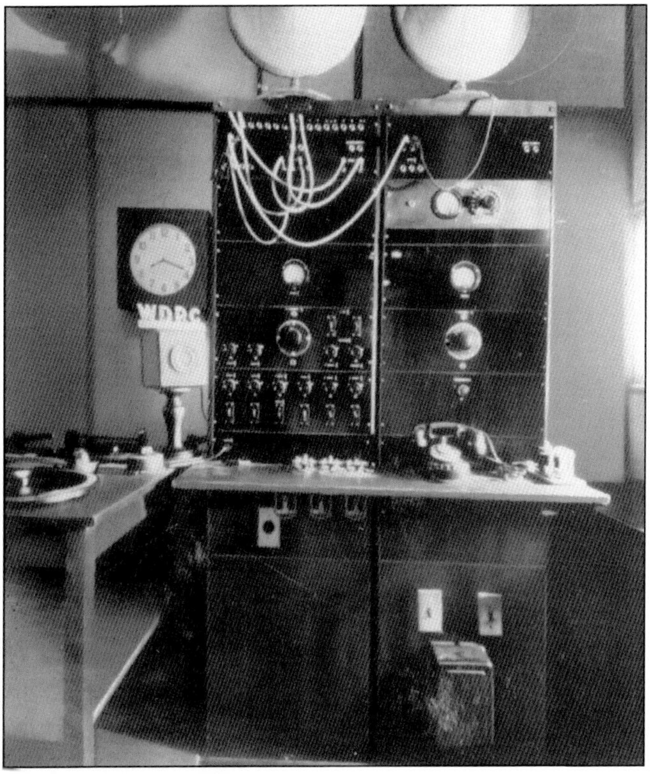


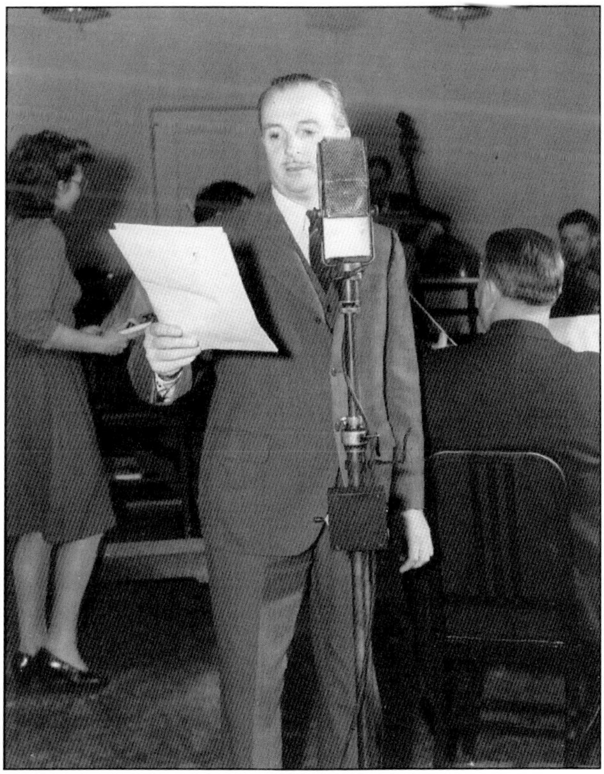

The rich baritone voice of Bernard L "Bunny" Mullins was one of the most listened-to voices in the 1930, 1940s, and 1950s on WTIC. At one time or another, he was an integral part of every important program on the station. Dramas, musical shows, special events, and commentaries—whatever the program, it took on a touch of class when Bernard Mullins had a role in it. (Courtesy of CBS Radio Inc.)

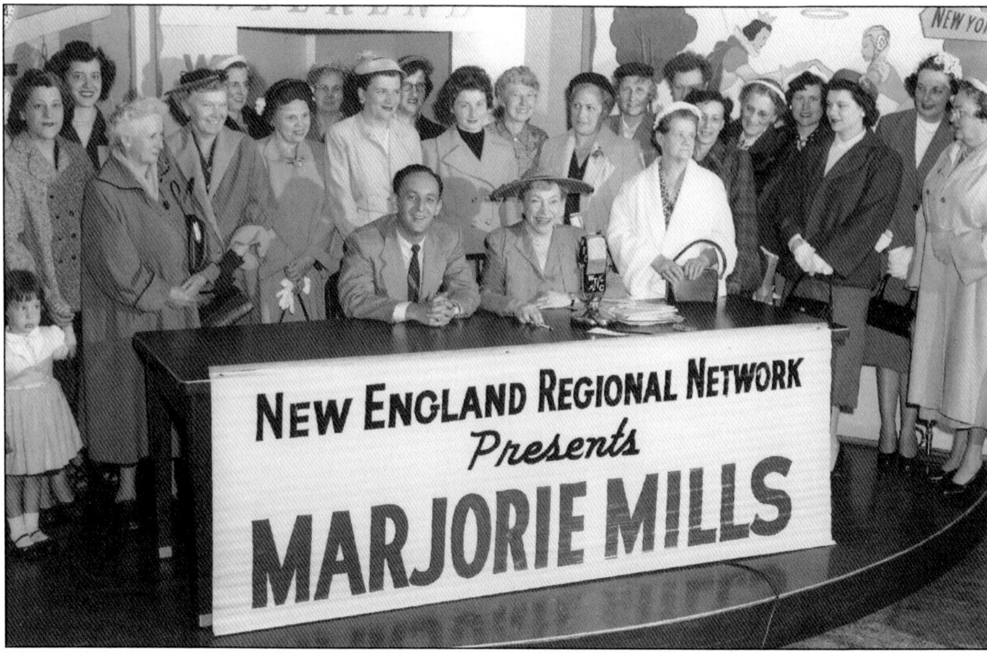


Throughout the 1940s and 1950s, *The Marjorie Mills Hour* was a popular program that could be heard on WTIC every weekday afternoon via the New England Regional Network. Here, Marge (seated, right), surrounded by some of her fans, visits the WTIC studios. WTIC's Floyd Richard (seated, left) handled the announcing chores. (Courtesy of CBS Radio Inc.)

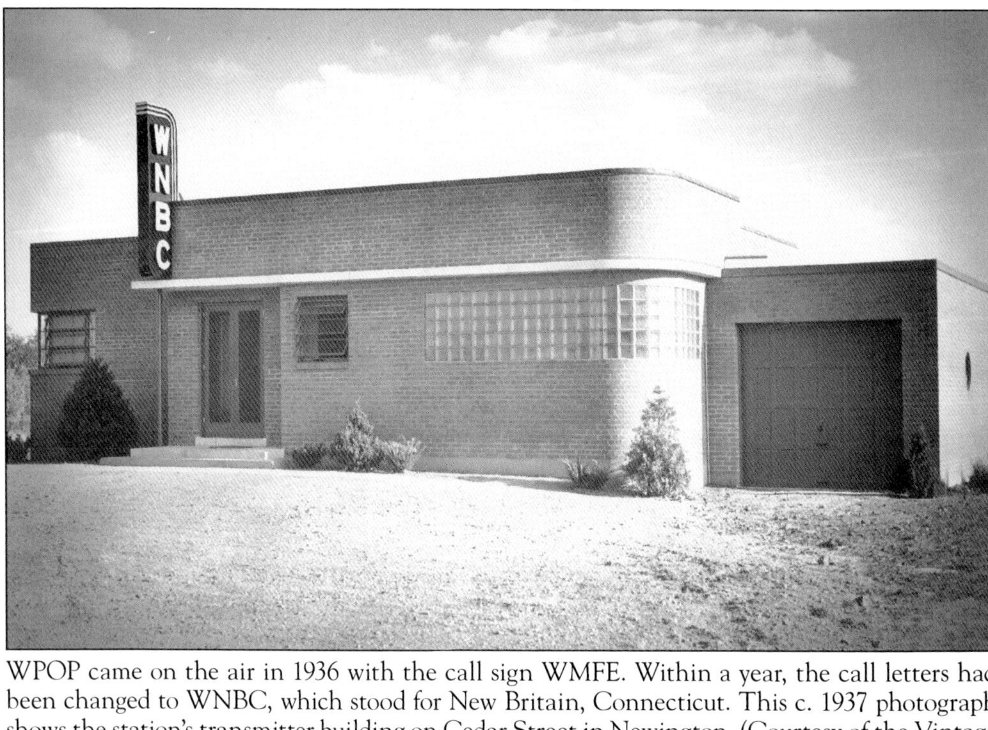


WPOP came on the air in 1936 with the call sign WMFE. Within a year, the call letters had been changed to WNBC, which stood for New Britain, Connecticut. This c. 1937 photograph shows the station's transmitter building on Cedar Street in Newington. (Courtesy of the Vintage Radio and Communications Museum of Connecticut.)

Nearly 1,000 letters surround Mona Lee of the Players Troupe in response to a single question asked of the radio audience by WTIC's Guy Hedlund. The question asked what types of plays the listeners preferred. No gifts, souvenirs, or free samples were offered. (Courtesy of CBS Radio Inc.)

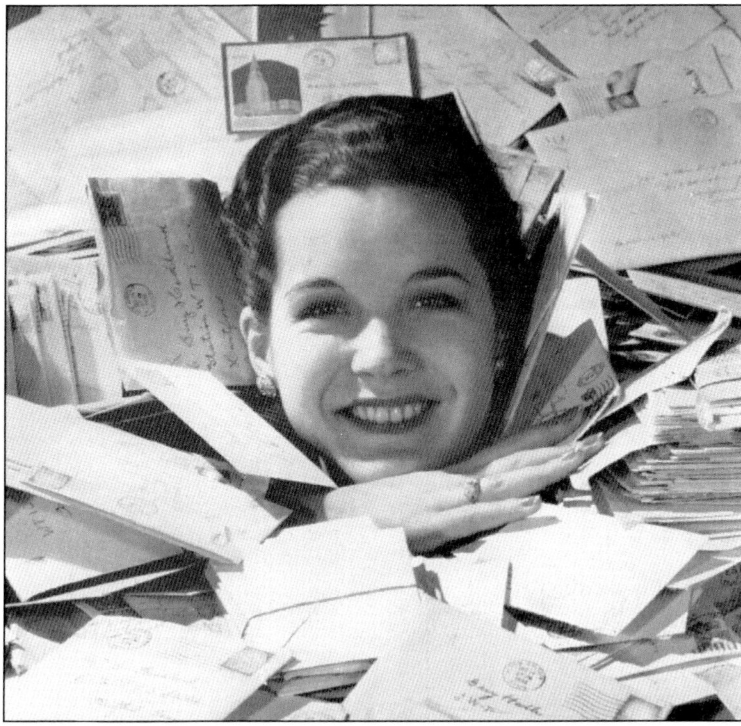

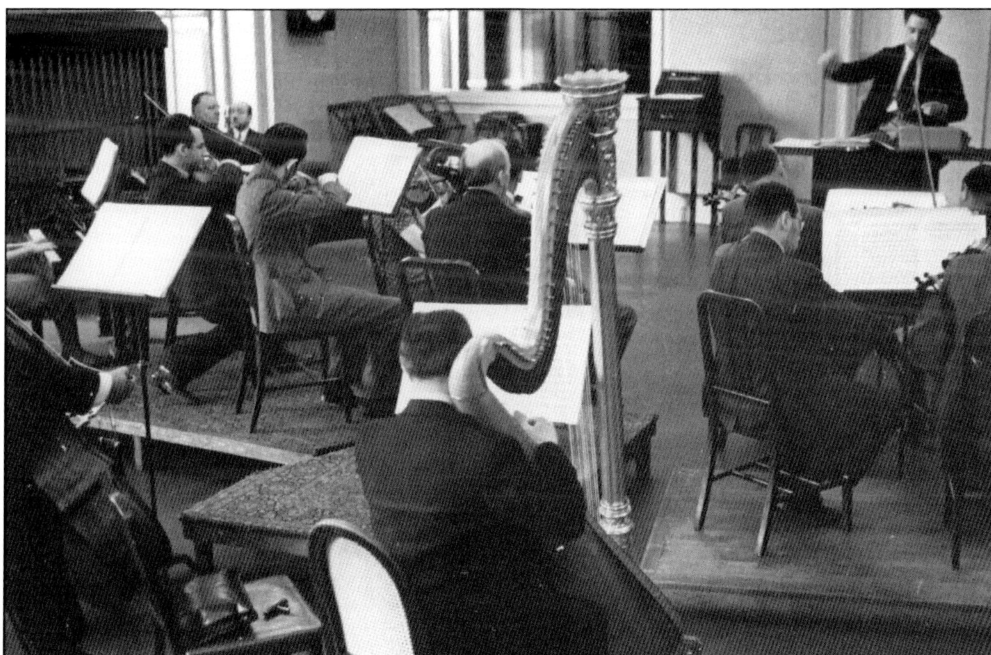

Moshe Paranov, who later went on to help found the Hartt School of Music at the University of Hartford, regularly conducted live music on WTIC. Many of the programs he conducted were heard nationwide on the NBC radio network, including the broadcast of *Encores*. Paranov is seen here conducting the WTIC string orchestra in Studio D for a program heard on Saturday mornings in the mid-1930s. (Courtesy of CBS Radio Inc.)

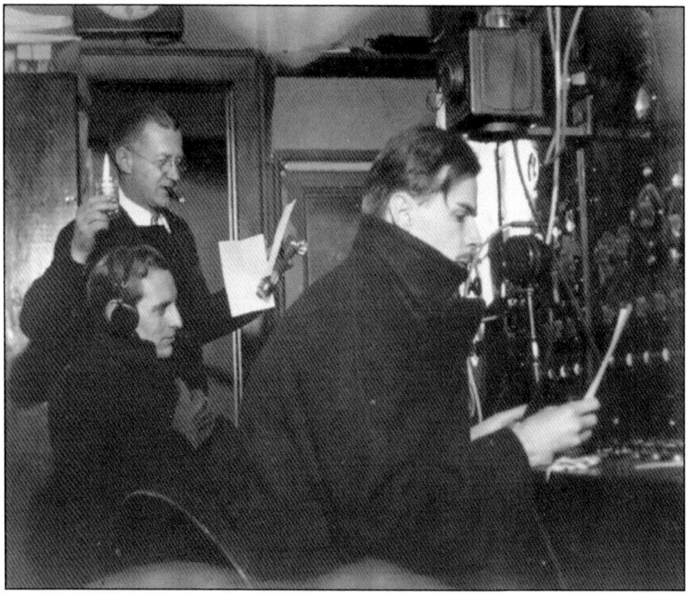

Radio has always had an important role keeping the public informed during emergencies. During the flood of 1936, people turned to radio as their only source of real-time information. In this image, WDRC announcers, from left to right, Sterling V. Couch, Ray Barrett (with headphones), and Harvey Olson report news bulletins by candle- and flashlight during the disaster. (Courtesy of WDRC.)

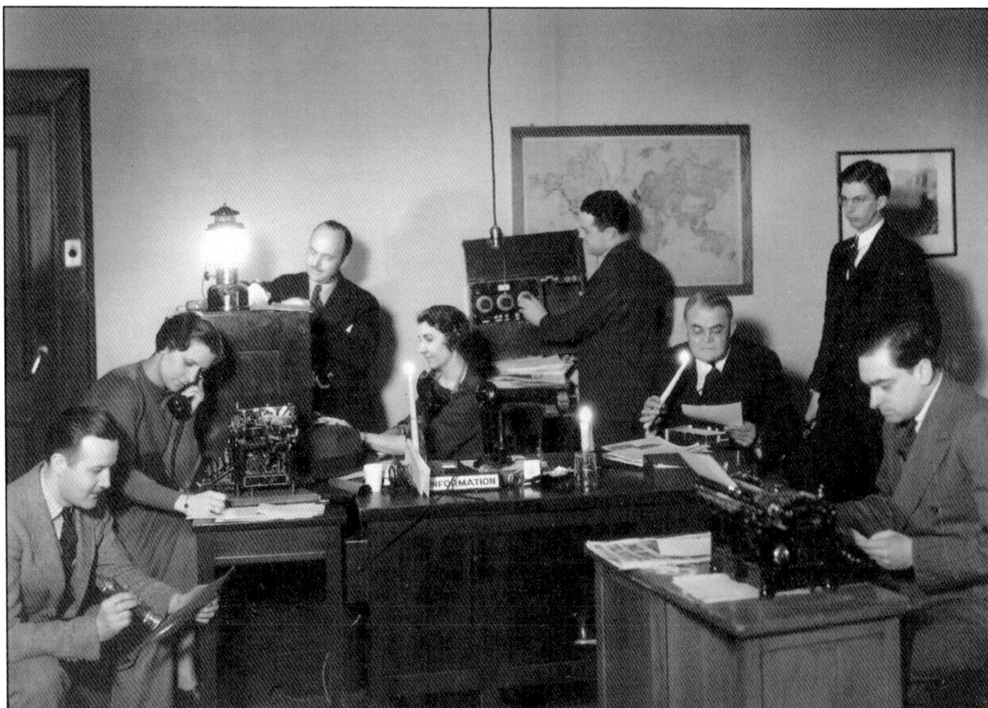

Without power for lighting during the devastating flood of 1936, WTIC's staff operated by gaslight, candlelight, and flashlight. Pictured are, from left to right, announcer George Bowe, secretary Mary Anderson, engineer Jack Murphy, receptionist Annette Stevens, engineer Ed Kingsley (at the controls), manager James F. Clancy, engineer Carl Noyes, and production manager Paul Lucas. WTIC was the source for important flood information and worked with municipal authorities as well as service agencies such as the Red Cross to aid victims of the flood. (Courtesy of CBS Radio Inc.)

Prizefighter Jack Dempsey, pictured at WTIC around 1933, was the boxing heavyweight champion of the world from July 4, 1919, to September 23, 1926. His rematch with Gene Tunney in 1927 produced the biggest gate to that date at a prizefight—more than $2.6 million. (Courtesy of CBS Radio Inc.)

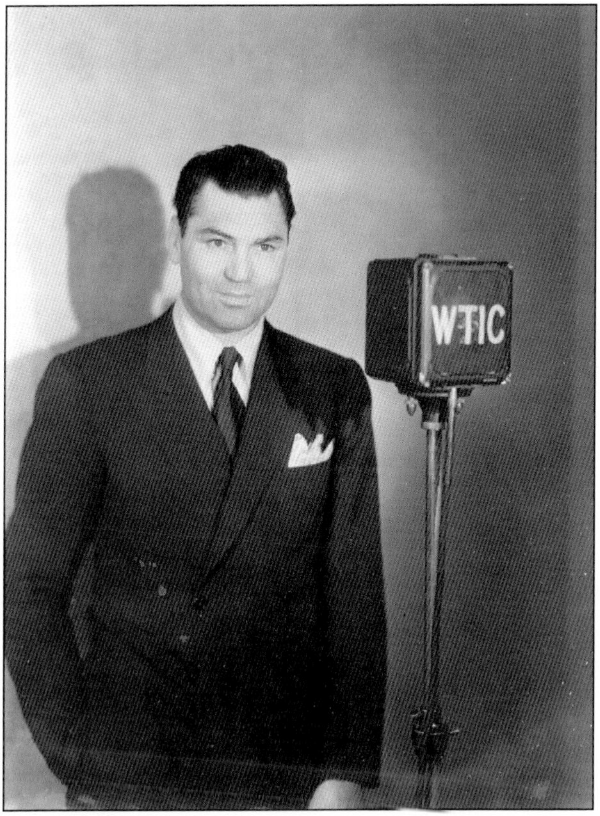


Prior to the invention of tape recording, most sound effects heard on the radio were produced live by specially trained operators. In this photograph, an unidentified WTIC sound effects man works with the some of the tools of his trade. (Courtesy of CBS Radio Inc.)

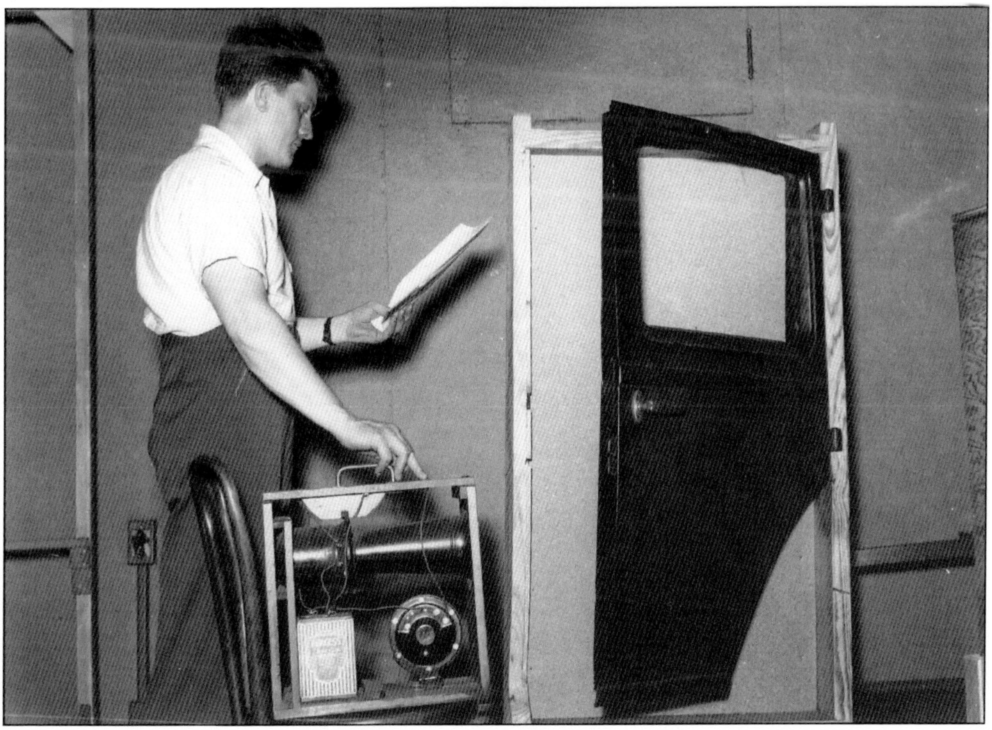

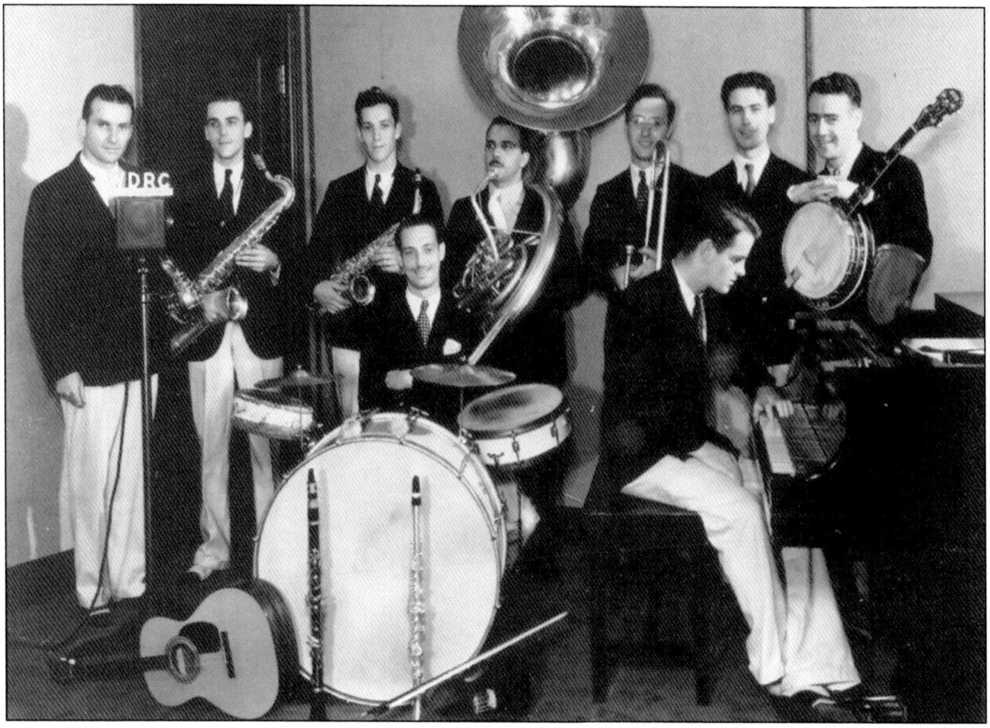


Band members pause for a snapshot before a live broadcast on WDRC around 1936. That same year, the station moved from the third floor of the Corning Building at 11 Asylum Street to the top floor of 750 Main Street. (Courtesy of WDRC.)

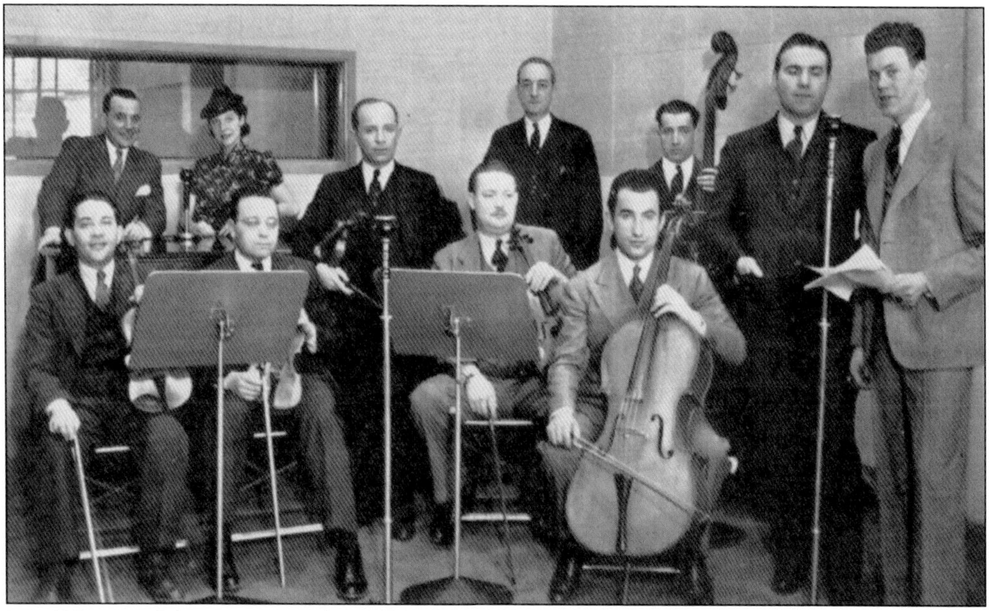

In 1937, one of the more popular WDRC programs was *Sunday Call*, which featured a musical ensemble conducted by Joseph Blume. The music was performed live from studios at 750 Main Street in Hartford. The man and woman standing in the upper left handled the dramatic commercials. (Courtesy of Daniel Blume.)

Andre Schenker, associate professor of history at the University of Connecticut, became WTIC's foreign affairs analyst in 1935. Professor Schenker kept listeners well informed as to the implications of international developments during the prewar period, World War II, and postwar years. His program, *History in the Headlines*, was heard nightly at 6:15 p.m. (Courtesy of CBS Radio Inc.)

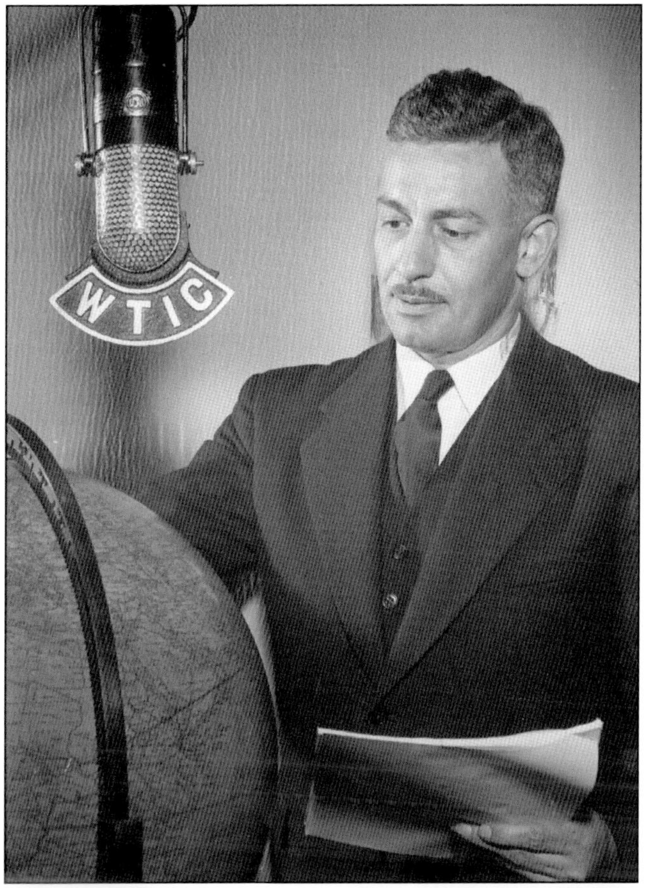


In 1938, WTIC's *Woman's Radio Bazaar* presented a variety of topics of interest to women and featured Gertrude Warner as hostess. In this photograph, Bud Rainey, facing Gertrude, serves as the emcee, who occasionally sang and recited an original piece of poetry. Seated to the left is announcer Bernard Mullins. To the right, behind the control room glass, are Ben Hawthorne and an engineer. (Courtesy of CBS Radio Inc.)

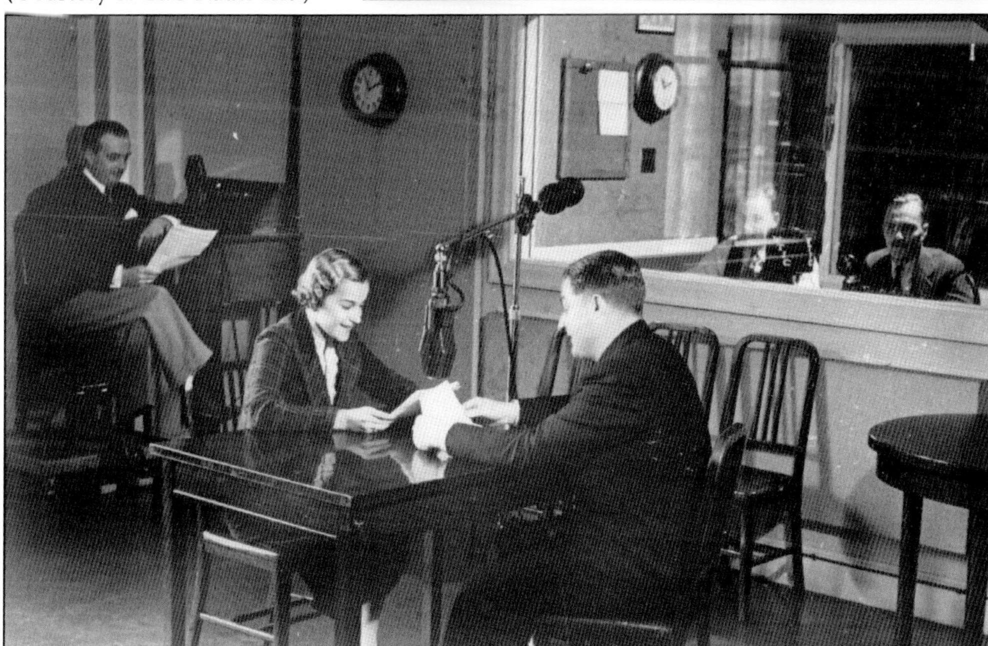

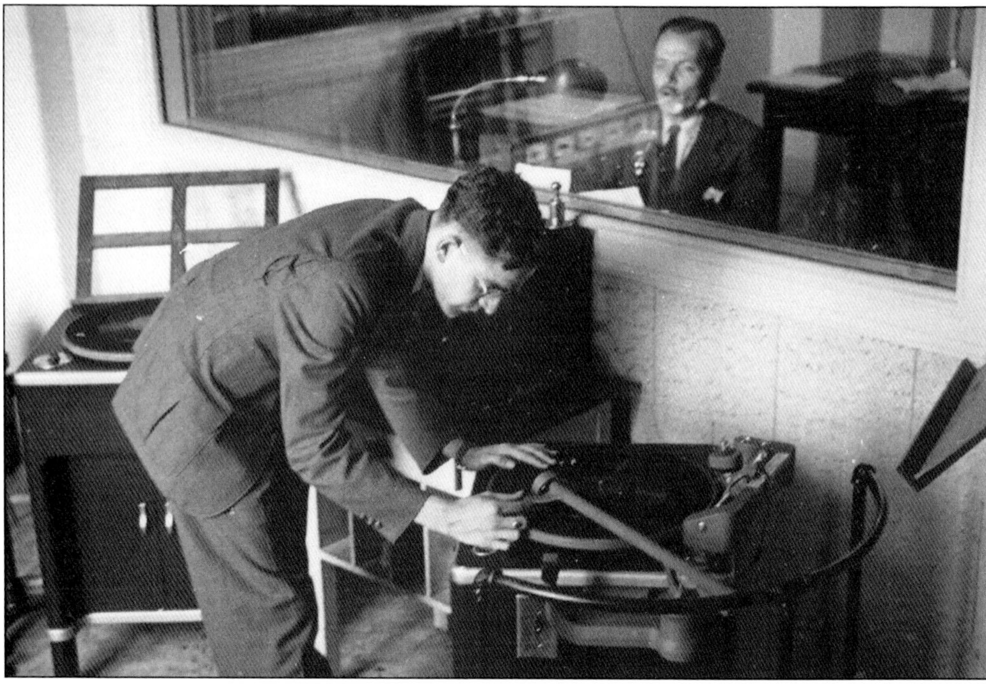

Bob Steele's predecessor Ben Hawthorne hosted WTIC's *Morning Watch* from 1934 to 1942 when he went into the Air Force. In this photograph, Ben is at the microphone while engineer Fred Edwards cues up a 78 rpm recording. (Courtesy of CBS Radio Inc.)

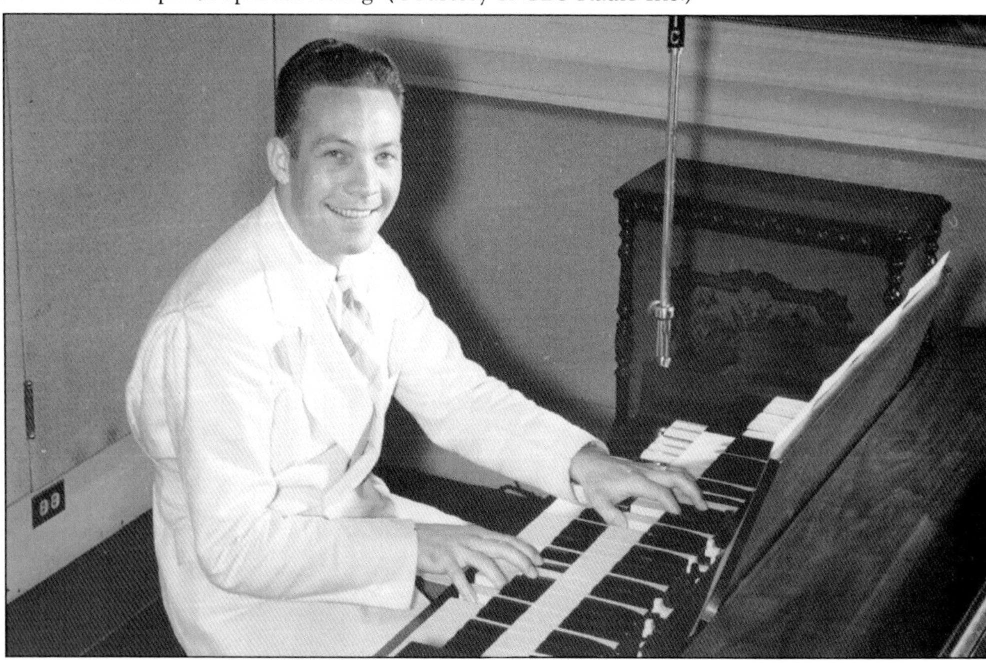

Hal Kolb served as the WTIC staff organist from 1938 until the late 1950s. A gifted musician, Hal created original mood music for all manner of programs, from drama to poetry and dramatic narrations. His daily program, *Medley Time*, featured one pair of hands playing organ, piano, and celesta, another broadcast first on WTIC. (Courtesy of CBS Radio Inc.)

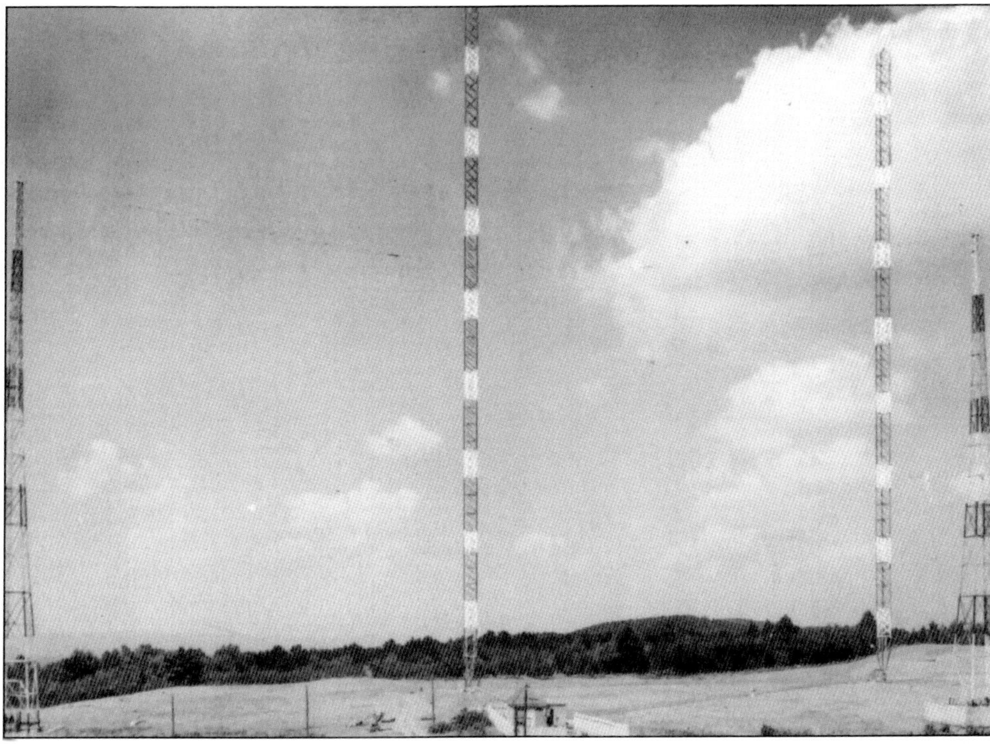

This is a rare photograph of both the original and the newer WTIC towers on Deercliff Road in Avon. In the foreground are the two original towers built in 1929 for WTIC's power increase to 50,000 watts. In the background are the two 1939 towers still in use by the station. (Courtesy of CBS Radio Inc.)

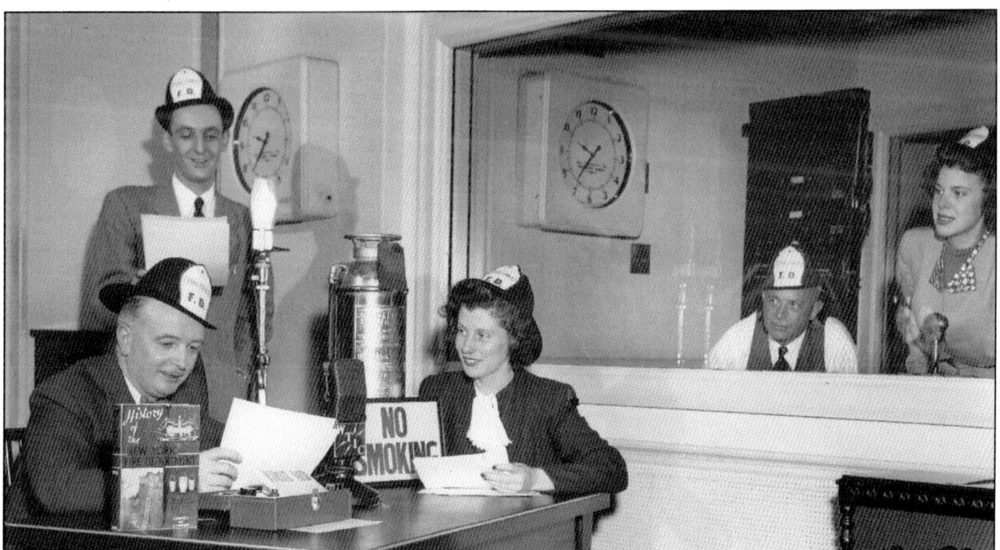


The topic was fire prevention during this broadcast of WTIC's *Radio Bazaar*. From left to right are Bernard Mullins, director of WTIC's public affairs programs; Floyd Richards; Betty Pattee, hostess; and engineer John Murphy in the control room with Inez Hansen. (Courtesy of CBS Radio Inc.)

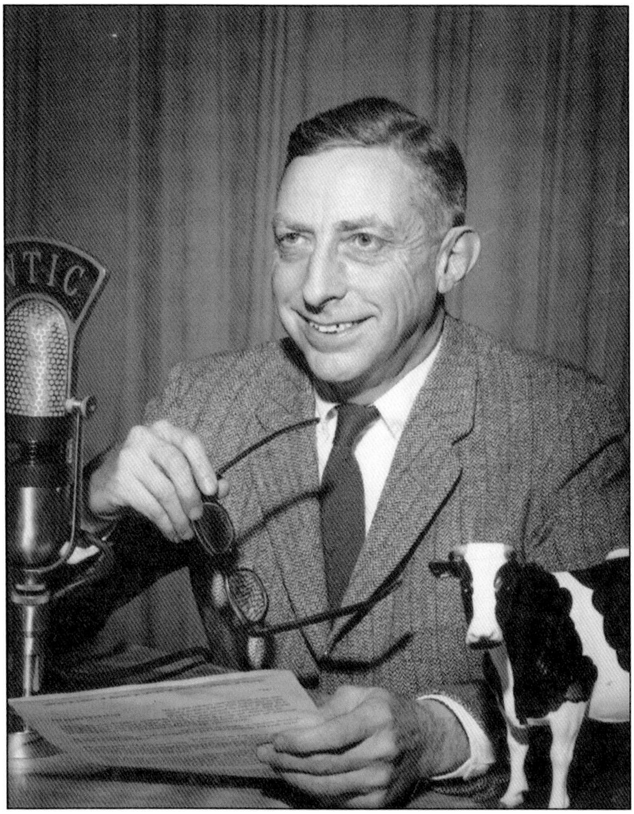

With his colorful Vermont twang in his speech, everybody thought WTIC's Frank Atwood must have been a native of the Green Mountain state. Actually, Frank was born in Granite Falls, Washington, and moved to Vermont as a youngster around 1939. (Courtesy of CBS Radio Inc.)

In this photograph is a collection of bells used by this WTIC announcer to add excitement to a live program. Current-day radio personalities would have this kind of sound effect available via a hard-drive playback system. (Courtesy of CBS Radio Inc.)

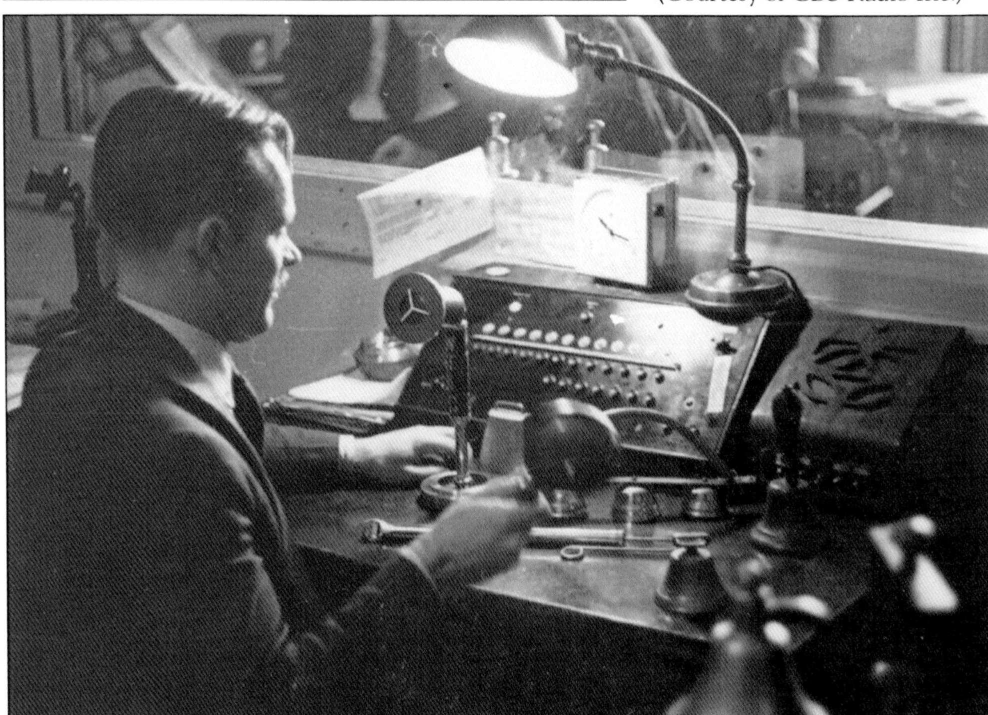

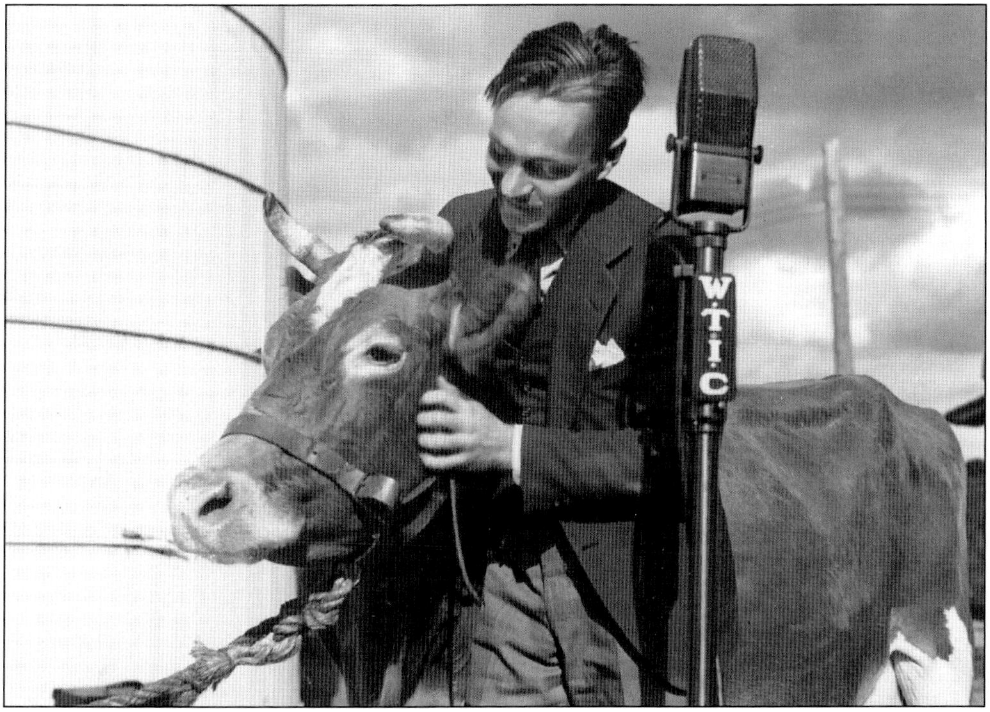


WTIC's morning man, Ben Hawthorne, broadcasts on location with the cohost of the *Morning Watch*, Bessie Bossie, around 1938. The cow represented the station's commitment to farm programming. Bob Steele became the host of the *Morning Watch* after Hawthorne went in the military in 1943. (Courtesy of CBS Radio Inc.)

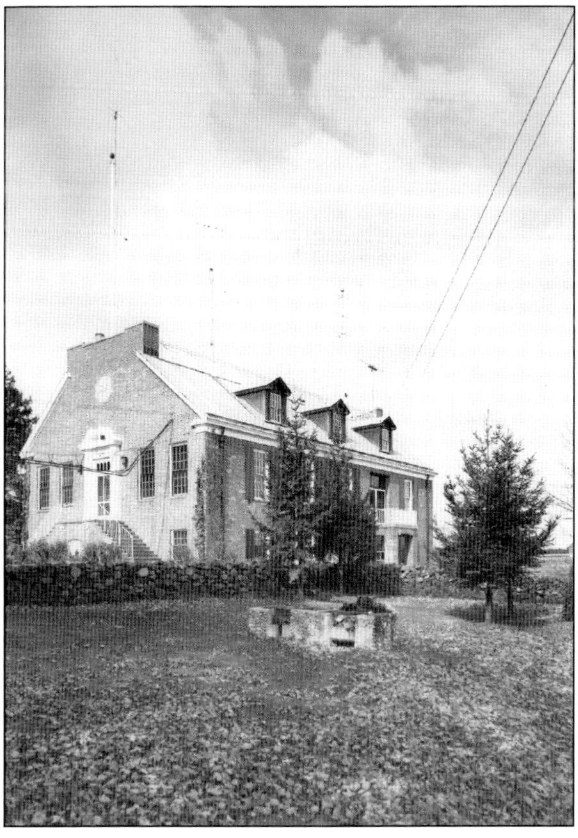

The WTIC transmitter building on Deercliff Road in Avon was reportedly designed to look like a New England mansion. The three-story structure contained the WTIC transmitting equipment, a complete electrical repair shop, and a dormitory for engineers who would get stranded at the site during severe weather. (Courtesy of CBS Radio Inc.)

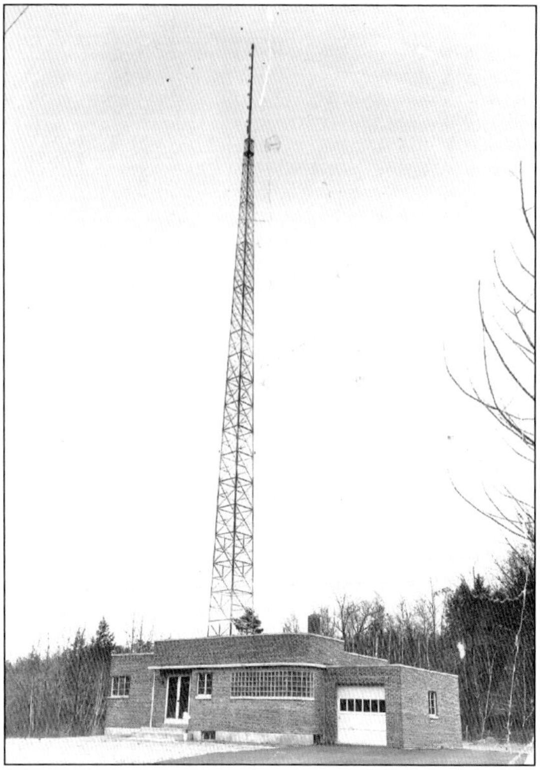

The WKNB-FM transmitter building and tower on Deercliff Road in Avon are pictured around 1939. After the station went off the air, the facility was used for another three decades by WHCT-TV, Hartford's channel 18. (Courtesy of the Connecticut Vintage Radio and Communications Museum.)

In 1939, this Studebaker President coupe was the latest thing in remote units and allowed WTIC to conduct man-on-the-street interviews. This was the same car that, six years later, roamed the streets of Hartford, rebroadcasting sounds of the victory on VJ Day, marking the end of World War II. Studio supervisor Al Jackson is seen testing the shortwave radio in the vehicle used to feed programs back to the studio. (Courtesy of CBS Radio Inc.)

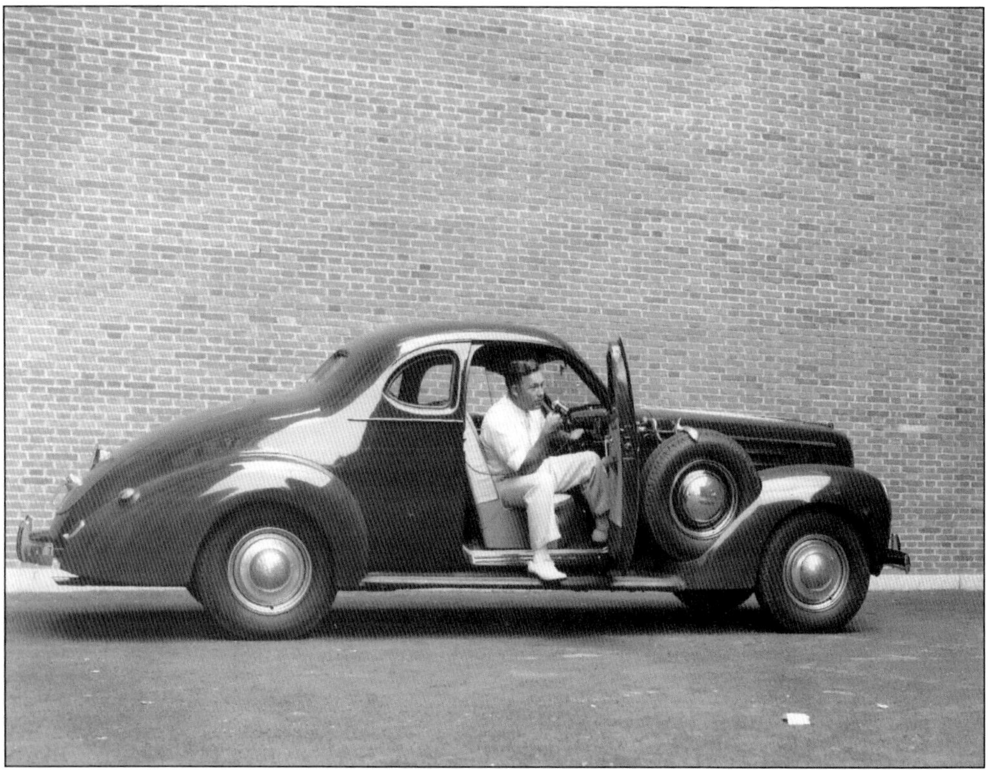

# *Three*

# THE 1940s

During the war years, newspapers and newsreels provided Americans with war news, but the very nature of these two types of media outlets meant that the news was often days, or even weeks, out of date by the time it was delivered stateside. Radio was the only medium at the time that could provide up-to-the-minute news and information about what was going on overseas. In fact, nothing could beat radio's immediacy, and reports from radio reporters at or near the front lines drew huge audiences.

The development of FM radio, invented by Maj. Edwin R. Armstrong in the 1930s, was hampered by the war, which severely slowed its implementation in the states. Nonetheless, Hartford's Franklin Doolittle received one of the first commercial FM licenses in 1940 and put an FM station on the air from Meriden's West Peak; it is still on the air today as WHCN.

The end of the war marked the beginning of the baby boom and an accompanying significant increase in consumer marketing and spending. Advertisers saw radio as the medium for getting the word out about their products to the masses, and this resulted in hundreds of new stations coming on the air in the late 1940s.

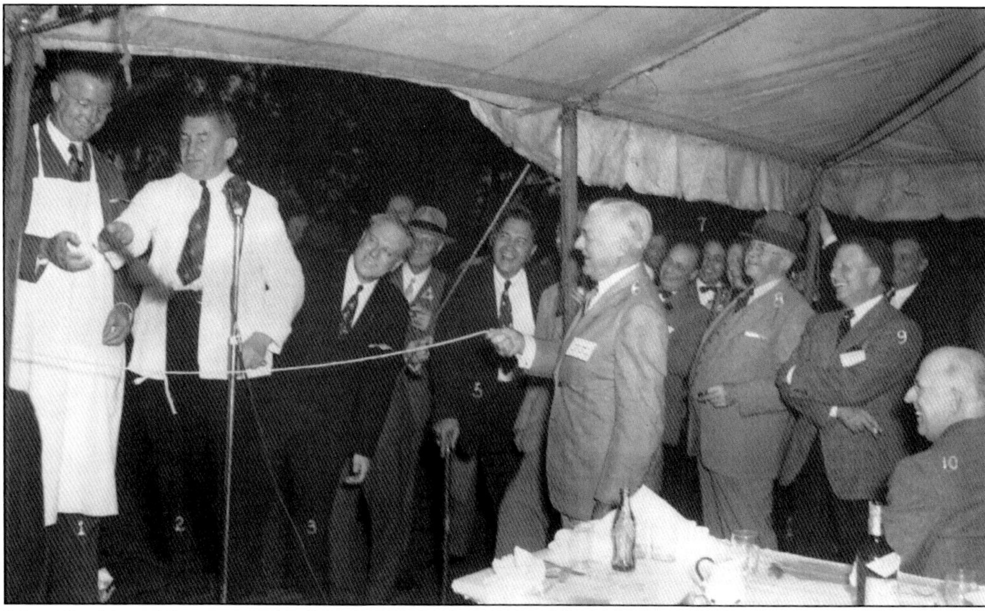

The Heublein Tower overlooking Hartford was used for several years in the late 1940s by the *Hartford Times* station, WTHT-FM. This postcard commemorates the occasion of making the public acquainted with the tower and its future use for radio-frequency modulation and television. From left to right are waiter Alden Mann, Gov. Raymond Baldwin, former governor John H. Trumbull, WTIC president Paul Morency, F. Gannett, and musicians L.F. Dettenborn, F.S. Murphy, and Robert O'Neill. (Courtesy of CBS Radio Inc.)

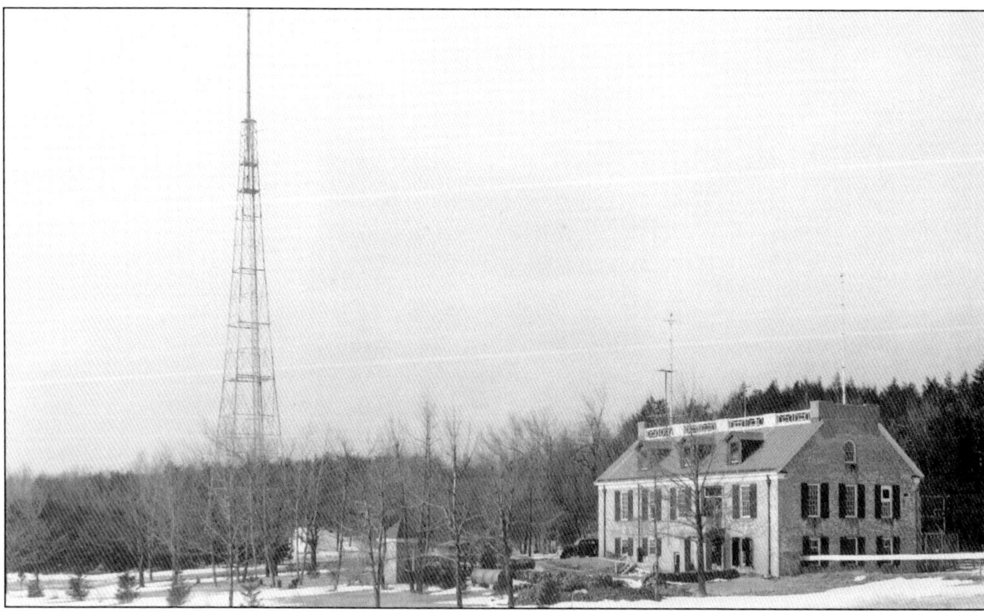

On February 5, 1940, the Travelers Broadcasting Service began operating experimental FM station W1XSO on 1 kilowatt of power and a wavelength of 43.7 megacycles (mc). In this rare 1942 image, one can see the original WTIC-FM tower on Deercliff Road on Avon Mountain. W1XSO, the second FM station in Hartford, spent time as W53H in 1941 and was granted WTIC-FM in 1944. (Courtesy of CBS Radio Inc.)

WTIC's Ross Miller, third from left, is pictured doing a remote broadcast on location at a local firehouse with several unidentified Hartford firefighters. The broadcast was part of a WTIC fire prevention program. Miller was with WTIC for four decades. (Courtesy of CBS Radio Inc.)

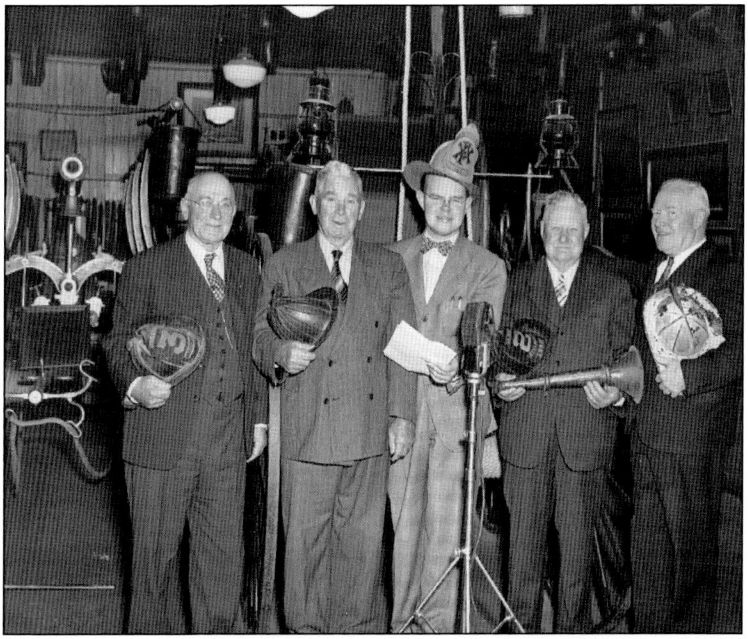

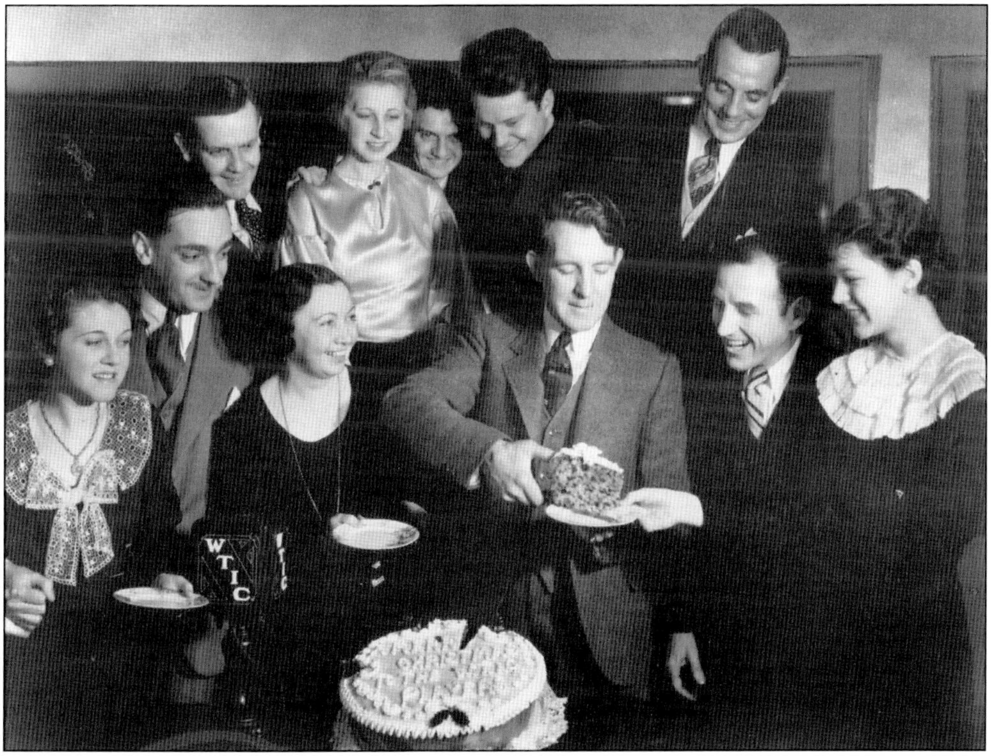

An important milestone in WTIC's history was reached on September 13, 1931. That was the date of the first presentation of the *WTIC Playhouse*, directed by former stage and screen star Guy Hedlund (first row, third from left). In this anniversary picture, Ed Begley looks on (first row, second from right) as Hedlund passes the birthday cake. Also identified is a smiling Michael "Eddie" O'Shea (second row, second from right). (Courtesy of CBS Radio Inc.)

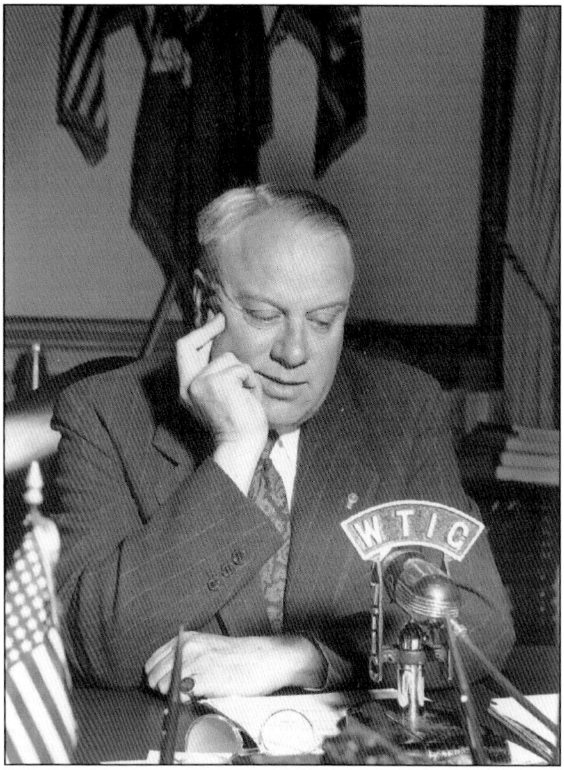


Gov. Raymond F. Baldwin, of Stratford, broadcasts over WTIC from his office at the state capitol. His reassuring voice was heard regularly during World War II and, in later years, as a US senator and chief justice of the Connecticut Supreme Court. (Courtesy of CBS Radio Inc.)

When World War II started, WTIC sales manager Irwin Cowper suggested the Morse code letter *V*, for victory, be used as the hourly time, tone. WTIC's Leonard Patricelli refined it to the opening notes of Beethoven's *Symphony No. 5*, and it went on the air on July 4, 1943. Pictured here is bandmaster Charles Messer conducting the Coast Guard Band on the program *United States Coast Guard on Parade* for NBC. (Courtesy of CBS Radio Inc.)

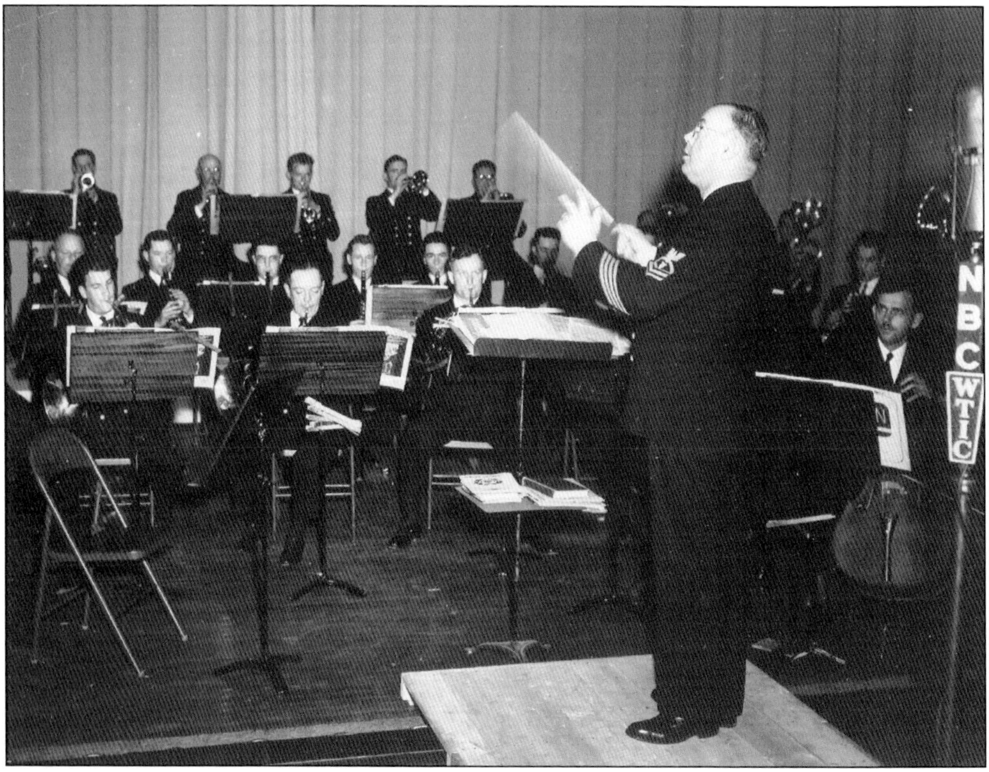

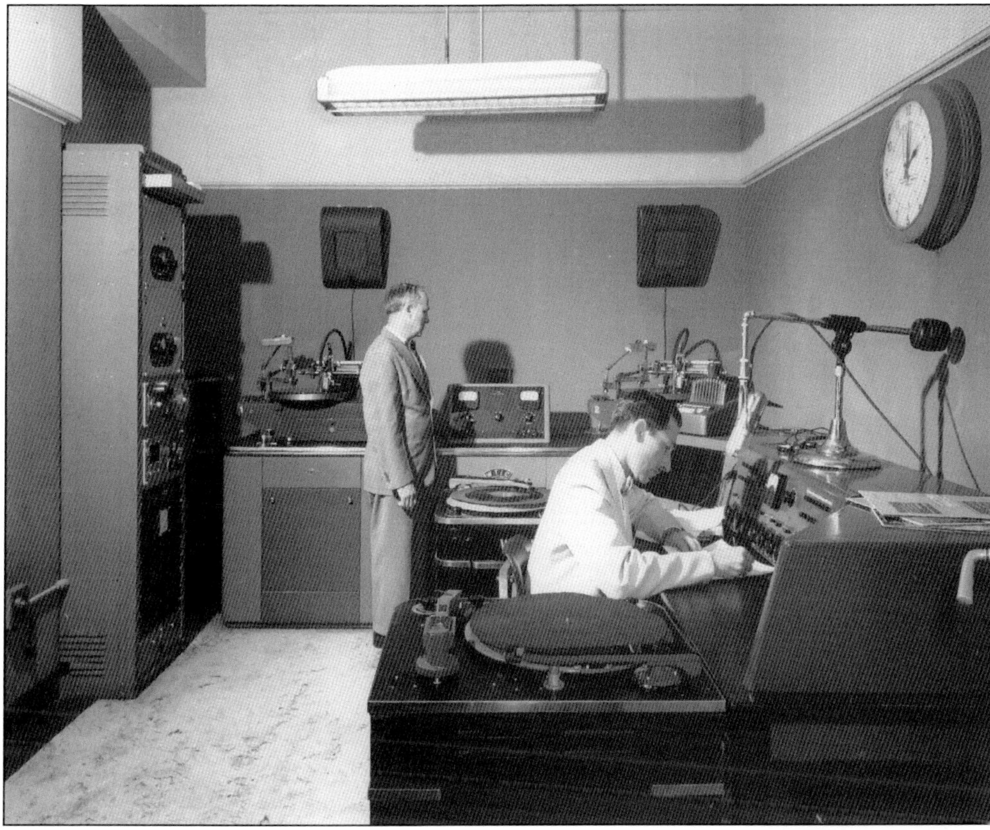

WTIC-FM began operations on February 5, 1940, almost 15 years to the day after WTIC (AM) first came on the air. Initially operating as an experimental station with the call sign W1XSO, the station became WTIC-FM on November 1, 1943. Standing at the controls is the station's chief engineer, Herman D. Taylor. The announcer at the desk is Bruce Kern. (Courtesy of CBS Radio Inc.)

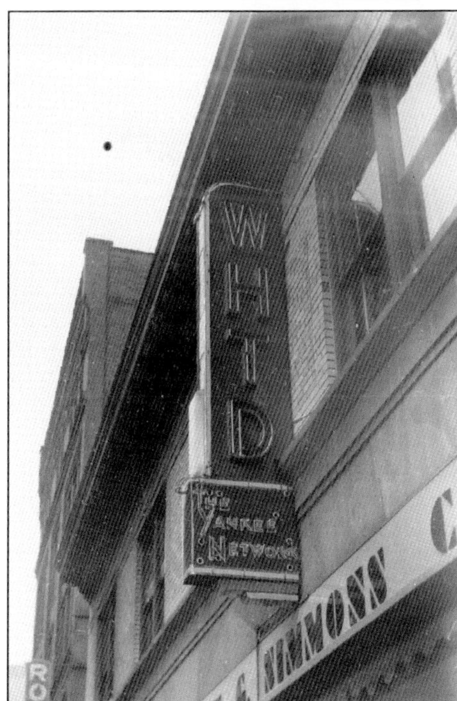


In the early 1940s, General Tire Corp. purchased both the Yankee Network and WHTD 1410 (now WPOP). Pictured is the sign in front of the station's studios at 54 Pratt Street in downtown Hartford. (Courtesy of the Vintage Radio and Communications Museum of Connecticut.)

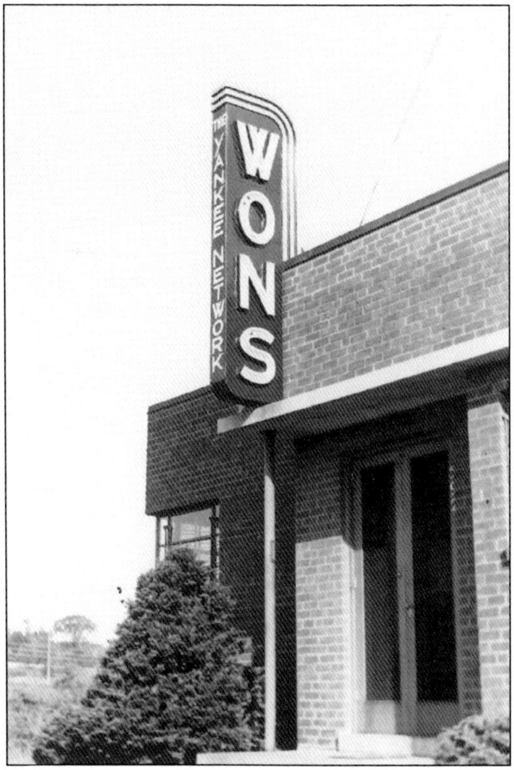


Proclaiming "Yankee Network" affiliation, this neon sign on the front of what is now the WPOP transmitter building on Cedar Street in Newington shows the station's call letters as WONS in 1946. WONS stood for "William O'Neill's Station." This call sign was used for only two years. (Courtesy of the Vintage Radio and Communications Museum of Connecticut.)

A program featuring happy on-air horseplay that became popular in 1946 was WTIC's *Variety Matinee*, broadcasting daily from 1:30 p.m. to 2:00 p.m. One of the few remaining live music shows, the program featured Rudy Martin and his studio orchestra with vocalists Mary Osborne, Len Collins, and Larry Mayo. In this photograph, Bateese himself (Harry Crimi) gets his ponytail clipped. Looking on, from left to right, are emcee Bob Tyrol, announcer Bruce Kern, the unidentified barber, Bateese, Mary Osborne, and Len Collins. (Courtesy of CBS Radio Inc.)

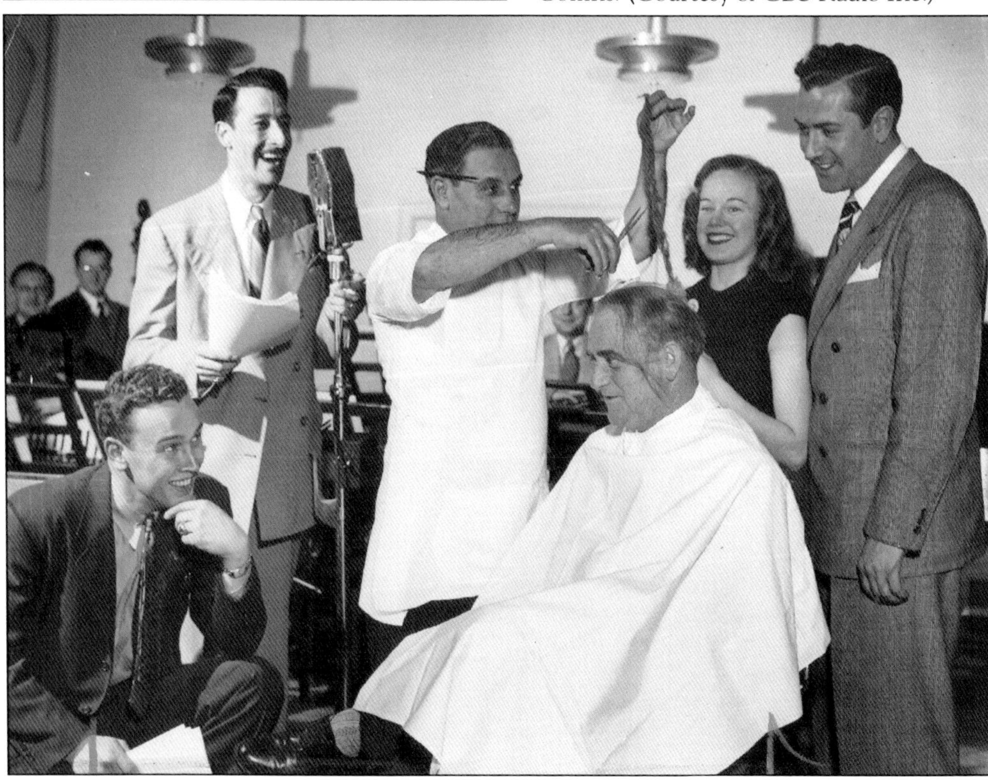

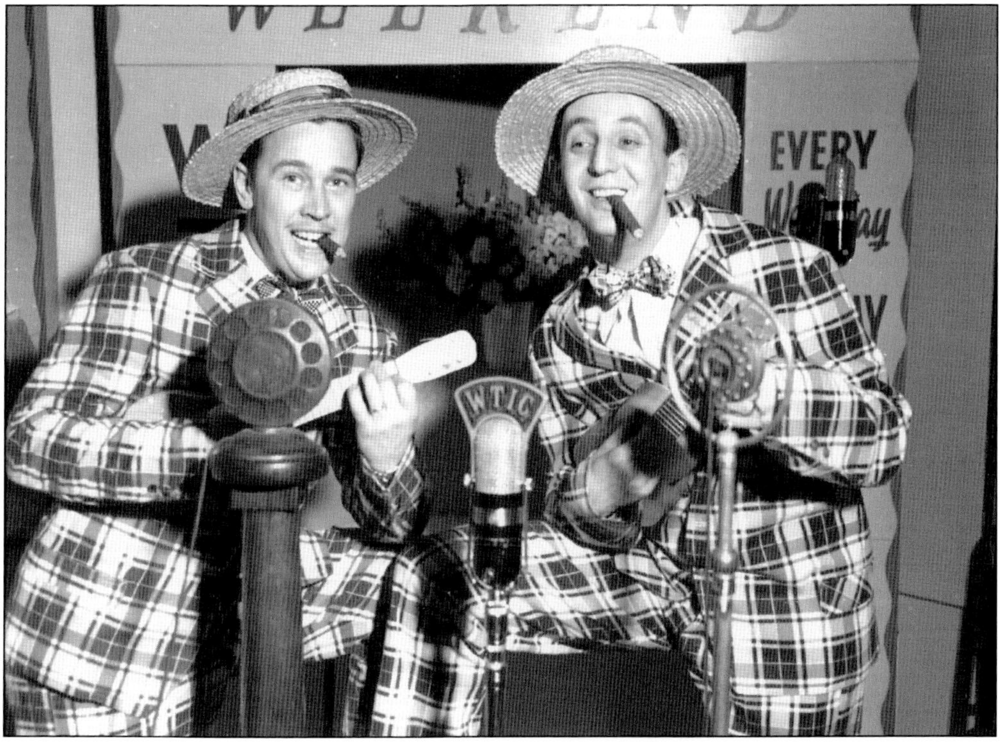


WTIC's *Cinderella Weekend* was one of the first audience participation shows. It premiered on August 4, 1947, and remained in the program lineup until May 1, 1953. The show originated from the Orchid Room at Ryan's Restaurant on Pearl Street. It became such a hit that announcers Bob Tyrol (left) and Floyd Richards adapted it for the stage and took it on the road around the state. (Courtesy of CBS Radio Inc.)

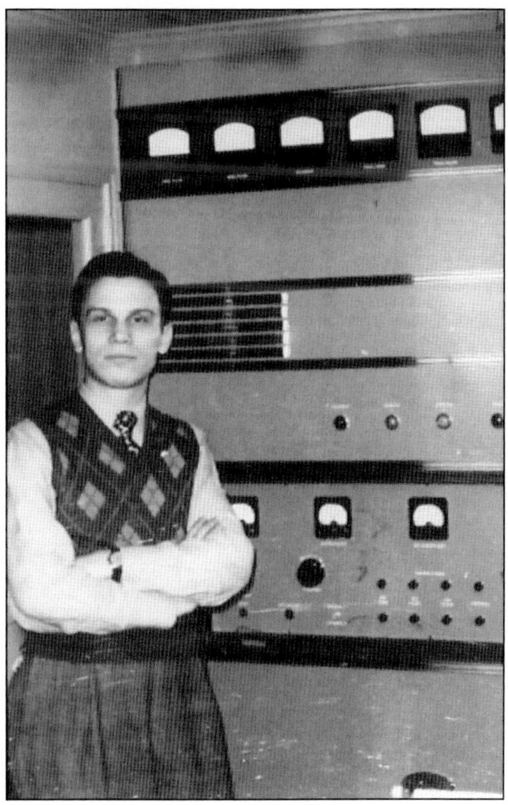

WKNB's first chief engineer, Charles Portia, stands in front of the brand-new 1,000-watt transmitter when the station first went on the air in 1947 from Cedar Street in Newington. The station call letters are now WRYM. (Courtesy of Charles Portia.)

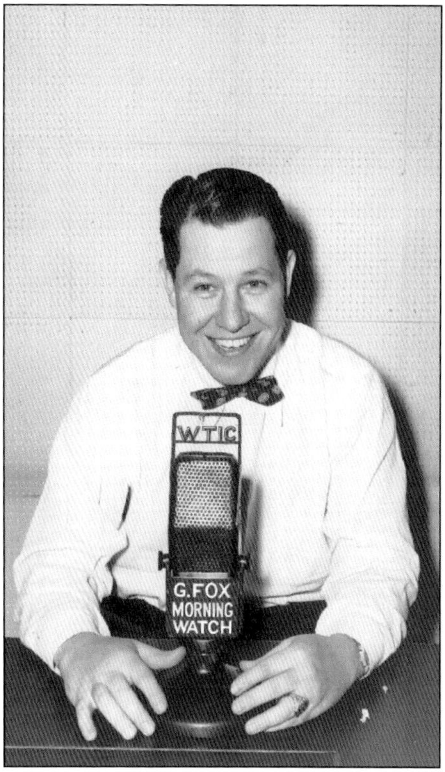


Bob Steele's *Morning Watch* program, sponsored for years by Hartford's G. Fox Company, was on WTIC for over six decades. For a period during its broadcast, it enjoyed some of the highest ratings of any program in the entire country. (Courtesy of Phil Steele.)

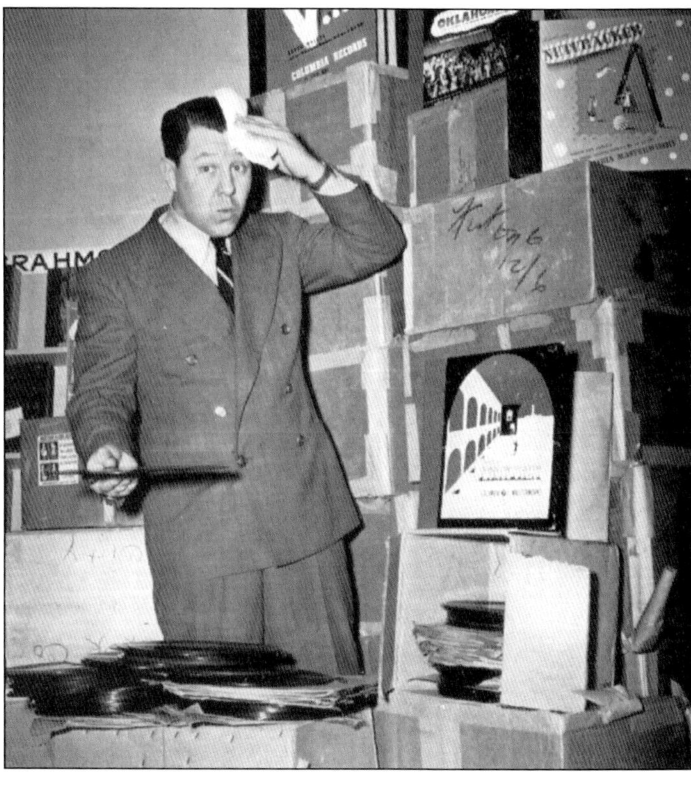

During his *Morning Watch* program, WTIC's Bob Steele requested phonograph records to be used on hospital trains bearing wounded servicemen returning from World War II. In one week, his fans donated more than 3,000 platters to the cause. (Courtesy of CBS Radio Inc.)

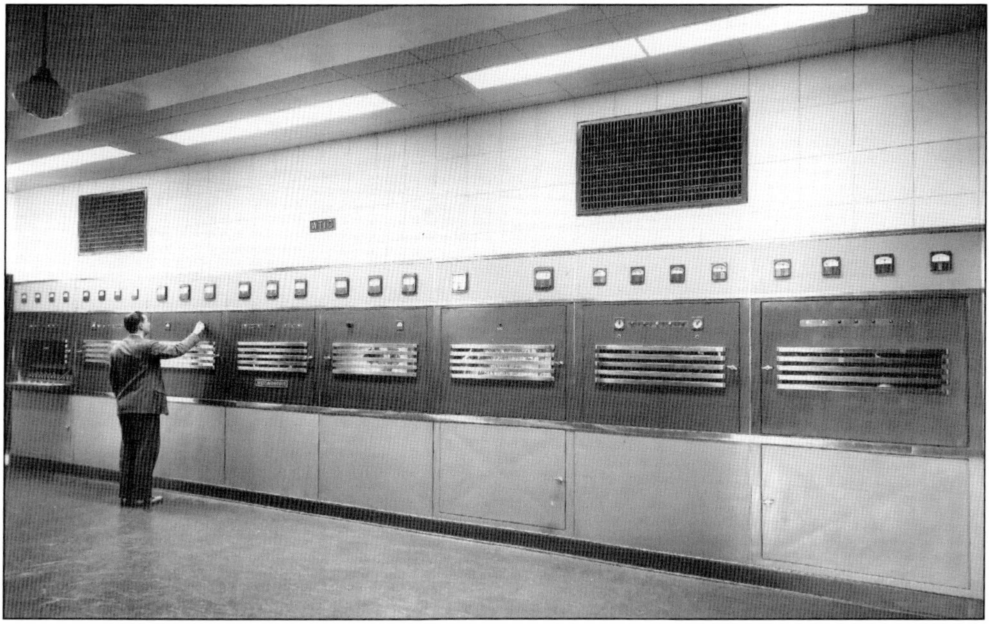

In 1947, the original WTIC 50,000-watt transmitter known as the RCA Old No. 1 was replaced with the huge Westinghouse transmitter shown in this photograph, at a cost of approximately $250,000. This transmitter was in use until the late 1960s. (Courtesy of CBS Radio Inc.)

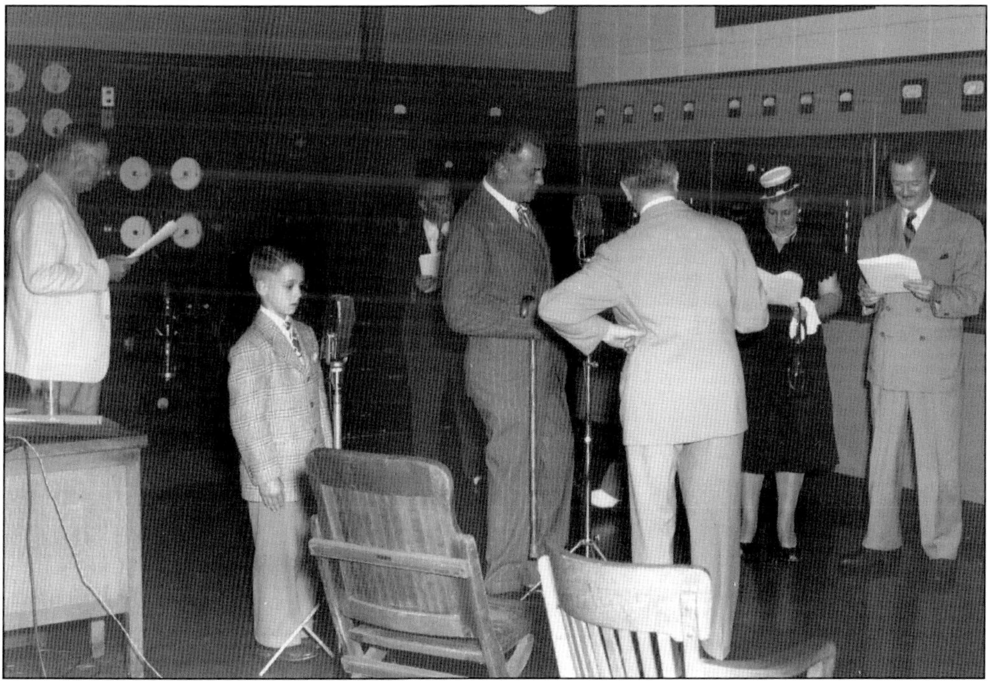

Eight-year-old Alan Scott waits his turn to speak on a program dedicating WTIC's newest transmitter in 1947. His father, WTIC engineer Carl Scott, died a few weeks before the installation was completed. From left to right are WTIC president Clayton Randall, Scott, transmitter supervisor William Coleman, WTIC vice president Paul W. Morency, Bernard Mullins, Mrs. Carl Scott, and George Bowe. (Courtesy of CBS Radio Inc.)

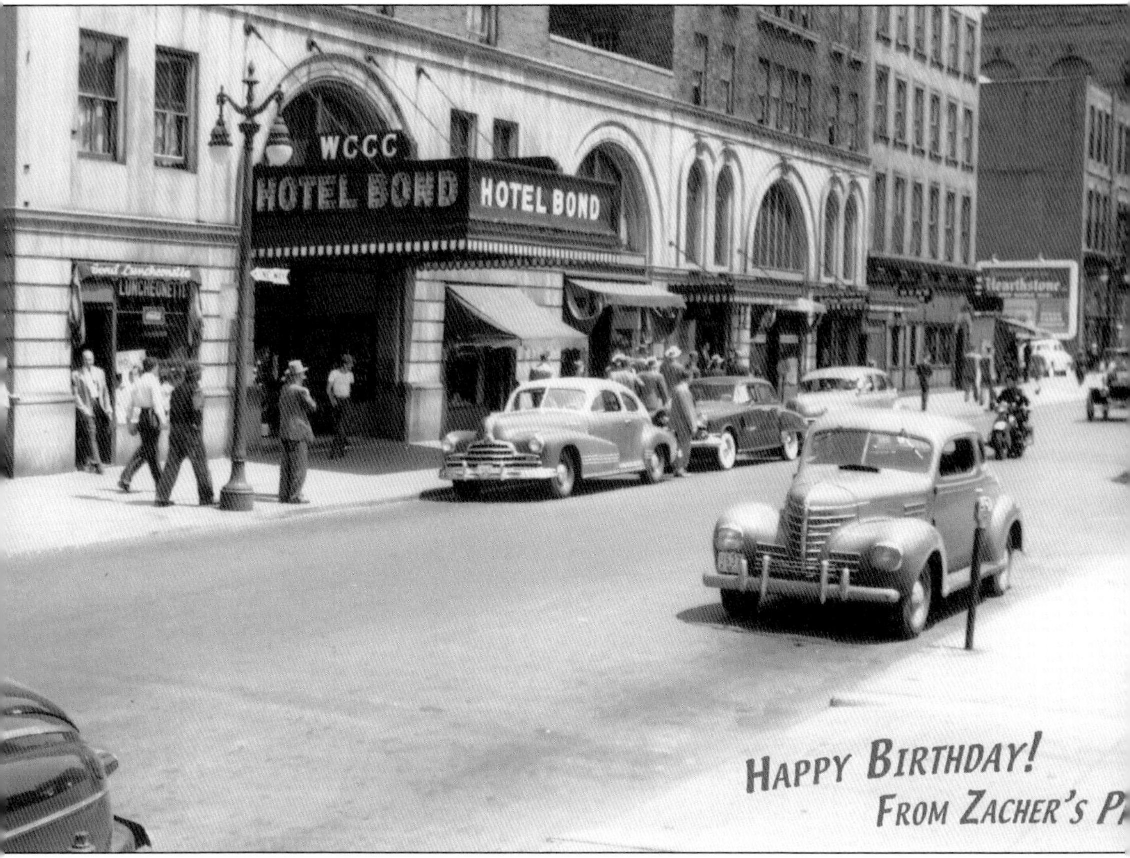


WCCC-AM 1290 signed on for the first time on October 26, 1947, from studios located in the basement of the Hotel Bond on Asylum Street in Hartford. The station was owned by the Savitt brothers—Bill, a well-known Hartford jeweler, and Maxx, a local judge. The call letters stood for "We Cover Connecticut's Capital." (Courtesy of WCCC.)

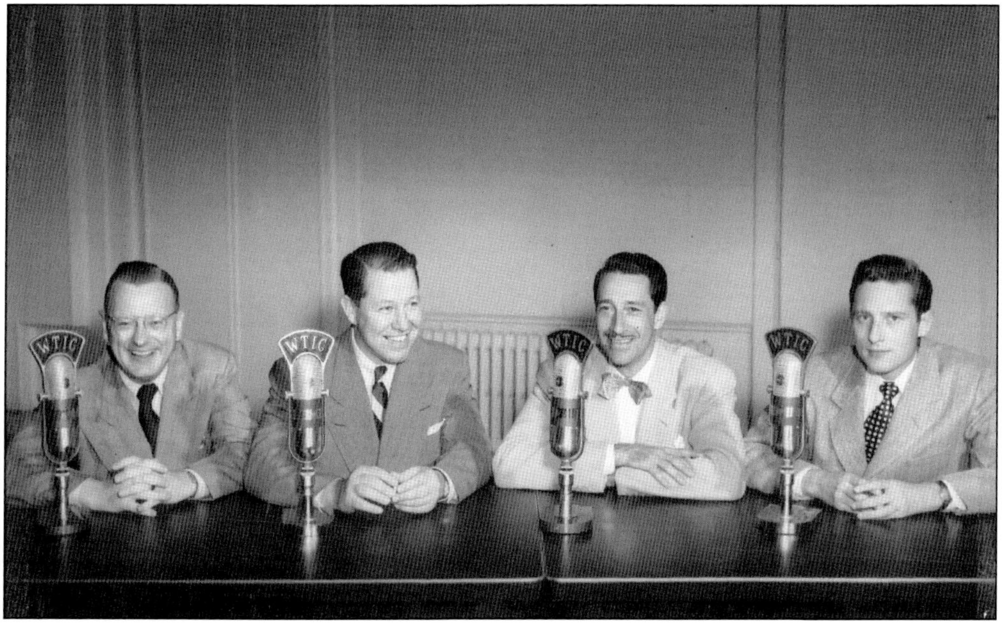


Four of WTIC's most popular announcers pose for a publicity shot in 1947. From left to right are WTIC's Ed Anderson, *Morning Watch* host Bob Steele, Bruce Kern, and Dick Westhrup. Steele was one of the station's most popular announcers and had a show on WTIC for six decades. (Courtesy of CBS Radio Inc.)

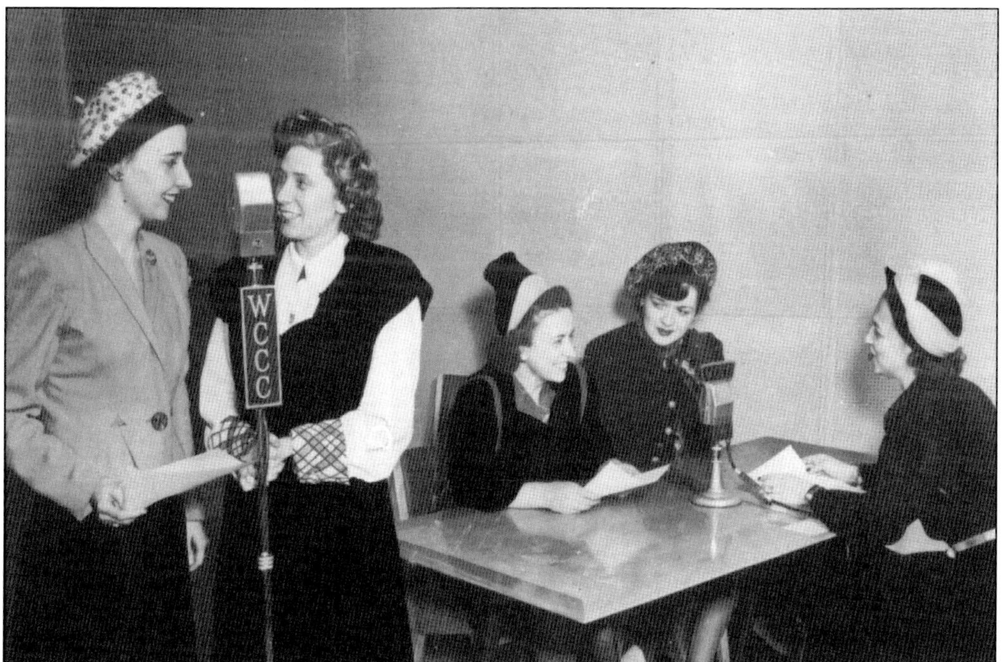


At the microphone around 1949, WCCC's "Miss Betty" (left) talks with Frances Cline of the advertising department of Worth of Hartford, a popular downtown retail store and station advertiser. Fashion counselors from Worth seated at the table include, from left to right, Mary Mayes, Gertrude Kaplan, and Frances Foley. (Courtesy of WCCC.)

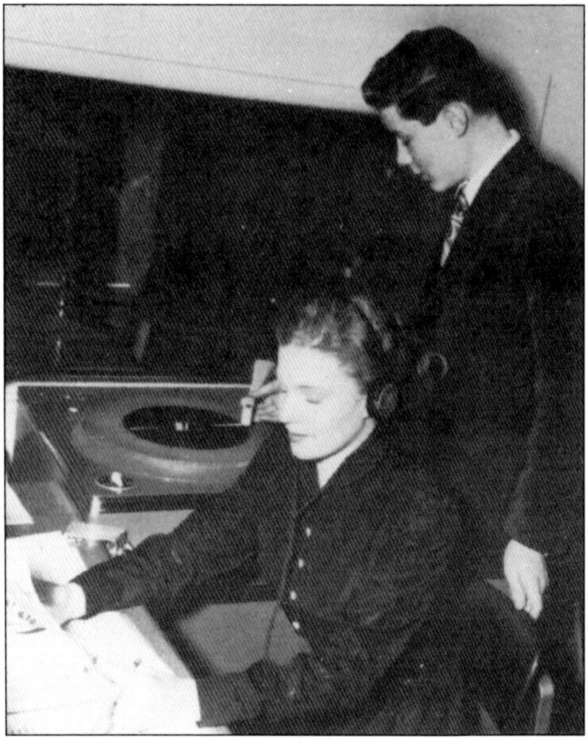

During the late 1940s, WCCC turned its studios over to students from area high schools for an hour every Sunday and Monday. The students chose their own tunes, announced them, and spun their own discs. In this photograph, two unidentified students are shown on the air on WCCC. (Courtesy of WCCC.)

WCCC's master of ceremonies Bob Sherman (left) takes contestants through their paces in the 1947 statewide spelling bee, a round-robin program in which five stations, members of the Connecticut Independent Broadcasting System, participated. At right is scorekeeper Emma Lou Kehler. (Courtesy of WCCC.)

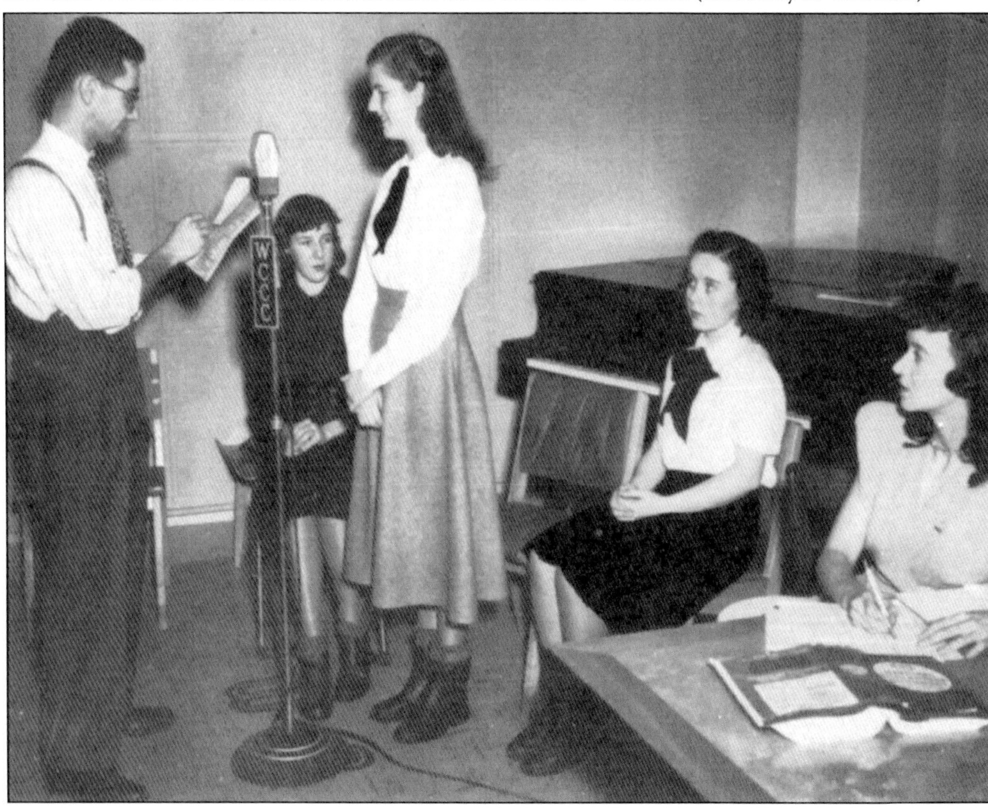

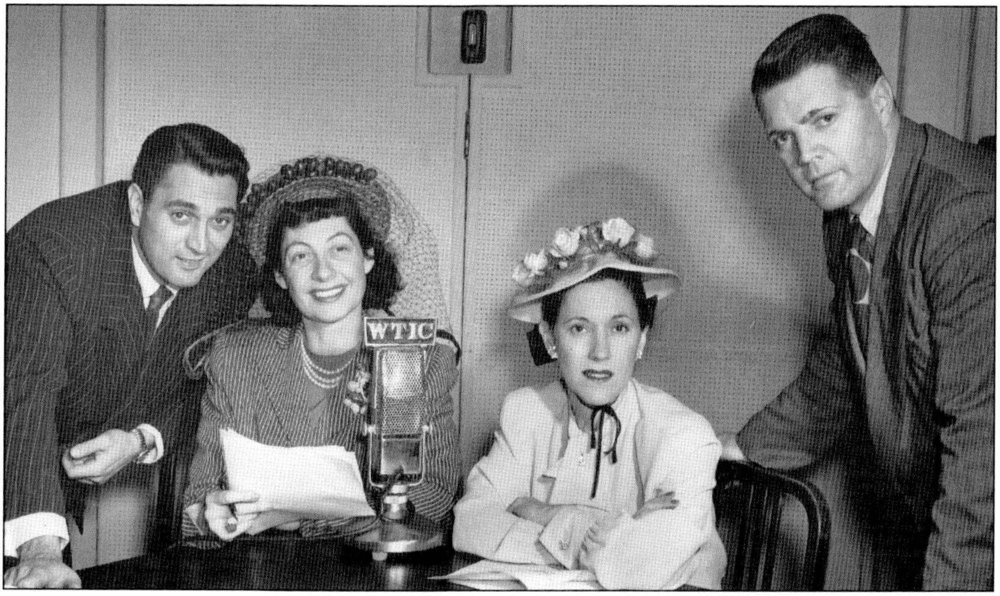


Charisma, interview technique, and an extensive acquaintance with an array of stars of Broadway and Hollywood gave Jean Colbert (third from left) an edge over other broadcasters when it came to getting guests for her show on WTIC. In 1947, Jean took over what was known as the *WTIC Radio Bazaar*. She is seen her in that same year with Robert Alda (left), the father of actor Alan Alda, and Ilka Chase when they were appearing in *There Goes the Bride*. Announcer Peter Stoner is at right. (Courtesy of CBS Radio Inc.)

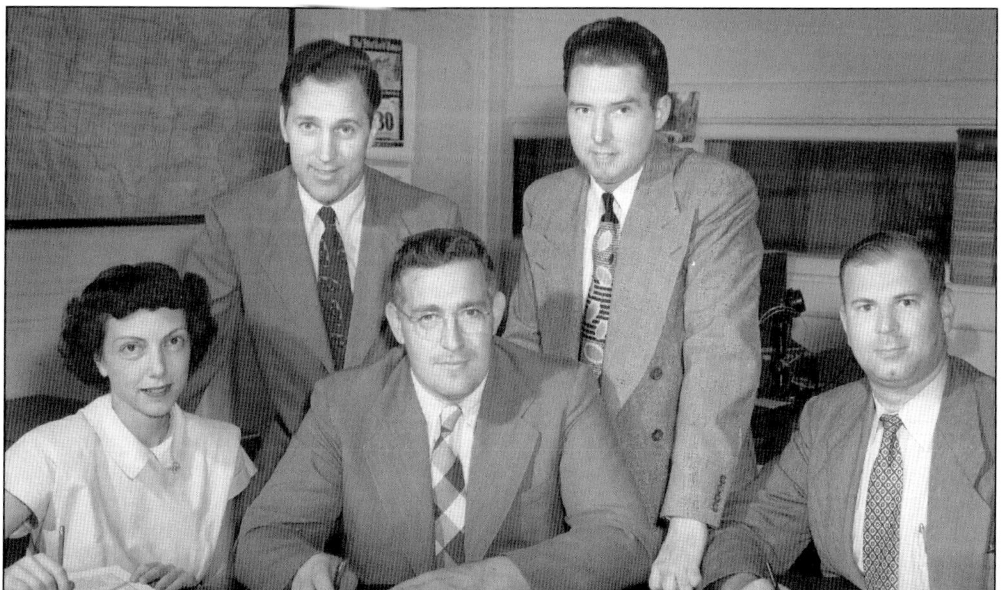

In the 1930s, most stations in Hartford got what news they had from their networks. WTIC began scheduling four daily, quarter-hour local-news programs in June 1935 at 8:00 a.m., 12:00 p.m., 6:00 p.m., and 11:00 p.m. Pictured here from left to right is the news staff of 1948: (seated) Gena Canestrari; Tom Eaton, WTIC's first new director; and Sydney Stewart, assistant news director; (standing) Forbes Parkyn and Don Gorman. (Courtesy of CBS Radio Inc.)

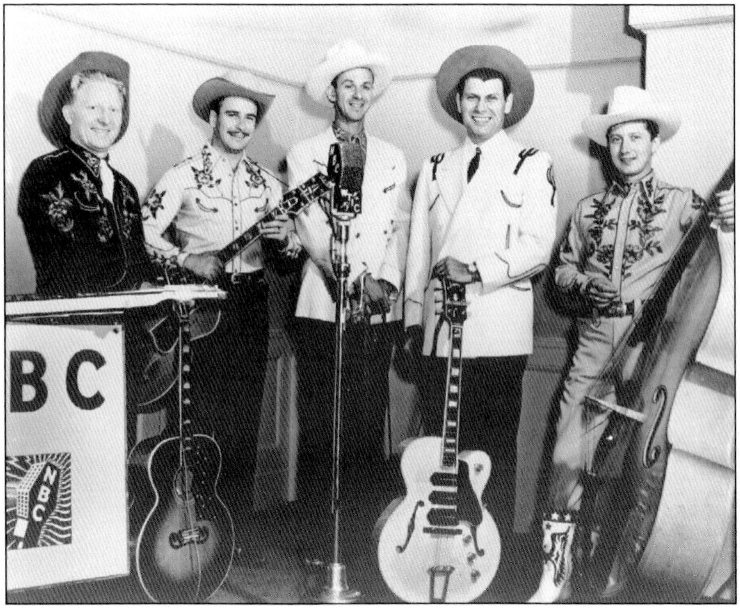


WTIC's Downhomers frequently came into the studio to do their daily program right off the road after entertaining somewhere in New England. For over four years, beginning in 1946, the Downhomers were heard on WTIC. From left to right are Shorty Cook, Rusty Rodgers, Slim Coxx, Guy Campbell, and Hank Gunder. (Courtesy of CBS Radio Inc.)

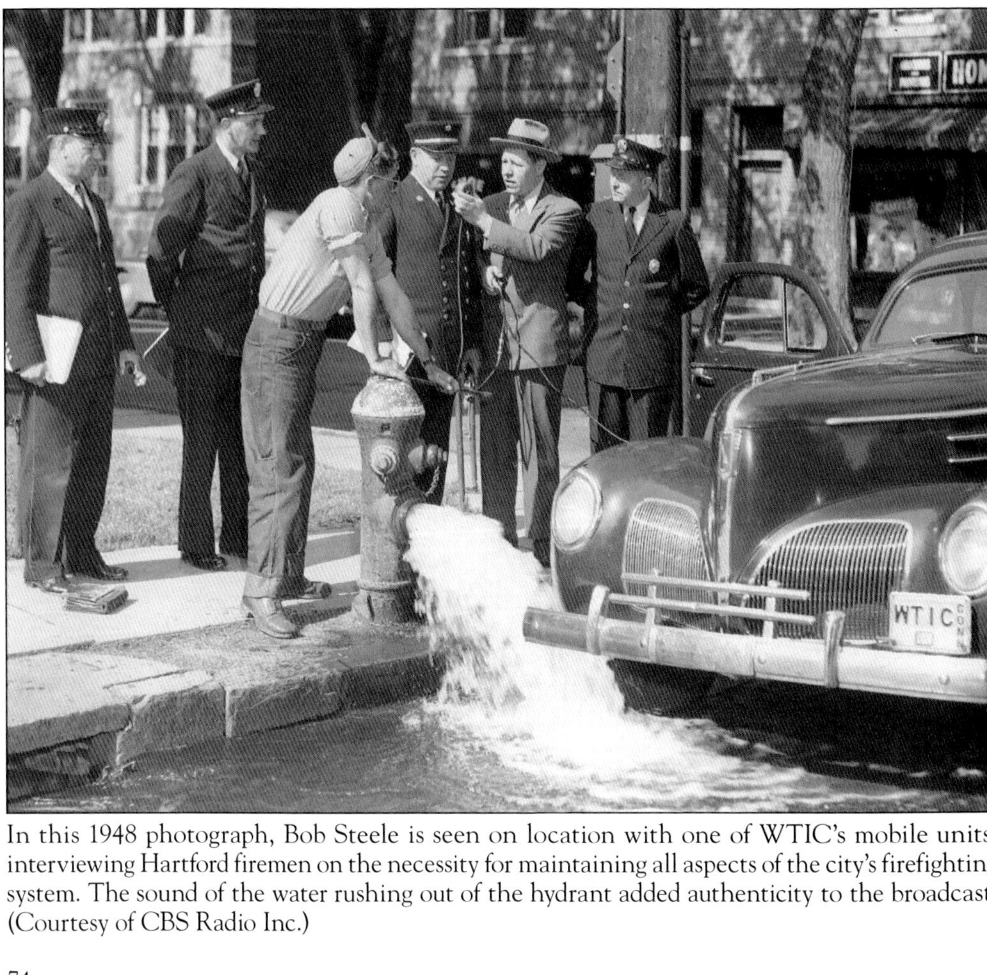


In this 1948 photograph, Bob Steele is seen on location with one of WTIC's mobile units, interviewing Hartford firemen on the necessity for maintaining all aspects of the city's firefighting system. The sound of the water rushing out of the hydrant added authenticity to the broadcast. (Courtesy of CBS Radio Inc.)

Ross Miller was WTIC's first afternoon–drive time personality. His first musical assignment was the weekly Saturday afternoon program *Juke Box Jingles* in late 1949. Ross rhymed many of the musical introductions to the popular music he played and, thus, became known as the "Jingle Jockey." The title of the show changed, too. As a result of a name change contest, *Ross the Musical Miller* emerged. (Courtesy of CBS Radio Inc.)

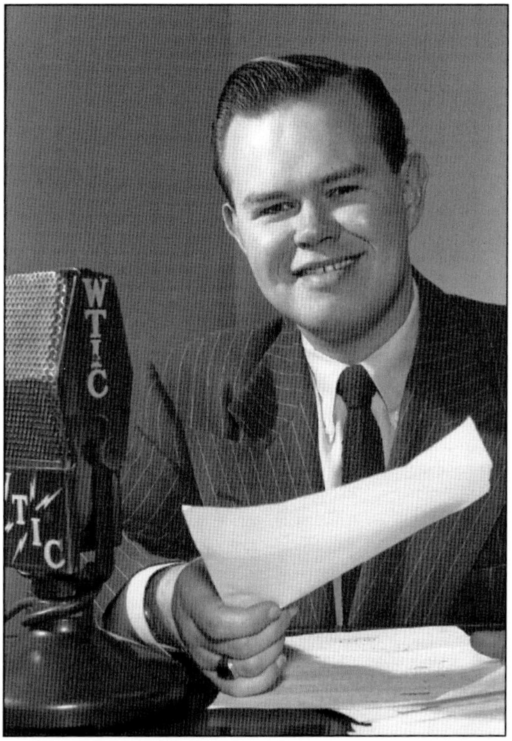

WTIC veterans of World War II returned to active Army duty to handle a special Mother's Day program from Fort Dix, New Jersey. From left to right are staff announcer Edward Anderson, formally with Armed Forces Network in Germany; supervisor of engineers Albert Jackson, who served with the Army Communications Service in France; producer Allen Ludden, who spent most of his war years in the Pacific area with the Special Services Division; and two unidentified men. (Courtesy of CBS Radio Inc.)

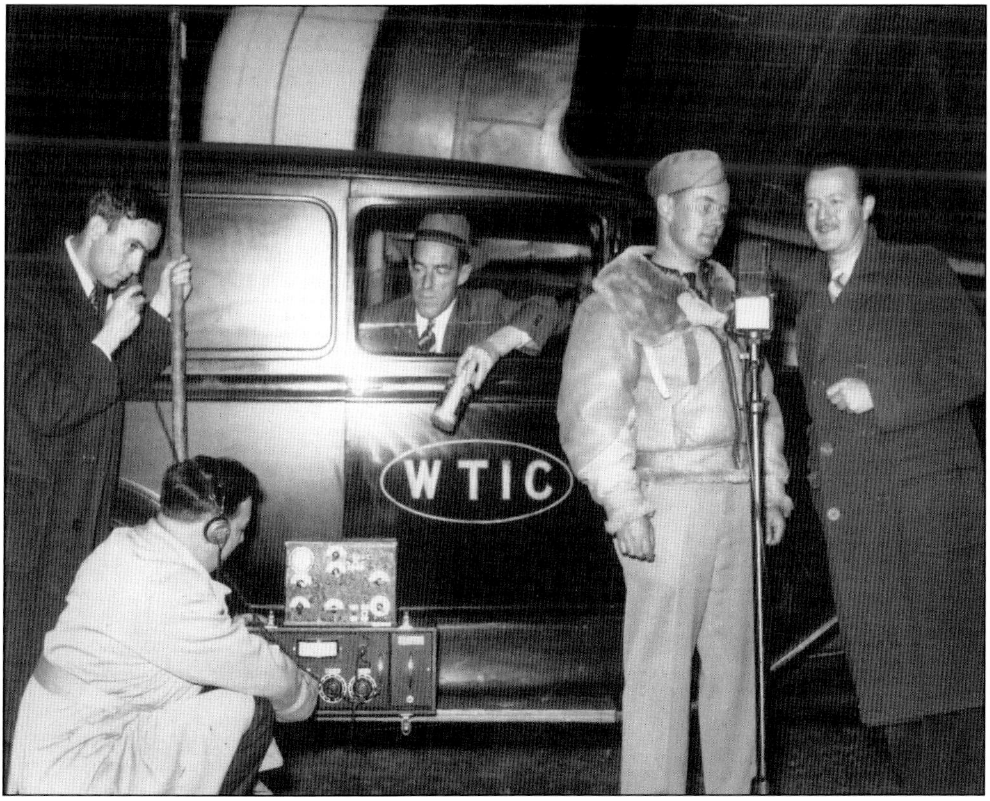

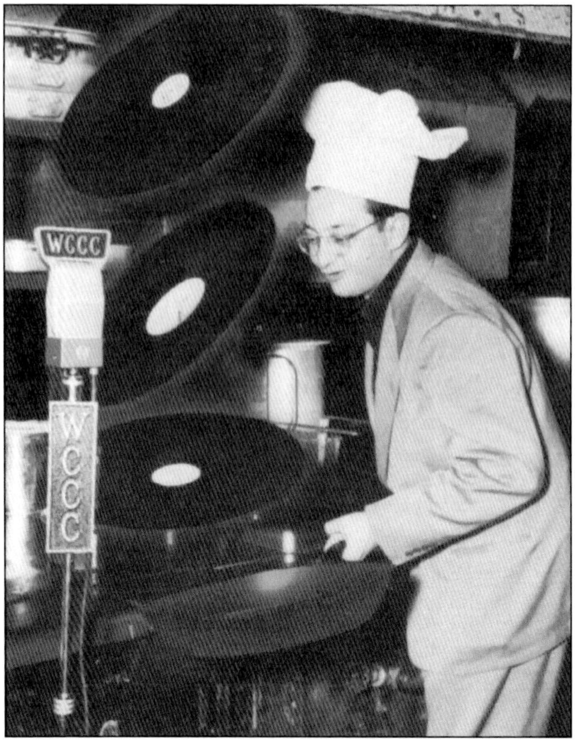


This promotional photograph shows Joe Girand, host of the popular *1290 Club* that aired on WCCC weekday afternoons in the early 1950s. Joe started in Hartford at WTHT, and after WCCC, he moved on to WDRC. WCCC's studios were in the basement of the Hotel Bond on Asylum Street in Hartford. (Courtesy of WCCC.)

A frenzy of activity at WTIC takes place on an election night as engineers connect reporters in the field to their respective assignment desks or engineers who would put them on the air live. Reporting election results took a large number of people and an amazing amount of equipment. (Courtesy of CBS Radio Inc.)

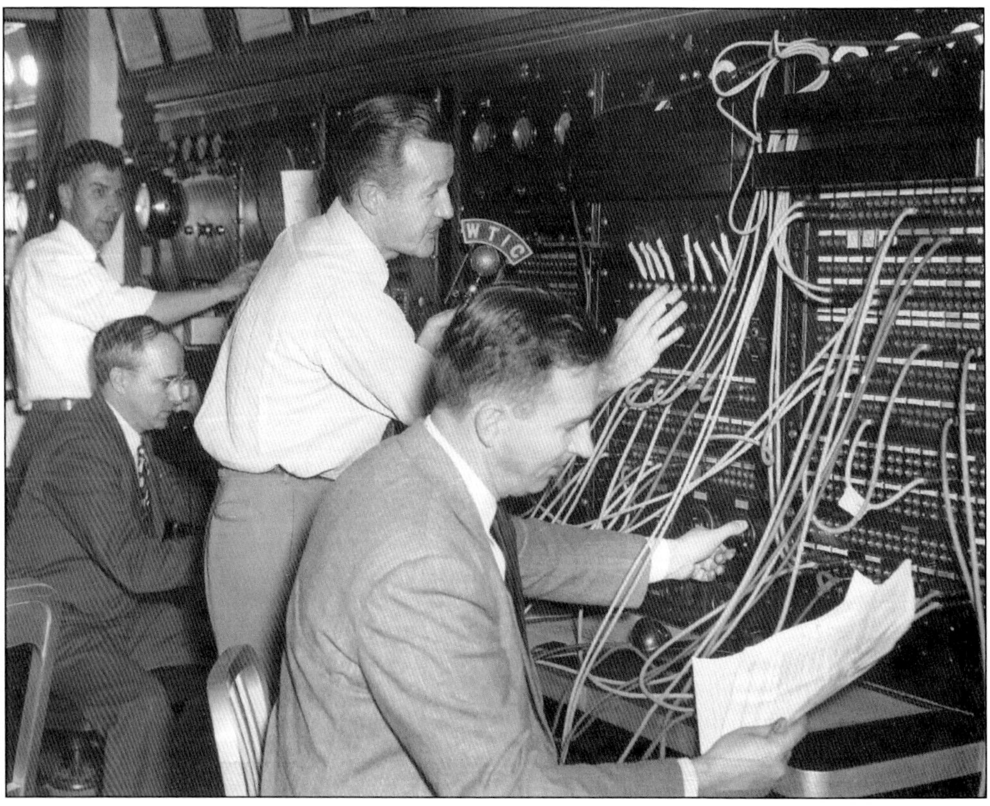

# *Four*

# THE 1950S

In the 1950s, the number of stations in the United Stated increased dramatically as listenership grew, and radio broadcasting was recognized as a powerful tool that allowed advertisers to reach the baby boom generation. Radio receivers became less expensive, and the transistor radio, reaching the US marketplace towards the end of the decade, helped increase listenership. Its small size sparked a change in radio-listening habits, for the first time allowing people to listen to radio anywhere they went.

AM radio was still the dominant mode during the 1950s, and some of the early FM stations, such as the *Hartford Times*'s WTHT-FM and WKNB-FM, would go silent during the period, the victim of apathy about FM on the part of some broadcasters and the general public. By and large, broadcasters did not yet see the potential of FM, and those that might have could not justify the added expense of programming their FM stations separate from the AM sister stations, so there was very little incentive for listeners to spend the extra money on FM receiving sets. FM's superior fidelity did start to appeal to hi-fi hobbyists who came to embrace the technology.

The 1950s saw television sets begin appearing in more and more homes across the nation. A good number of the most popular radio shows made the transition to television, forcing radio stations to develop new local programming. Many experts thought the invention of television would severely cut into radio listenership, but as the next decade would show, radio would reinvent itself and continue to be a major part of American life.

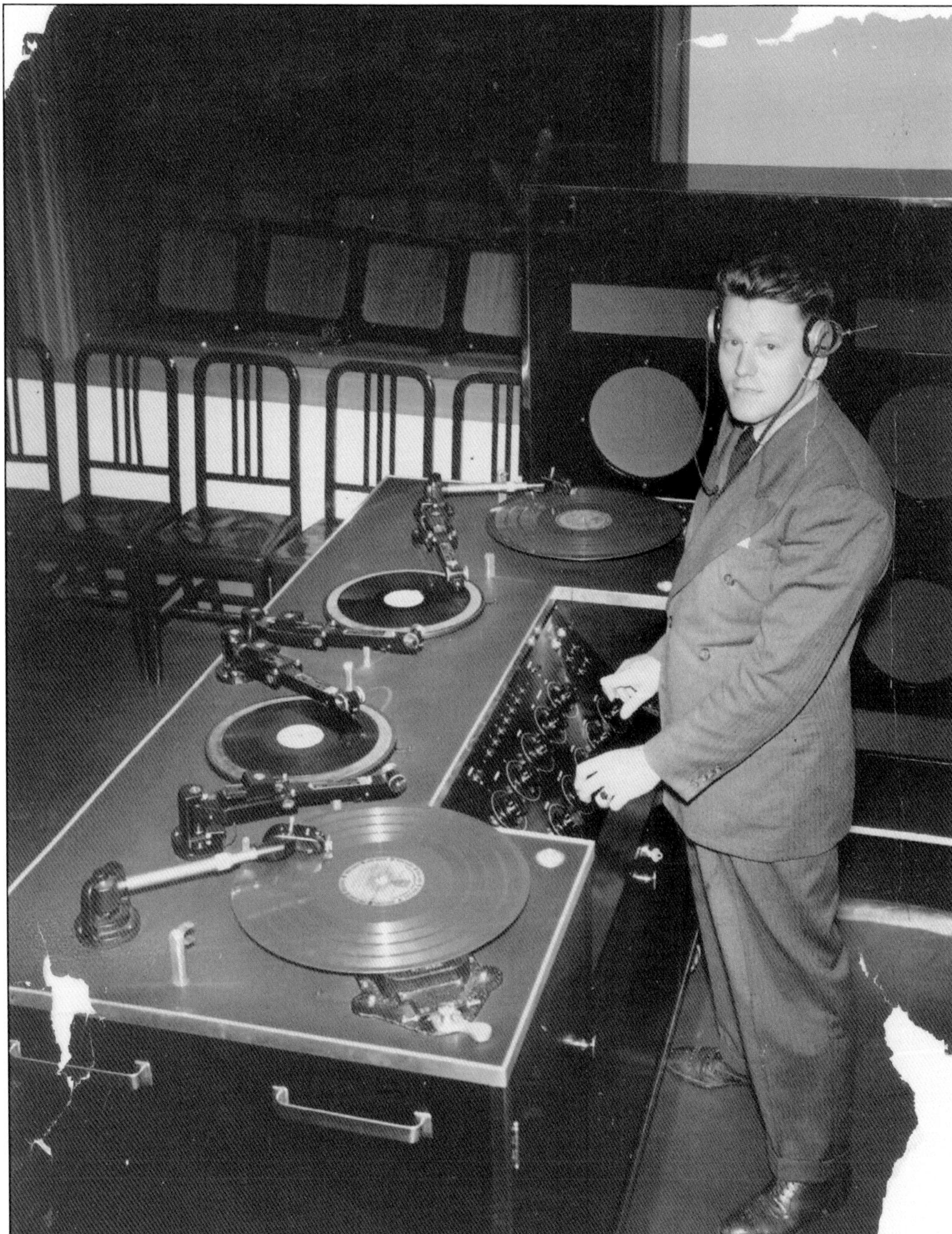

During the production of radio drama programs for WTIC, sound effects man Eddie O'Shea used the large device shown in this image to play back, on cue, various prerecorded sounds such as windows and doors, bells and whistles, chains, wheels, and wind. Some effects not available on records, like footsteps and gunshots, were created manually. (Courtesy of CBS Radio Inc.)

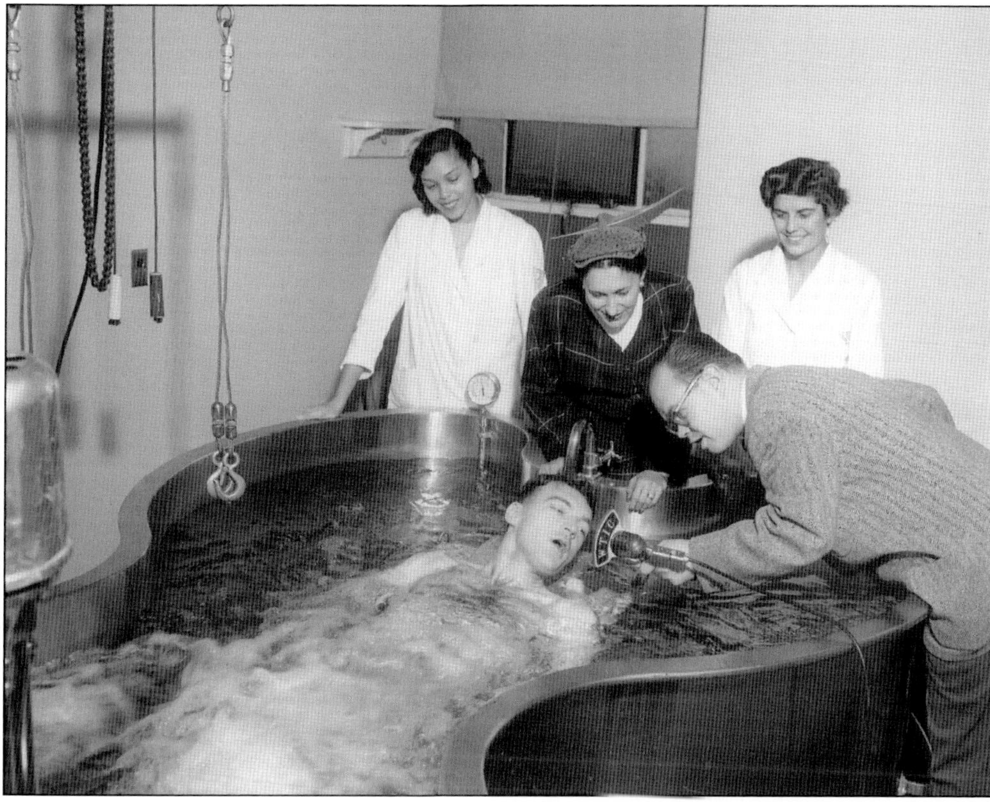

*The Jean Colbert Show* was responsible for many special programs, among them the feature "Know Your Community Hospital." WTIC listeners were given insights into services available at their local hospitals as Jean and her announcer, Ross Miller, originated broadcasts on location. In this photograph, taken November 12, 1951, listeners are learning about physical therapy available at the McCook Memorial Hospital in Hartford. Two therapists look on as Colbert leans over a Hubbard tank, listening to a patient's response to Miller's questions. (Courtesy of CBS Radio Inc.)

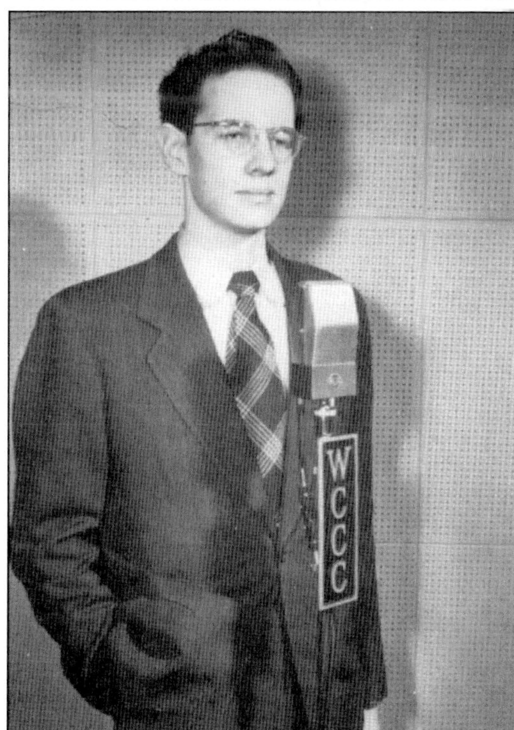


Ivor Hugh started at WCCC in 1947 as host of *The Concert Hour* program. He later became the music director and stayed with the station until 1965. He produced the very popular morning show from WCCC's studios in Hartford's Hotel Bond for years. Presently, he can be heard weekday evenings on WJMJ. (Courtesy of WCCC.)

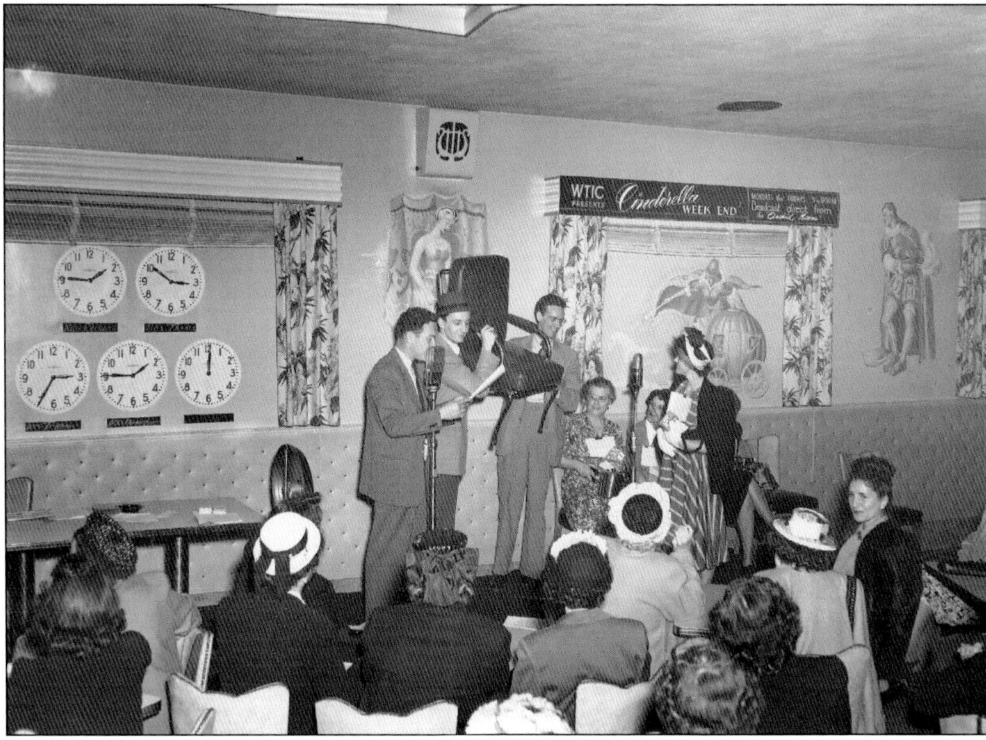


WTIC's popular *Cinderella Weekend* program was one of the first audience participation shows. It premiered on August 4, 1947, and remained in the lineup until May 1, 1953, the year this photograph was taken. The show originated from the Orchid Room at Ryan's Restaurant on Pearl Street. It became such a hit that announcers Bob Tyrol (left) and Floyd Richards (second from left) adapted it for the stage and took it on the road around the state. (Courtesy of CBS Radio Inc.)

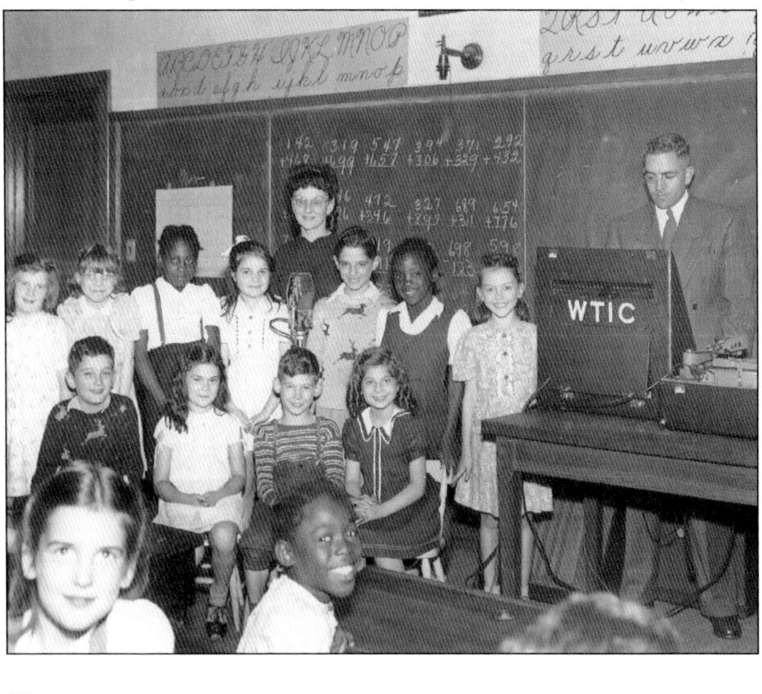


Over the years, WTIC has been a big booster of education, airing hundreds of programs on both public and secondary school topics. In this photograph, WTIC is on remote, broadcasting live from a Hartford public school classroom. Fred Edwards explains the intricacies of broadcasting to the children. (Courtesy of CBS Radio Inc.)

WTIC *Morning Watch* host Bob Steele (left) and Bob King, assistant supervisor of music at the Hartford station, pose for a publicity shot. Ten years later, WCCC's owner Bill Savitt would use a similar pose in the television commercials for his jewelry store. (Courtesy of Phil Steele.)

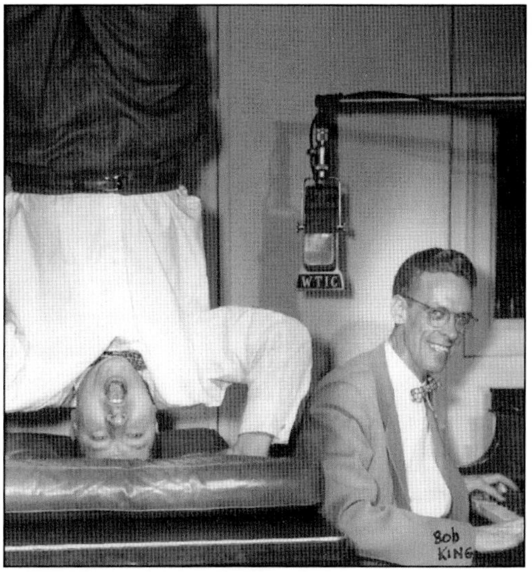


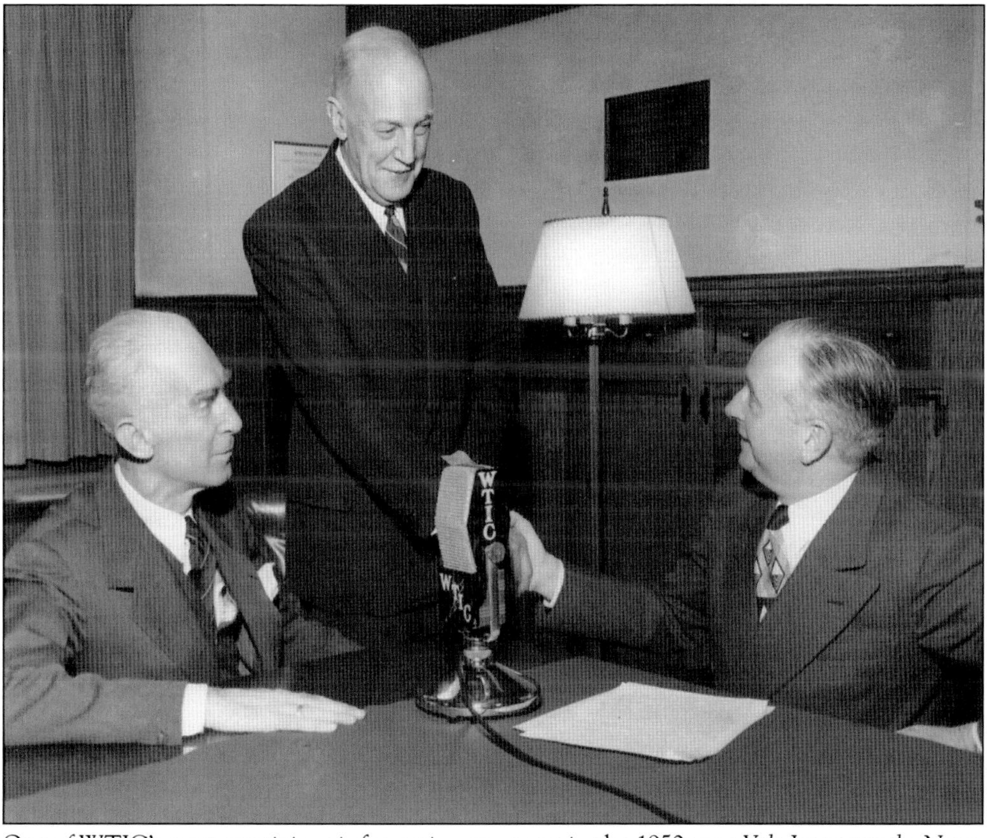


One of WTIC's most prestigious information programs in the 1950s was *Yale Interprets the News*. Established in 1941 with WTIC's Bernard Mullins as host, the program presented prominent members of the Yale faculty providing a background on the world's news. Broadcasting from the campus of Yale University, the program concluded in 1955. In this photograph, from left to right, are Arnold Wolfers, master of Pierson College and professor of international relations at Yale; Yale president Charles Seymour; and Bernard Mullins. (Courtesy of CBS Radio Inc.)

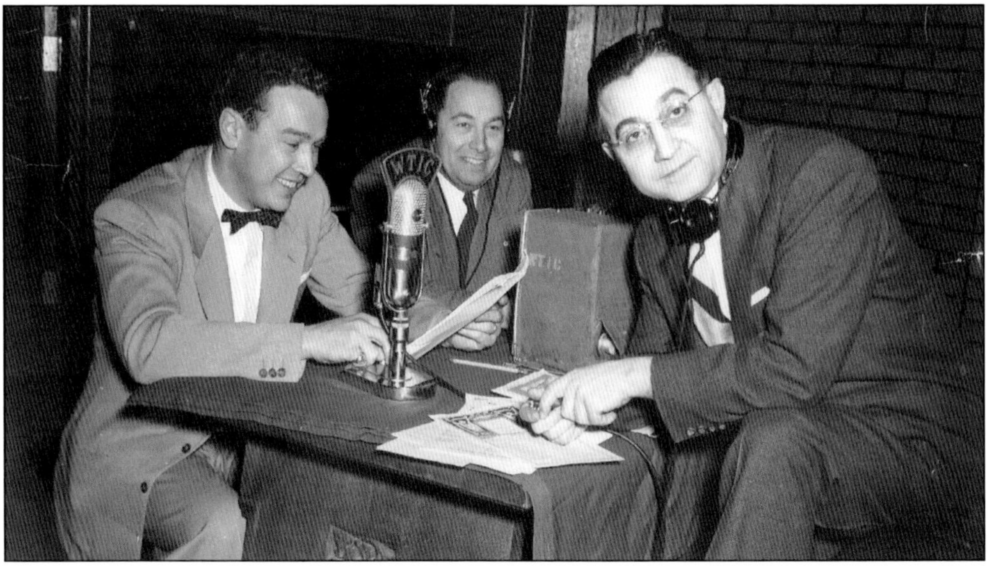

Every Sunday afternoon each winter during the 1950s, listeners to WTIC and the New England Regional Network heard college glee clubs direct from the campuses of such schools as Amherst, Brown, and Wesleyan. *Songs from New England Colleges* ran from 1949 to 1952. The on-the-road production crew in this image consists of announcer Bob Tyrol (left), engineer Al Jackson (center), and producer Leonard Patricelli, who would later become president of the station. (Courtesy of CBS Radio Inc.)

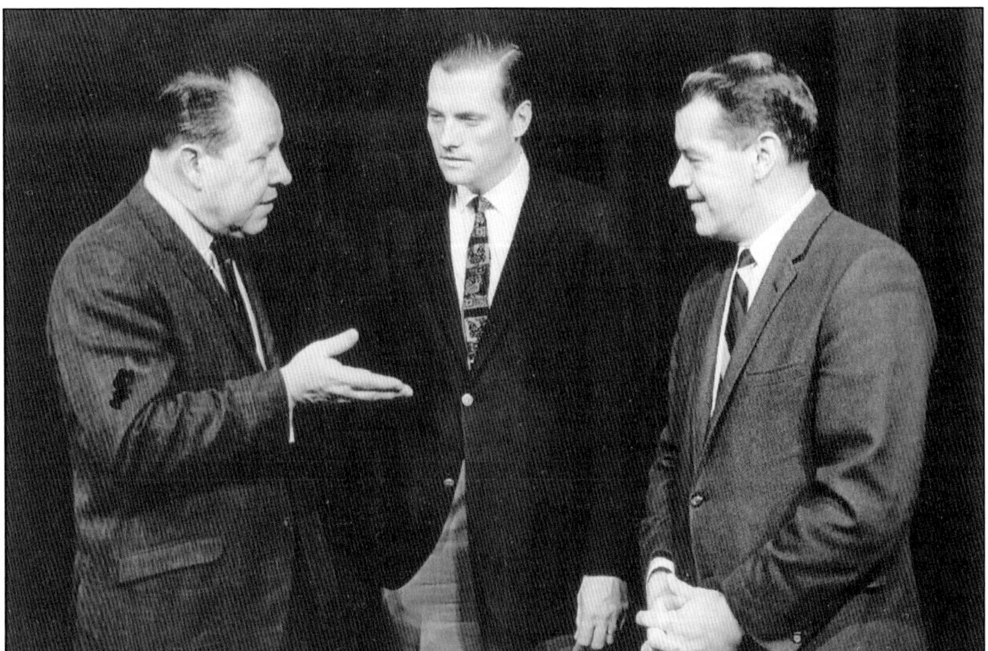

WTIC chief announcer Bob Steele (left) discusses programming with fellow announcers Dick Bertel (center) and Bill Hansen. As chief announcer, Steele was involved with many aspects of the station's programming and served as a resource for WTIC's other announcers. (Courtesy of CBS Radio Inc.)

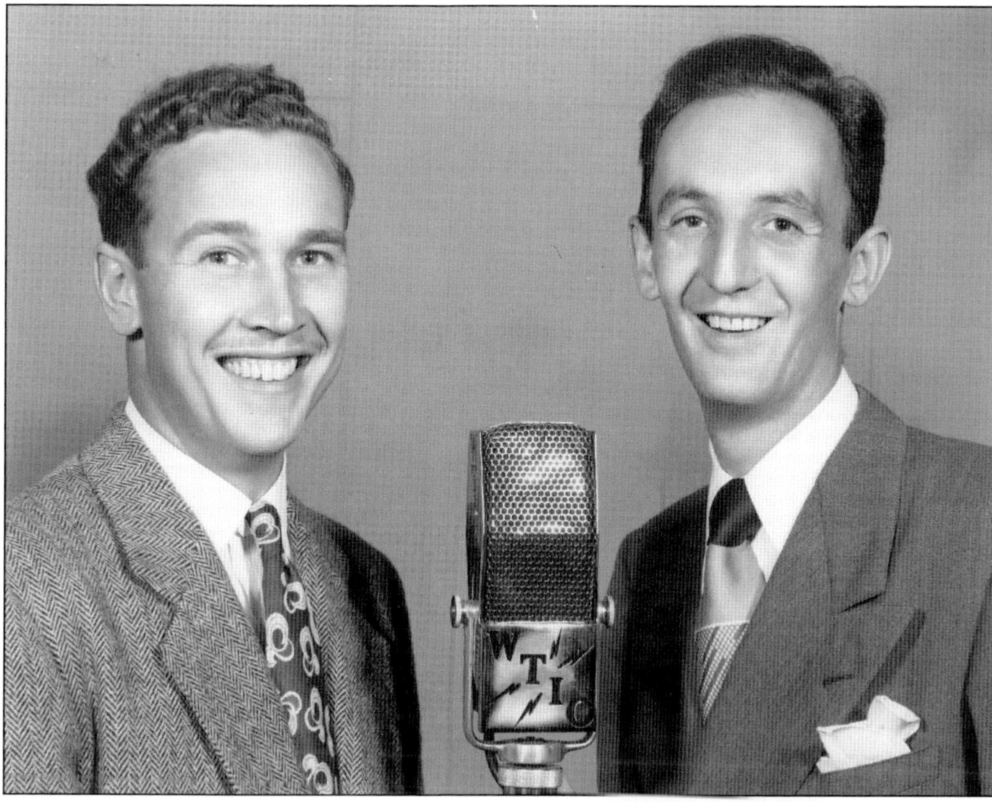


WTIC's Floyd "Hap" Richards (right) poses with *Morning Watch* host Bob Tyrol. Floyd was a jack-of-all-trades at WTIC and did many shows over the years, including stints of the popular *Mike Line* show. Ben hosted the morning show until he went into the service in 1943 and was replaced by Bob Steele. (Courtesy of CBS Radio Inc.)

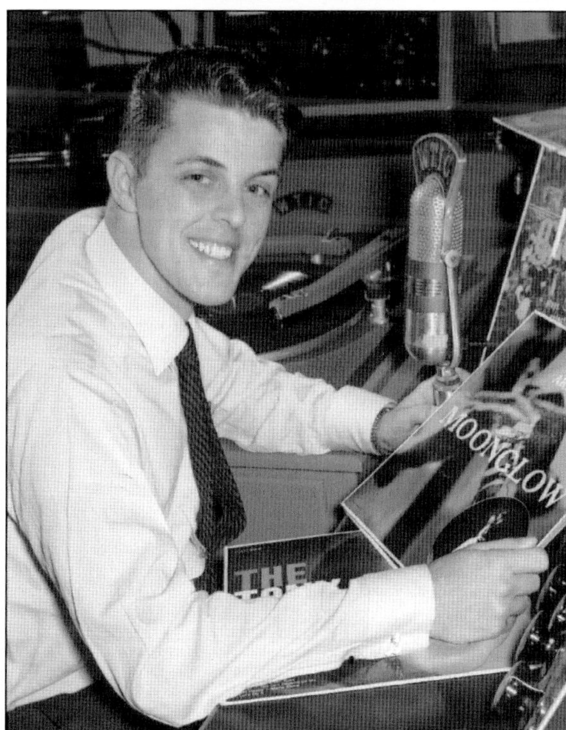


WTIC's Bill Hennessey has worked at just about every station in Hartford during his career, which has lasted more than four decades. He is seen here on the air at WTIC. (Courtesy of CBS Radio Inc.)

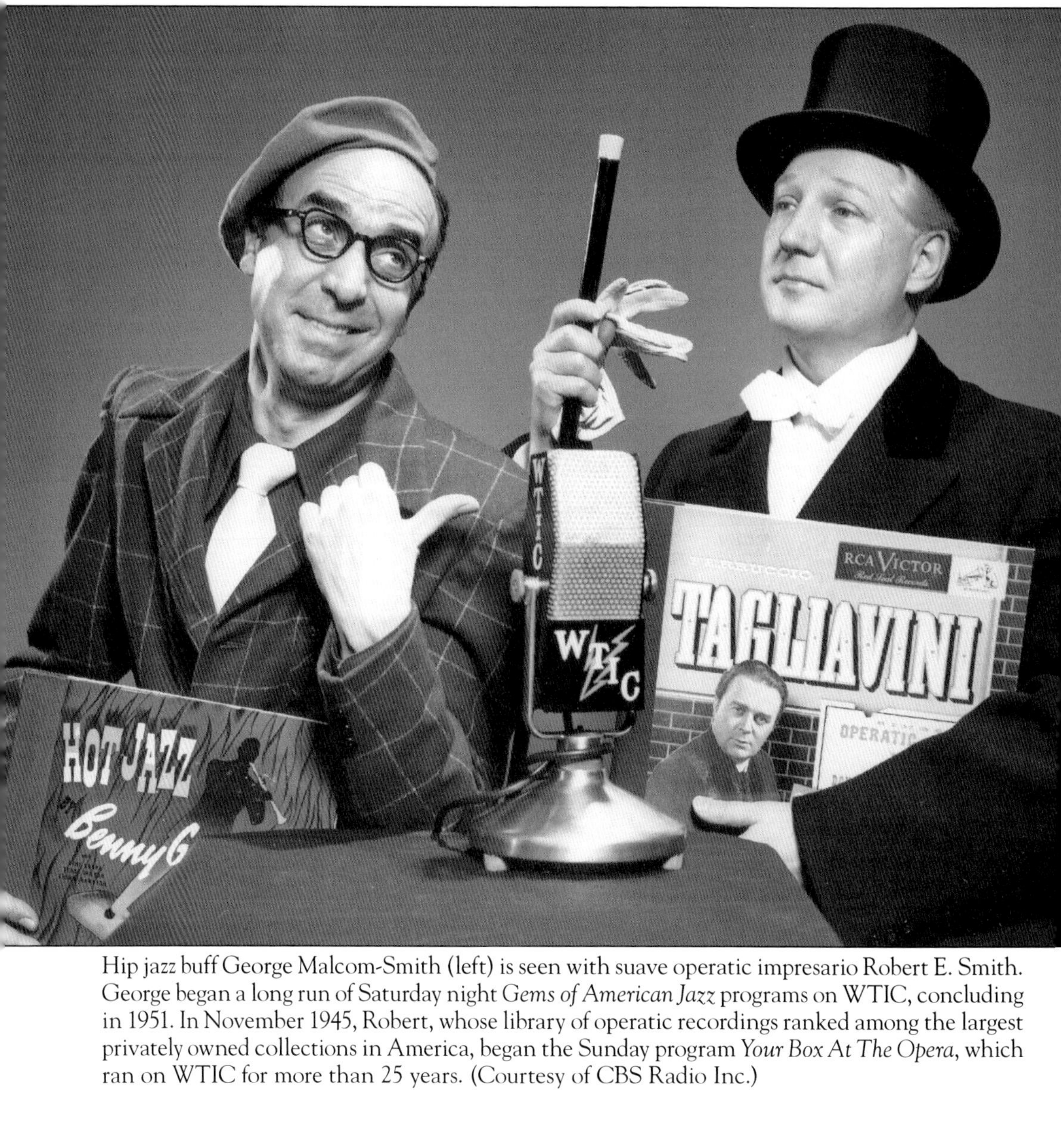


Hip jazz buff George Malcom-Smith (left) is seen with suave operatic impresario Robert E. Smith. George began a long run of Saturday night *Gems of American Jazz* programs on WTIC, concluding in 1951. In November 1945, Robert, whose library of operatic recordings ranked among the largest privately owned collections in America, began the Sunday program *Your Box At The Opera*, which ran on WTIC for more than 25 years. (Courtesy of CBS Radio Inc.)

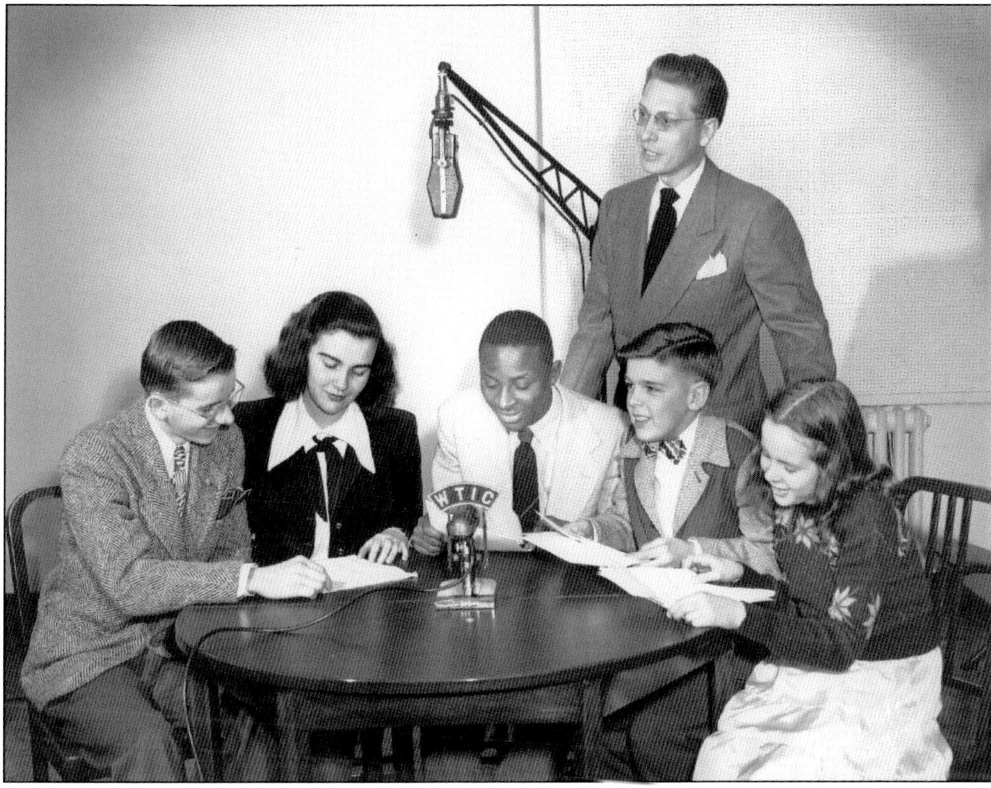


In 1947, Allen Ludden (standing) was WTIC's chief continuity writer and host of the award-winning youth program *Mind Your Manners*. A decade later, Ludden was nationally famous as master of ceremonies of television's *College Quiz Bowl*. Through the 1960s and 1970s, Ludden hosted one of television's most famous game shows, *Password*. He was married to actress Betty White from 1963 until his death in 1981. (Courtesy of CBS Radio Inc.)

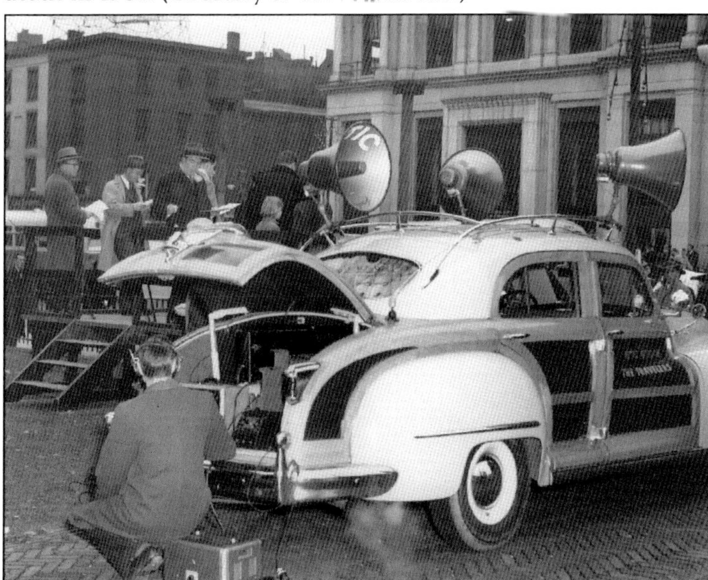

This WTIC remote crew covers a political rally in downtown Hartford. WTIC's ability to get out into the community to report important events over the years was second to none. (Courtesy of CBS Radio Inc.)

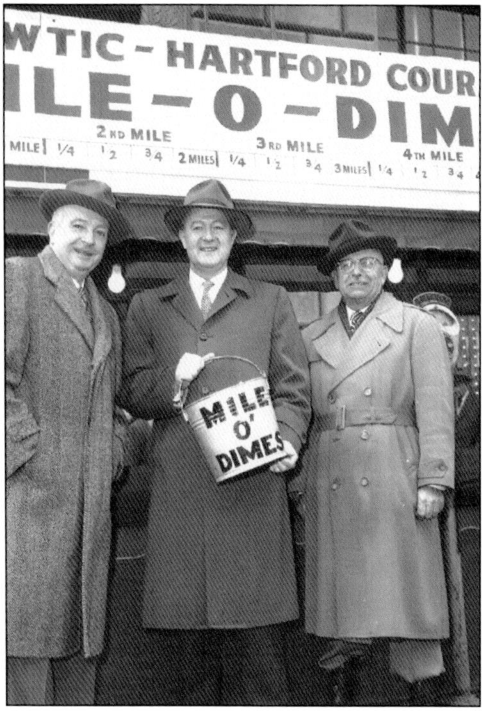


In 1941, WTIC and the *Hartford Courant* joined forces in the fight to conquer infantile paralysis with a program called *Mile O' Dimes.* In 1955, the WTIC-Hartford Courant *Mile O' Dimes* had raised $1,131,939.39 after 15 years of fundraising. Pictured here, from left to right, are Bernard Mullins, director of the *Mile O' Dimes* effort and longtime WTIC personality; George Bowe, production director; and Jack Murphy, engineer-operator and custodian of the *Mile O' Dimes* booth. (Courtesy of CBS Radio Inc.)

In 1954, the Travelers Insurance Company created the Travelers Weather Research Center for insurance underwriting purposes. A popular offshoot of the center was the Travelers Weather Service, which provided the people of southern New England with regular forecasts on WTIC. Pictured here, Milt Barlow, the founder of the weather center and service, pioneered probability forecasts. (Courtesy of CBS of Radio Inc.)

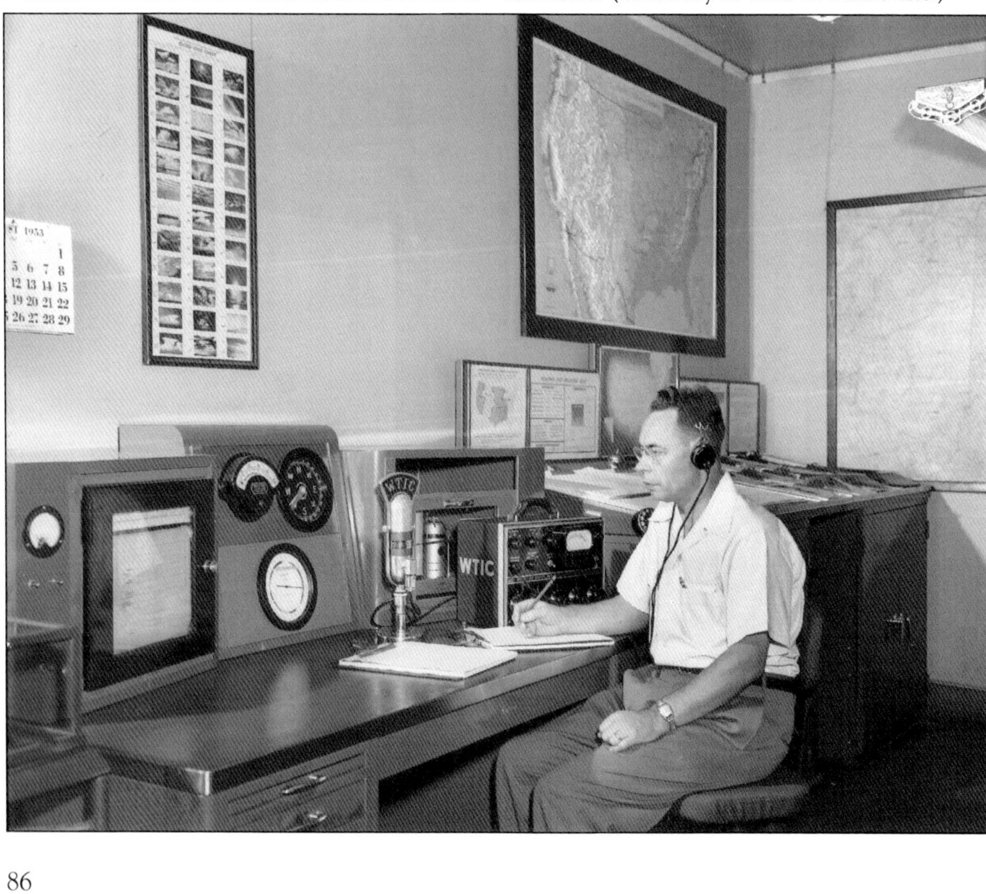

Leonard J. Patricelli joined the WTIC staff in 1929 as a scriptwriter and eventually became the first full-time continuity writer in New England. He became program manager in 1943, vice president of television programming in 1957, vice president and general manager in 1963, and executive vice president in 1966. In 1967, Patricelli became president of Broadcast Plaza Inc. In 1978, he was named chairman of the board, holding that position until his death in 1982. (Courtesy of CBS Radio Inc.)

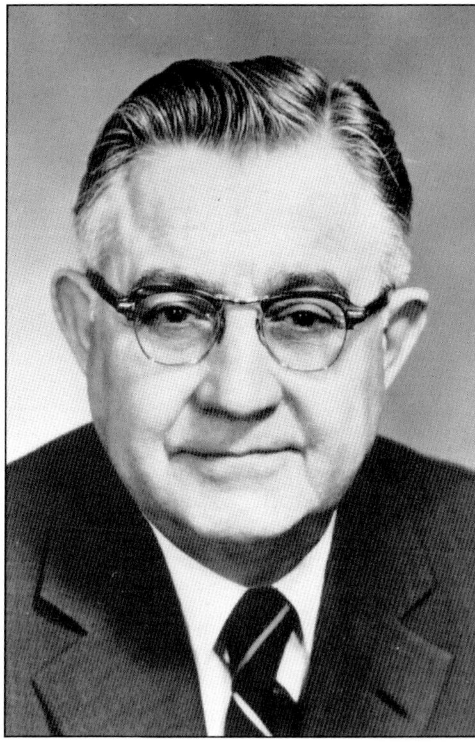

Wesleyan University's station, WESU, can trace its roots back to two students living in Clark Hall who were inspired by the Brown University station in 1939. They fed a record player into a small transmitter that, in turn, used the campus water pipes as an antenna. The station, originally WES, was assigned the WESU call letters in 1950. In this 1953 image, two student broadcasters are on the air in the basement studio. (Courtesy of Wesleyan University Library, Special Collections and Archives.)

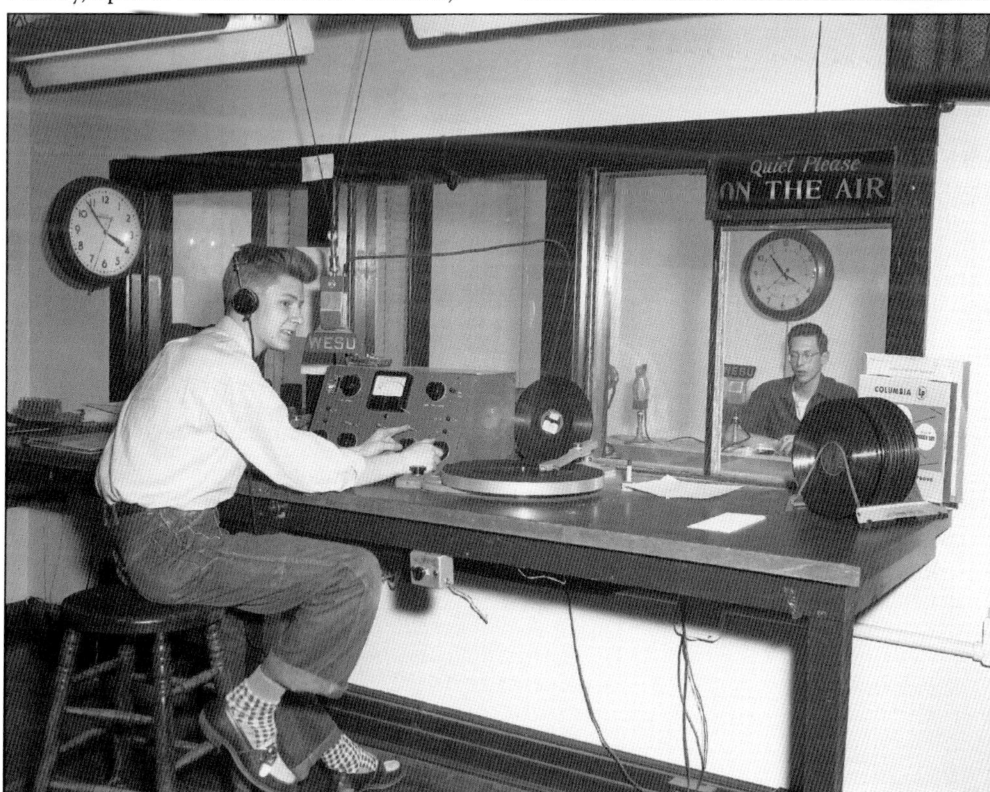

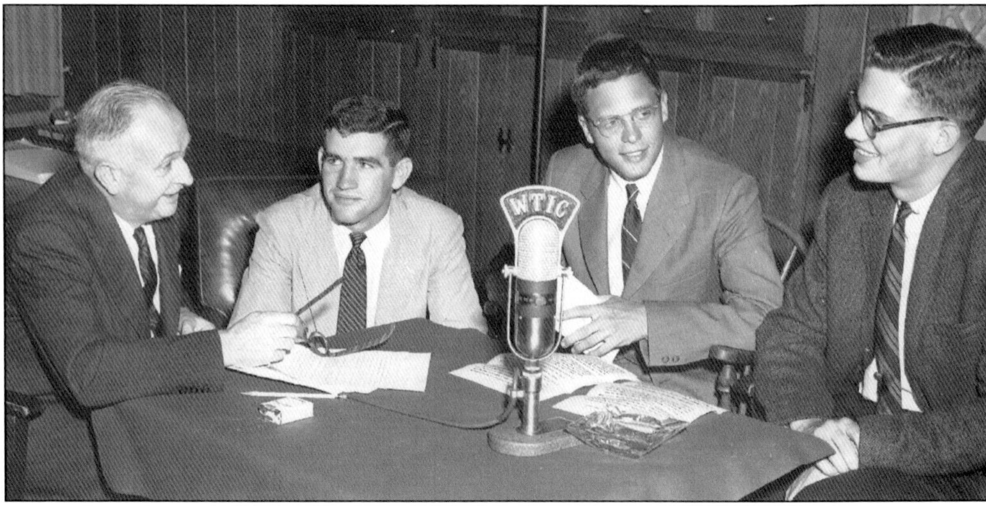


Three Yale seniors of the class of 1954 discuss their views on education during WTIC's *Yale Interprets the News* program. Participants in the panel discussion are, from left to right, moderator Bernard Mullins; Edward J. Molloy, a star football player; G. Gaddis Smith, chairman of the *Yale Daily News*; and George Jacoby Jr., president of the Yale Phi Beta Kappa chapter and a member of the varsity fencing team. (Courtesy of CBS Radio Inc.)

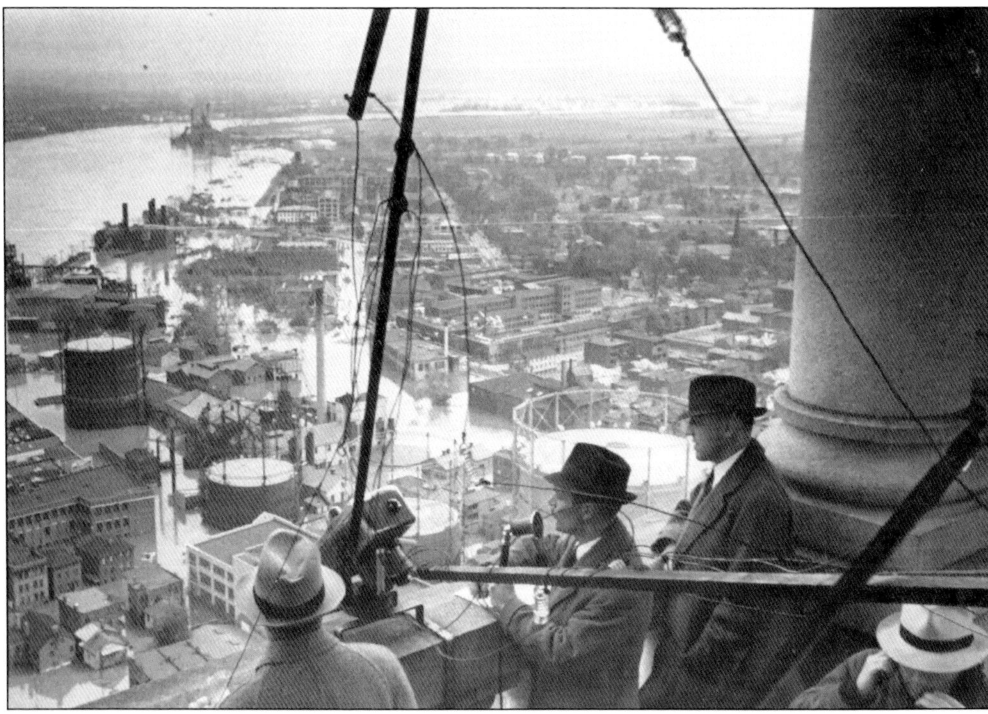

Radio stations played a key role during the great flood of 1926 by providing news and information to the state's residents. In this picture, newscasters from WTIC, including Tom McCray (right) broadcast from the observation deck of the Travelers Tower in downtown Hartford. This view is facing the southeast. The Park River can be seen overflowing its banks in the center of the photograph, and the South Meadows power plant and Brainard Field are visible in the upper frame of the photograph. (Courtesy of CBS Radio Inc.)

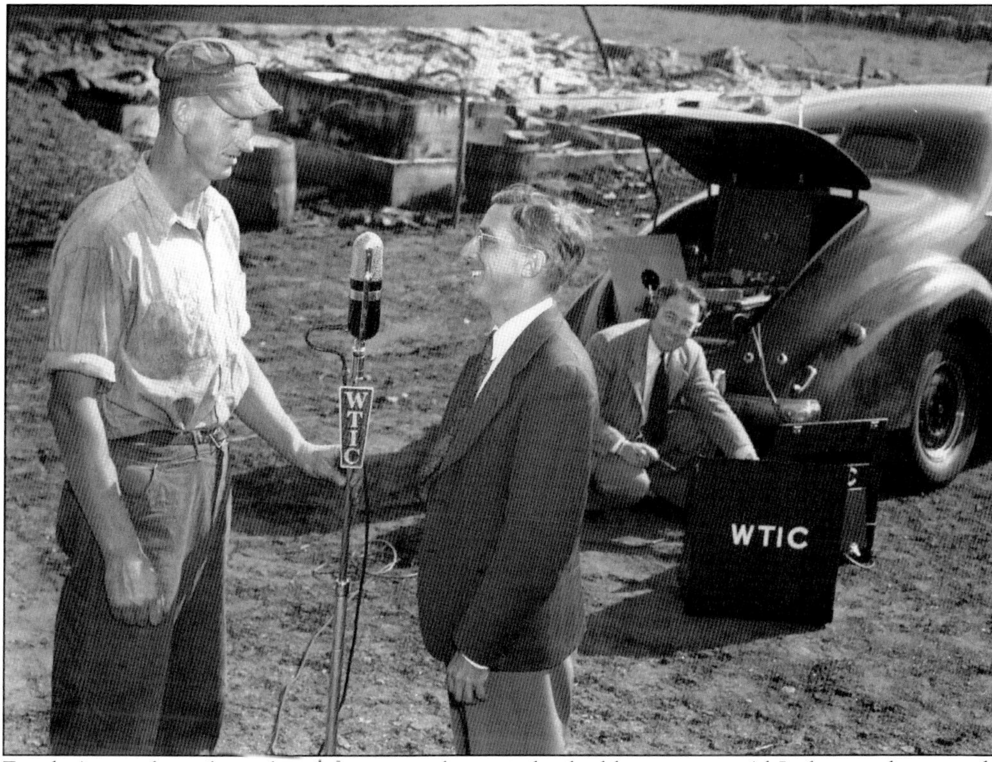


Frank Atwood, to the right of the microphone, is backed by engineer Al Jackson, who records the program on a 16-inch aluminum disk. The recorder is carefully set in the trunk of the old Studebaker. To assure quality, the recorder had to be level. This 1950s remote is at the scene of a barn fire in eastern Connecticut. Atwood is talking with an unidentified farmer whose barn has recently burned. The topic of the program was farm safety. (Courtesy of CBS Radio Inc.)

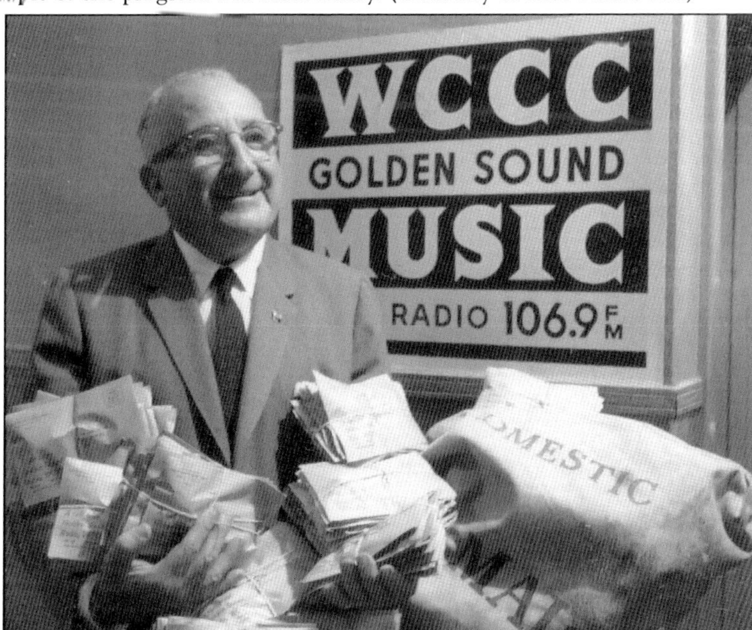


In this 1961 photograph, well-known Hartford jeweler Bill Savitt is seen with some of the mail generated by his popular AM radio station, WCCC. Sister station WCCC-FM had only been on the air for two years when this photograph was taken. (Courtesy of the Connecticut Historical Society.).

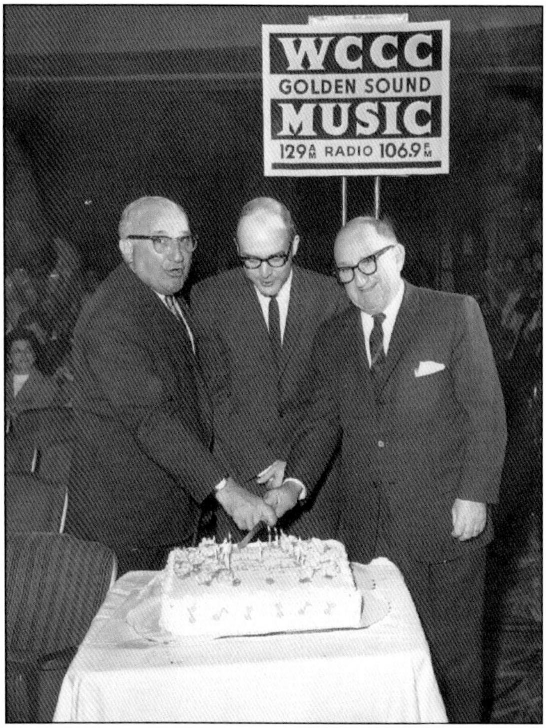


Bill (left) and Max Savitt (right) celebrate the birthday of their radio station, WCCC, with the lighting of a special cake. More than 400 people came to the party at Hartford's Strand Theater, where a special late-morning showing of *Mary, Mary* took place. WCCC-FM had only been on the air for a year or so when this photograph was taken. The man in the center is unidentified. (Courtesy of the Connecticut Historical Society.)

WTIC's Jean Colbert interviews former first lady Eleanor Roosevelt around 1957. Years later, Jean would tell friends that out of the hundreds of interviews she had done with dignitaries, actors, and recording artists, this was her favorite. (Courtesy of CBS Radio Inc.)

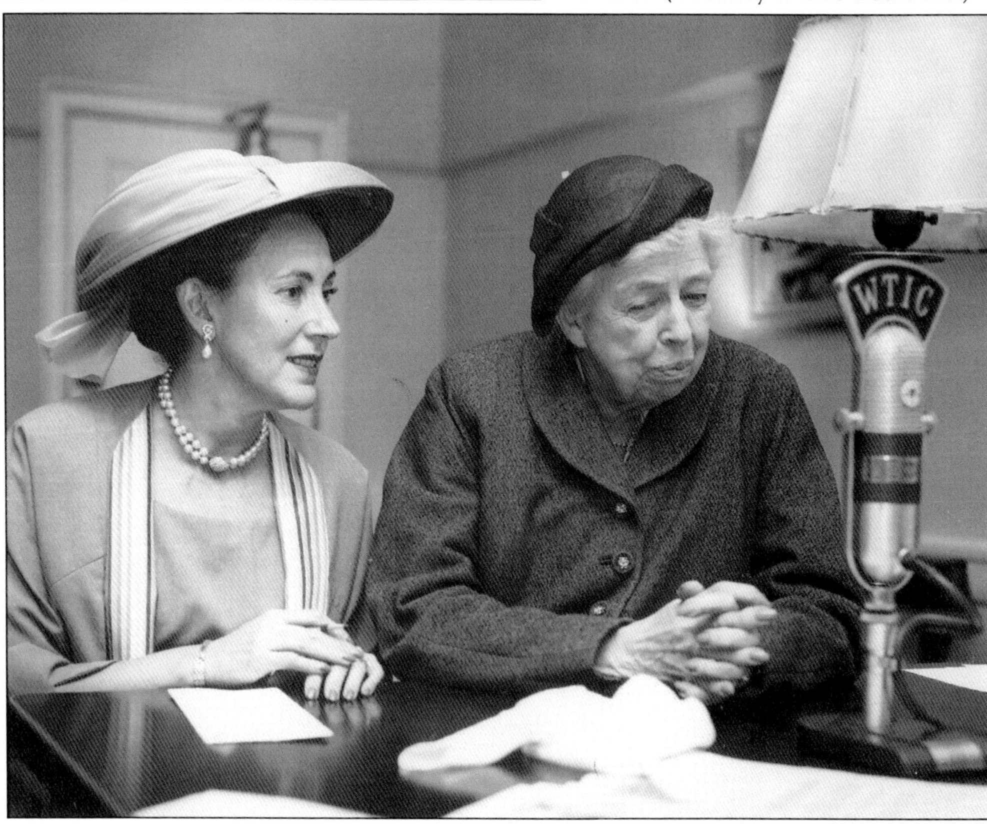

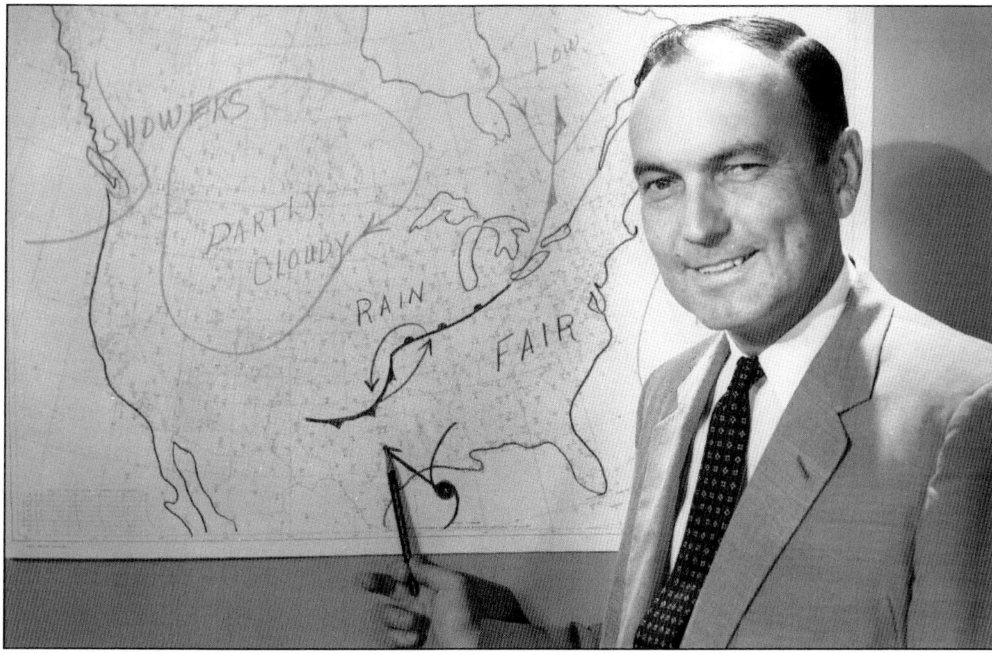


Milt Barlow of the US Weather Bureau is pictured at Bradley Field, preparing the 7:25 a.m. WTIC weather forecast for the *Bob Steele Show*. He was one of the first meteorologists hired by the Travelers Weather Service when it began providing forecasts and other weather information exclusively for WTIC on February 14, 1955. (Courtesy of CBS Radio Inc.)

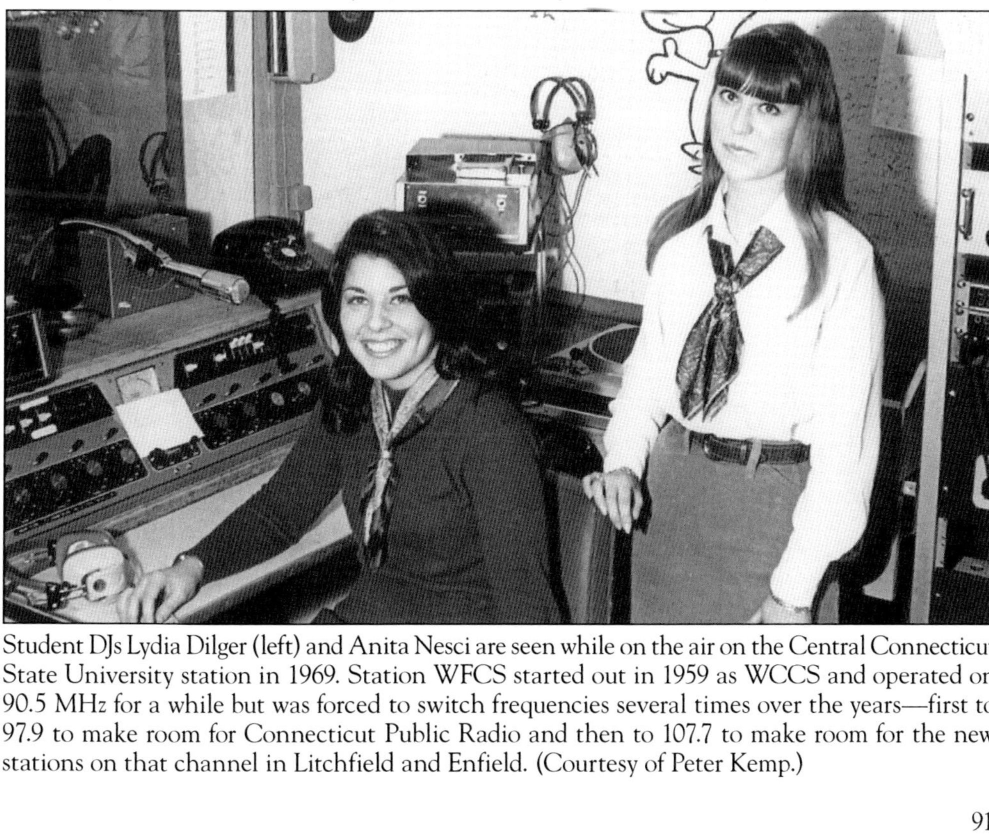

Student DJs Lydia Dilger (left) and Anita Nesci are seen while on the air on the Central Connecticut State University station in 1969. Station WFCS started out in 1959 as WCCS and operated on 90.5 MHz for a while but was forced to switch frequencies several times over the years—first to 97.9 to make room for Connecticut Public Radio and then to 107.7 to make room for the new stations on that channel in Litchfield and Enfield. (Courtesy of Peter Kemp.)

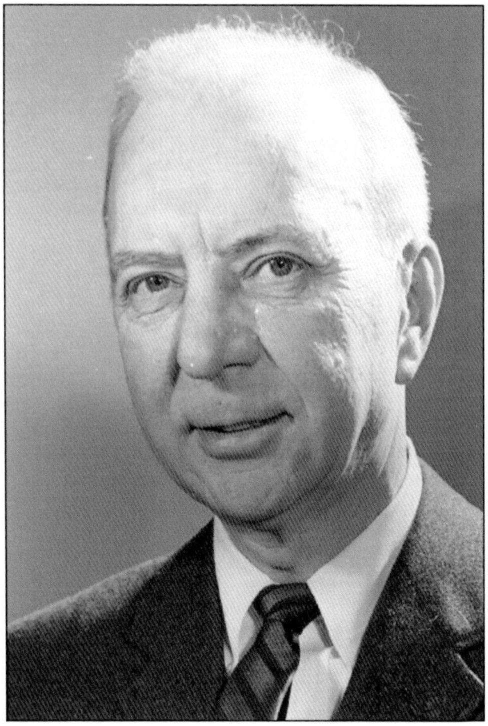

Walter Johnson left the Travelers Indemnity Company to become WTIC's first regular announcer in 1925. He was the station's only announcer for the good part of a year and reportedly wore a tuxedo to work during that time. Thirty years later, he is pictured here as vice president and general manager of WTIC. (Courtesy of CBS Radio Inc.)

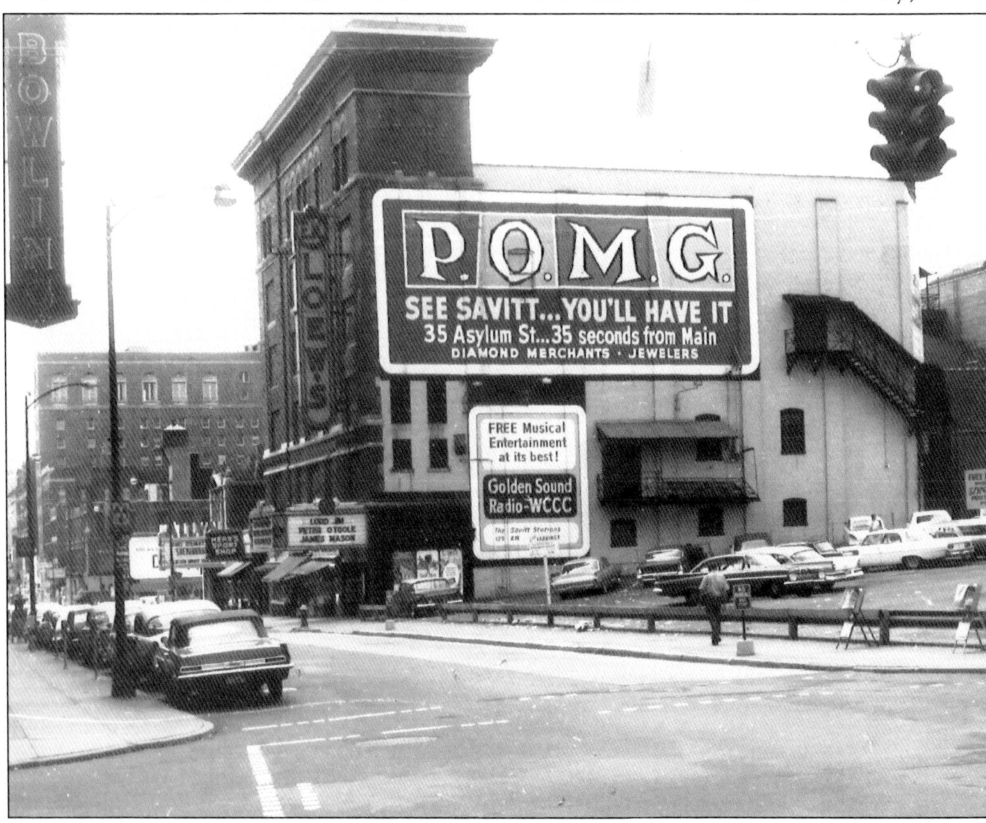


An advertisement for "Golden Sound Radio 'WCCC'" can be seen on the side of a building at the corner of Trumbull and Asylum Streets in Hartford around 1958. Also visible is a prominent advertisement for the jewelry store owned by the station's founder, Bill Savitt. "POMG" stood for "Piece of Mind Guaranteed." (Courtesy of the Connecticut Historical Society.)

# *Five*

# THE 1960s

Rock and roll came to the airways in force in the 1960s, and WDRC adopted a Top 40 format in 1960—the first station in Hartford to do so full-time. WDRC was a pioneer in the new Top 40 format and rode the British Invasion to national success. DJs were once again household names, and radio became part of an entirely new generation. It was not long before WPOP switched to Top 40, which resulted in a competitive environment that made both stations stronger.

Radio was still relied upon to provide the news, and a number of Hartford radio stations had large news staffs during this time. Some AM stations still refused to broadcast new music and suddenly faced new competition from FM stations that would play it.

College radio started coming into its own in the 1960s, helped along by the progressive music scene. Station's such as Trinity College's WRTC and the University of Hartford's WWUH were some of the first in the country to play what was known then as underground or progressive rock music. Towards the end of the decade, a number of commercial FM stations decided to play progressive rock. Hartford's WHCN switched from classical music to rock in 1969, helped in part by some of the folks who had put WWUH on the air the prior year.

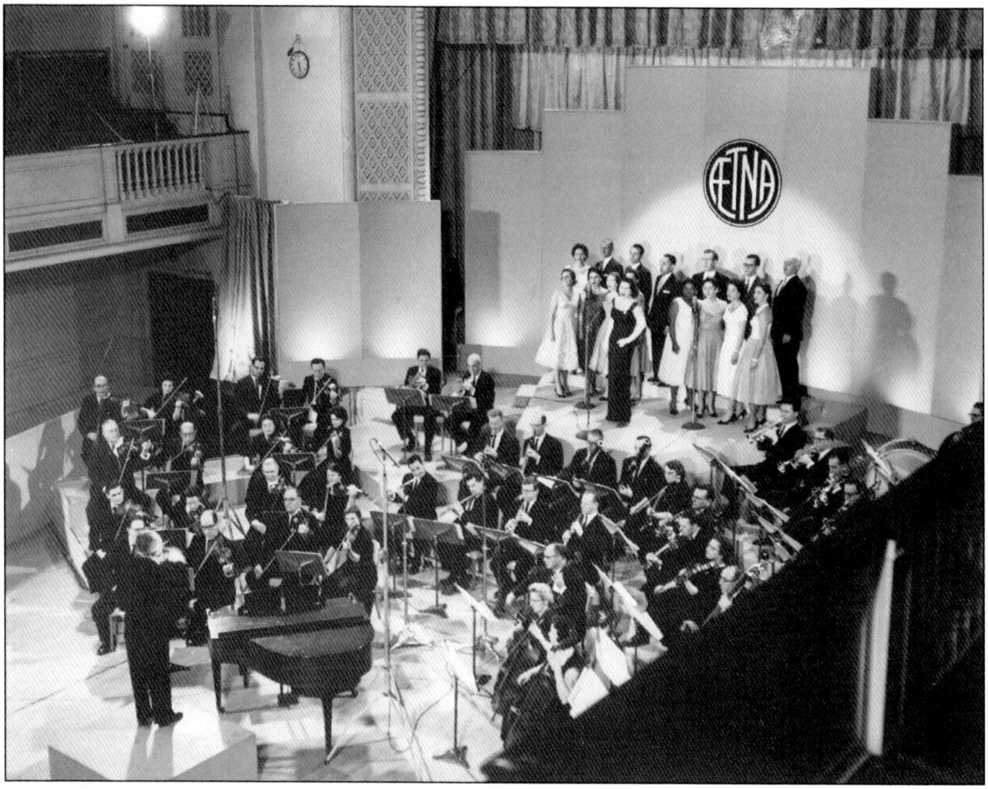


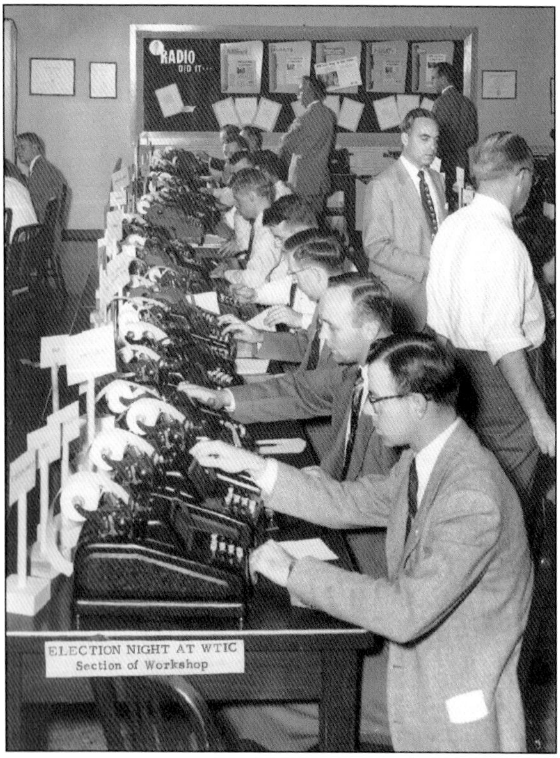


This photograph shows a live WTIC broadcast from the Aetna Theater. During one of these broadcasts in 1962, three members of the same family were reportedly on the radio on different Hartford stations simultaneously. Joseph Blume was performing on violin in the Hartford Symphony on WTIC, while son Jerry Blume was doing his regular show on WDRC, and Joseph's other son, Dan Blume, was doing his regular jazz show on WBMI. (Courtesy of Daniel Blume.)

Many listeners turned to radio to keep them informed on election night. In this 1962 image, WTIC staffers use mechanical calculators to manually tally the results of the various statewide and local races. The numerical results were then given to producers who incorporated them into the scripts read by the announcers. (Courtesy of CBS Radio Inc.)

In white tie and tails is Robert E. Smith, host of the *Theater of Melody*, one of WTIC's most popular weekday morning programs. The show began in 1947 and enjoyed a longer run than any of the Broadway shows it featured. For more than a quarter of a century, Bob Smith displayed his knowledge and love of Broadway and Hollywood musicals, introduced by his distinctive theme, "The Music of the Spheres." After WTIC-FM switched formats in the mid-1970s, *Theater of Melody* was aired on WWUH at the University of Hartford. (Courtesy of CBS Radio Inc.)

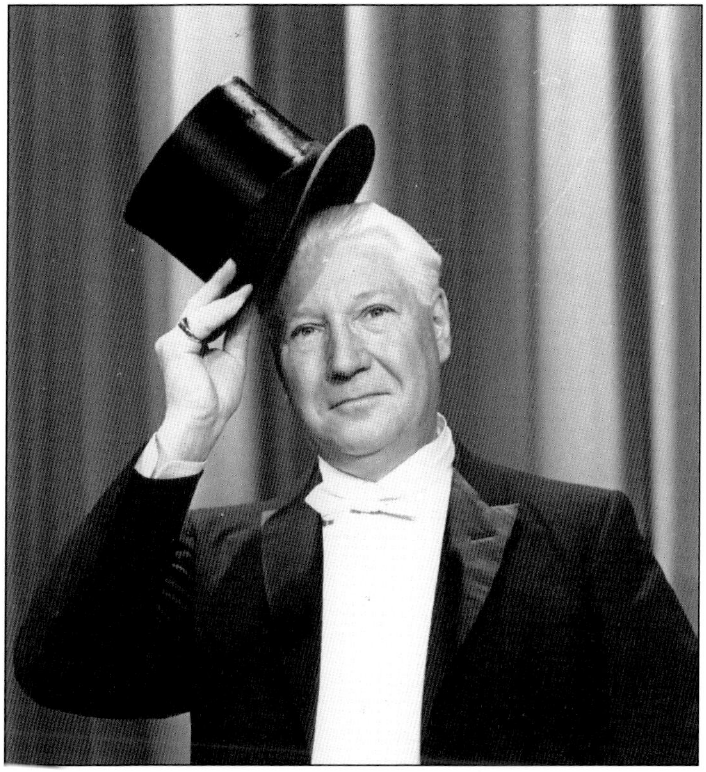

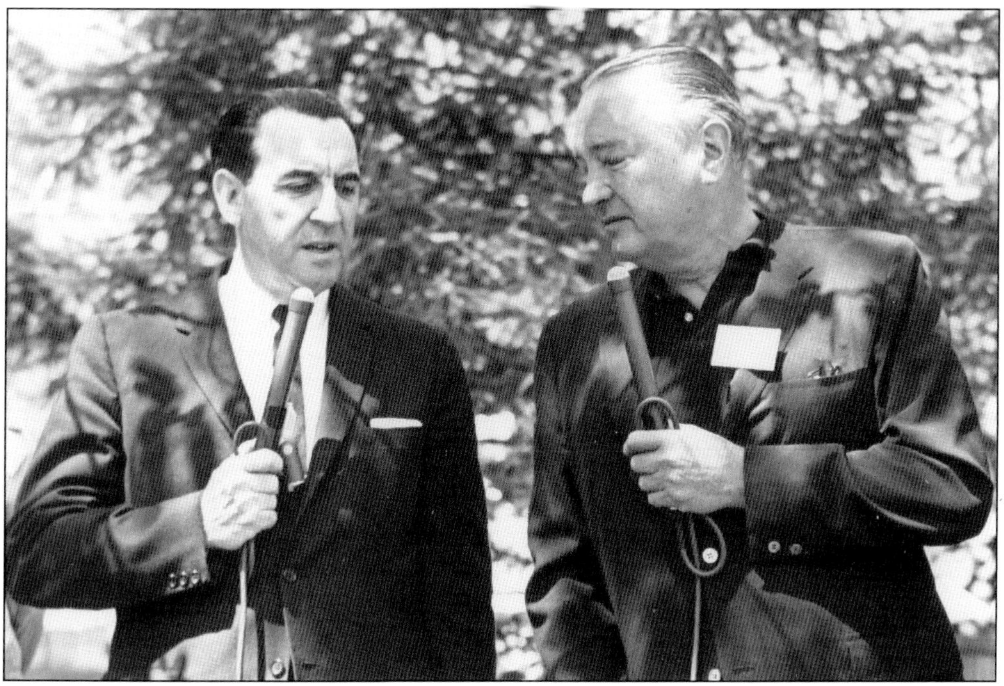

Gov. John Dempsey (left), the state's chief executive from 1961 to 1971, is shown here with WTIC's first president, Paul W. Morency, during a 1962 remote broadcast from the state capitol. (Courtesy of CBS Radio Inc.)

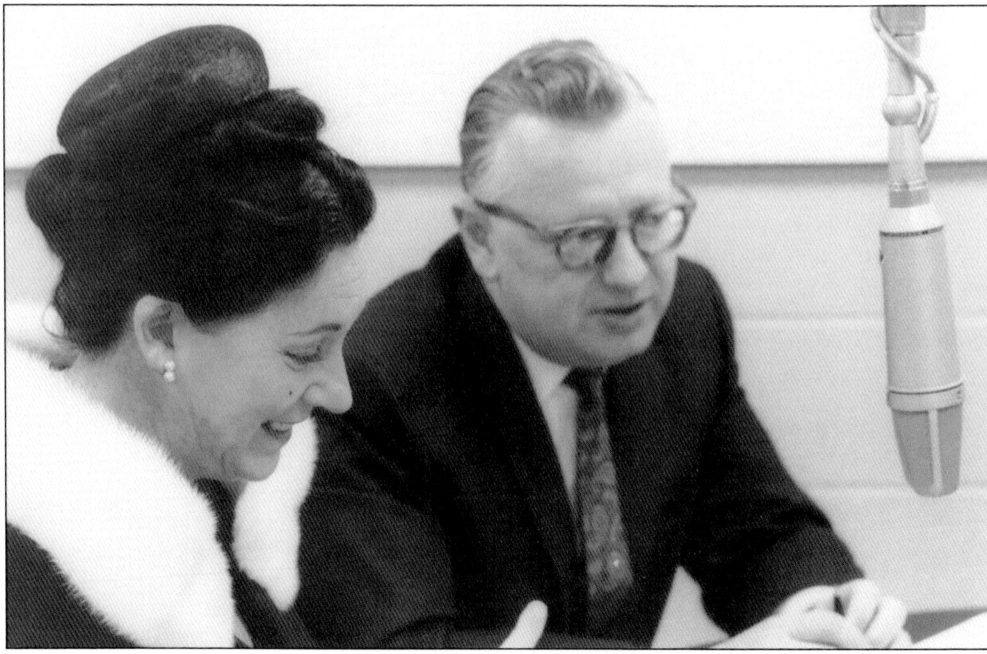

WTIC's *Jean Colbert Show* was hosted by its star for over 25 years. During that record run, the program featured two WTIC announcers as cohosts—Ross Miller for the first seven years and Ed Anderson for the last 18 years. A loquacious character and skilled interviewer, Ed (shown here with Jean) anchored the show during Jean's girdling jaunts. (Courtesy of CBS Radio Inc.)

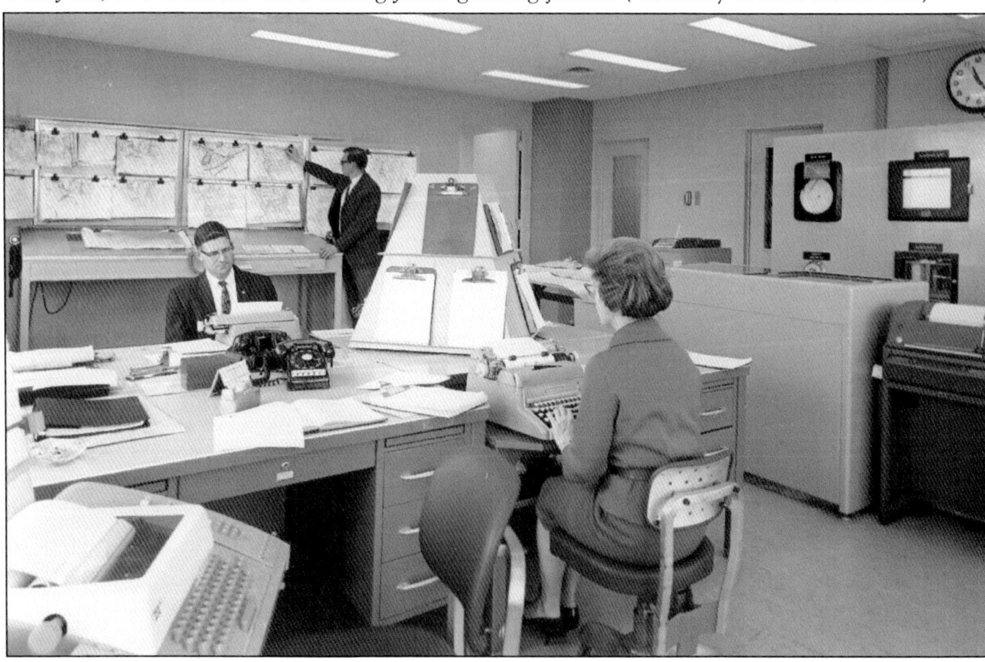

The Travelers Weather Research Center was created in 1954 by WTIC's parent, the Travelers Insurance Company, for insurance underwriting purposes. Pictured here is the weather service office around 1960. Meterologist Jim MacDonald is the man at the typewriter. (Courtesy of CBS of Radio Inc.)

WTIC's *Mike Line* was a very popular afternoon call-in show where listeners could ask questions and give answers. Bill Hennessey and Floyd Richards were the regular hosts of the show, while Bob Ellsworth would fill in from time to time. (Courtesy of CBS Radio Inc.)

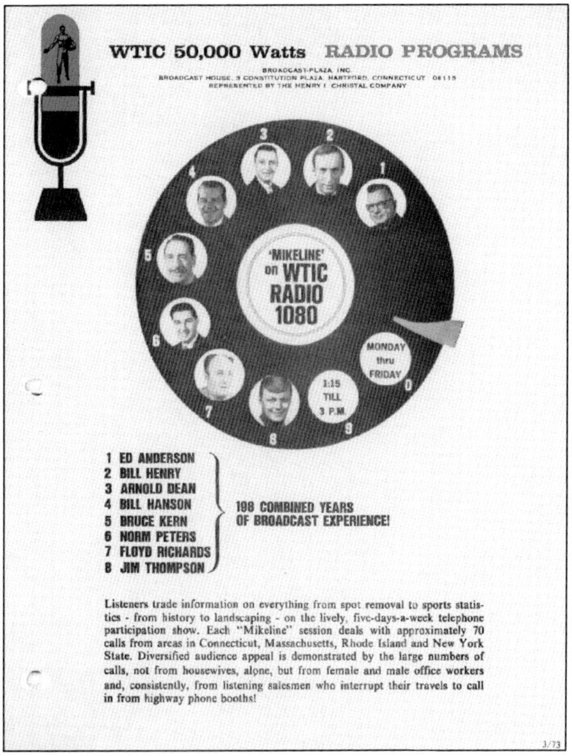


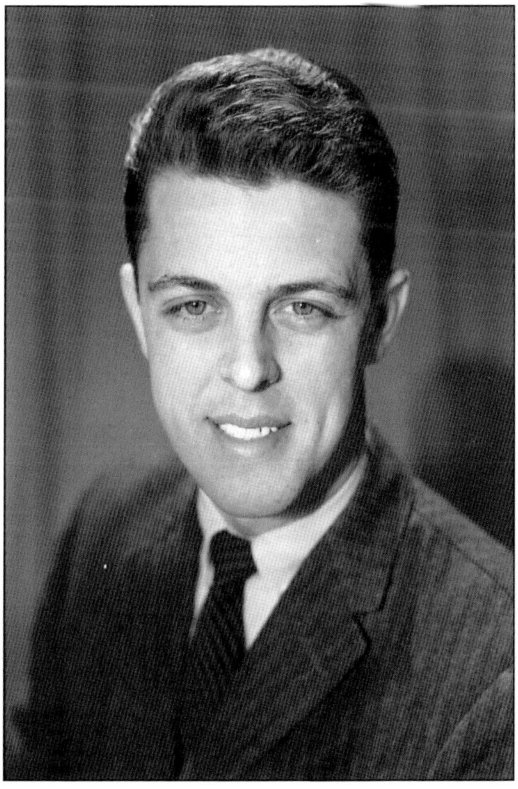

WTIC's Bill Hennessey was best known for his midday show at WTIC in the 1950s and 1960s called *Hennessey—That's Me*. During his more than 40-year career, Hennessey worked at just about every station in Hartford. (Courtesy of CBS Radio Inc.)

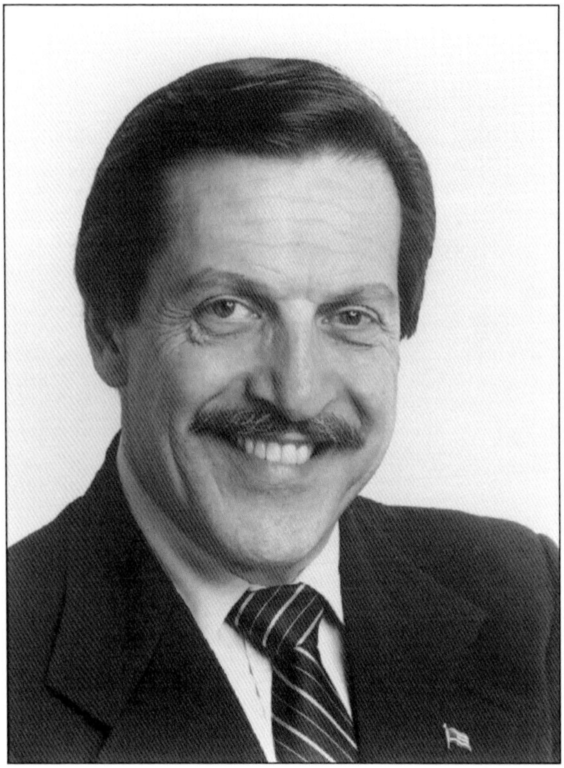

Bob Ellsworth was on WTIC during the 1950s and 1960s. He hosted an afternoon musical program but is best known as the TV/3 11:00 p.m. news anchor. Ellsworth was an expert at fielding listeners' questions during the call-in program. (Courtesy of CBS Radio Inc.)

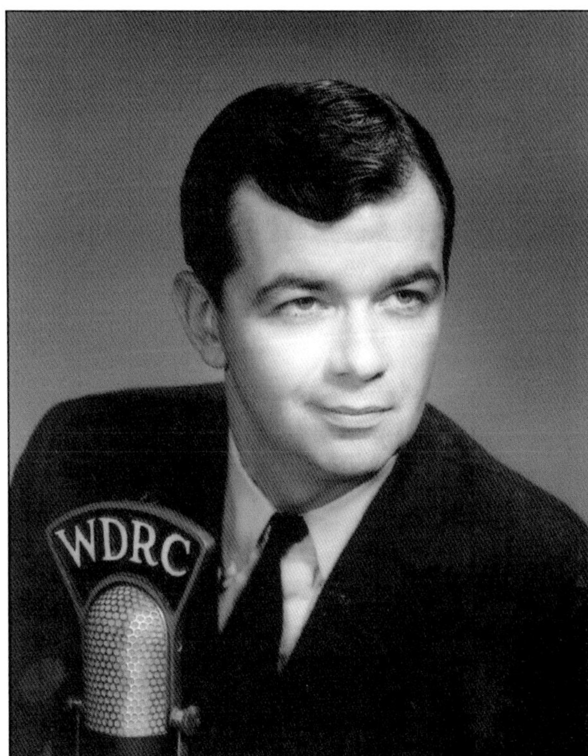


Dick Robinson has one of the most recognizable names (and voices) in Hartford radio. He hosted one of the most popular shows during the 1960s on WDRC. This is his WDRC publicity photograph. (Courtesy of WDRC.)

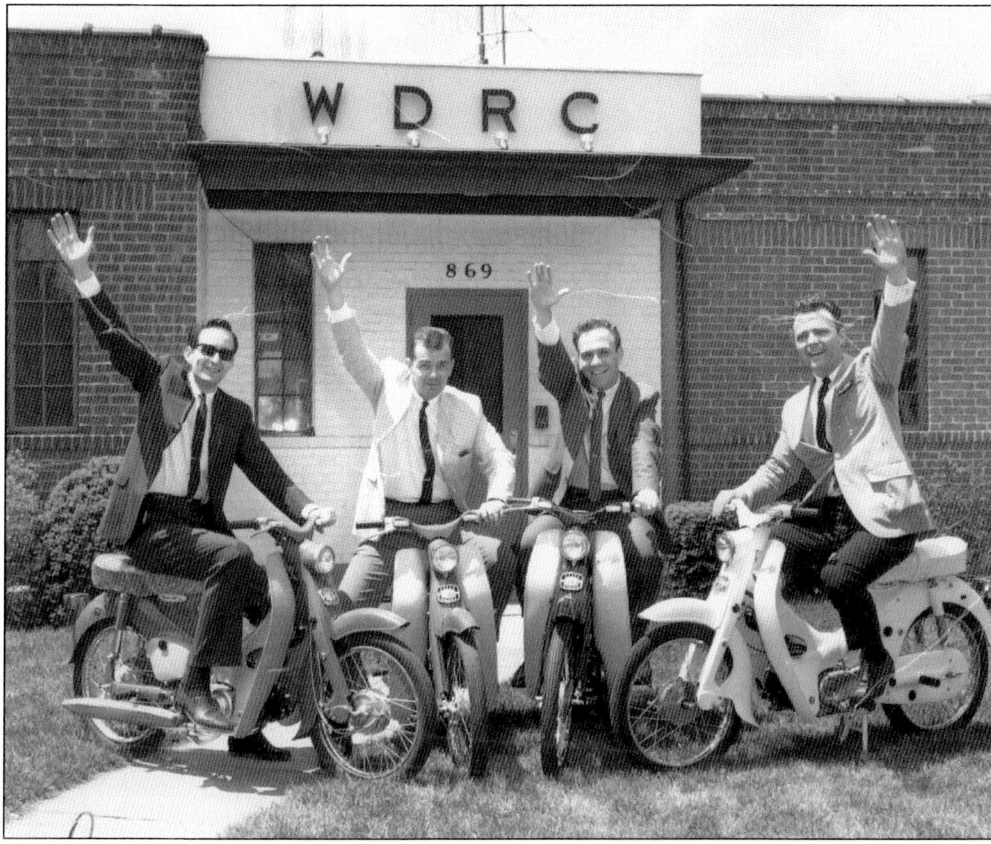


Pictured here are four WDRC on-air personalities who were popular in the mid-1960s. From left to right are "Long" John Wade, Dick Robinson, Jim Nettleton, and Ron Landry. This publicity shot was taken outside the station's studios on Blue Hills Avenue in Bloomfield. (Courtesy of WDRC.)

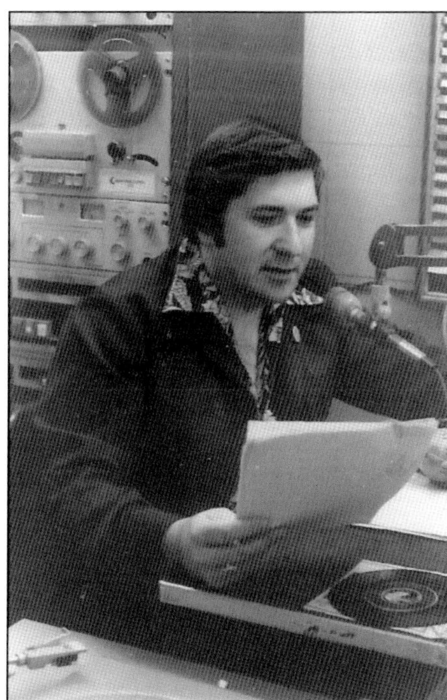

Lucio Ruzzier spent many years on the air on WRYM in Newington before purchasing Hartford's 1550 (formally WEXT), which became WRDM under his ownership. After selling WRDM, he purchased WRYM in Newington. Ruzzier also served as a board member of the Connecticut Broadcasters Association. In this c. 1978 photograph, Ruzzier is on the air at WRYM. (Courtesy of WRYM.)

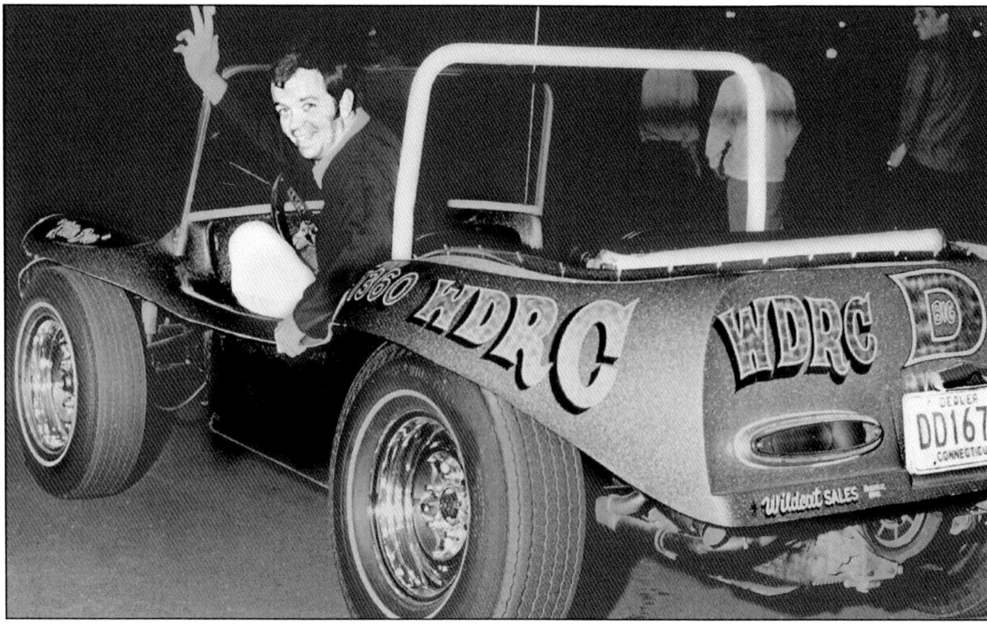


"The station with the beach reach" was a popular slogan heard on WDRC in the 1960s, and in its competition with rival WPOP, WDRC always tried to come up with interesting ways to draw attention to itself. In this photograph, WDRC's Dick Robinson is seen in the WDRC dune buggy at the Connecticut shore in 1968. (Courtesy of WDRC.)

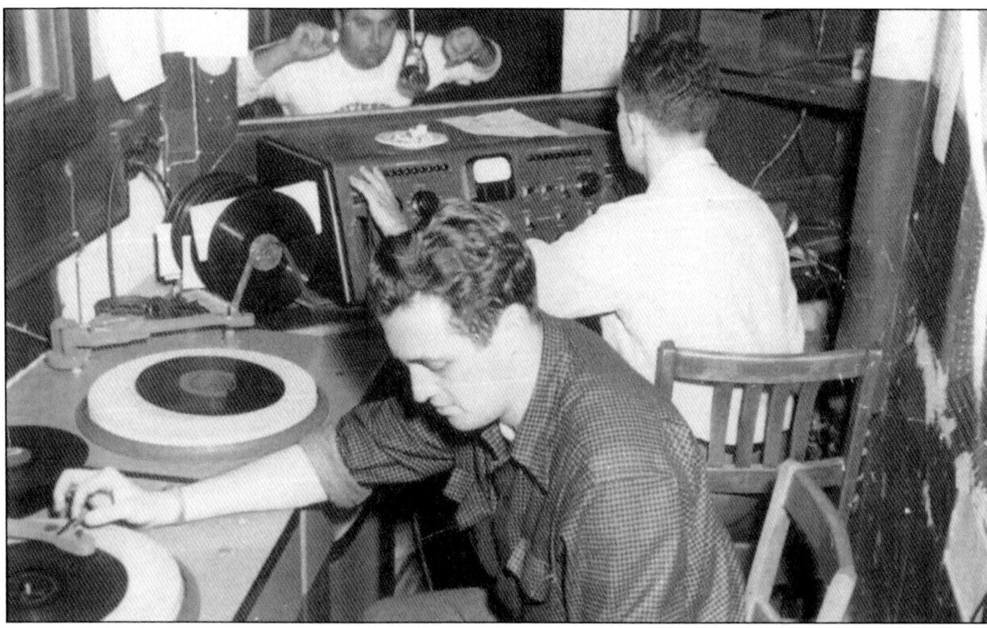

This 1953 photograph shows the WHUS studio in Koons Hall on the University of Connecticut campus as it looked before the station's move to the student center. Jack Guckin (left) is at the turntable, and Mike Drechsler is behind the glass signaling an unidentified engineer at the console. WHUS was the one of the first stations in the state, coming on the air in 1922 as WABL from Storrs. Around 1931, the call letters were changed to WCAC, which stood for "Connecticut Agricultural College." Later, the calls were changed to WHUS. (Courtesy of Michael Drechsler.)

# *Six*

# The 1970s

In the early 1970s, FM radio had yet to prove itself as its listenership was just a small fraction of the AM audience. The success of FM was hampered by the fact that, during this period, many stations were just simulcasting their AM programming on their co-owned FM stations. The higher cost of FM receivers as compared to AM was also a factor in the slow growth of FM.

The popularity of rock music among the nation's youth helped turn more people on to the unique programming offered by some FM broadcasters. By the mid-1970s, there were no longer just two formats—Top 40 on AM and progressive rock on FM; soft hits, old rock, new rock, classic rock, country, disco, soul, Latino, and even more was heard on the airwaves. Each station had only a small percentage of the audience, which allowed advertisers to put their money where potential consumers would hear their messages.

The proliferation of inexpensive satellite technology allowed hundreds of new radio networks to emerge, mostly offering music formats. Small stations plugged these music networks into their automation systems and tried to make a go of it with very small staffs.

By the end of the decade, FM had caught on, helped along by the popularity of rock and disco music.

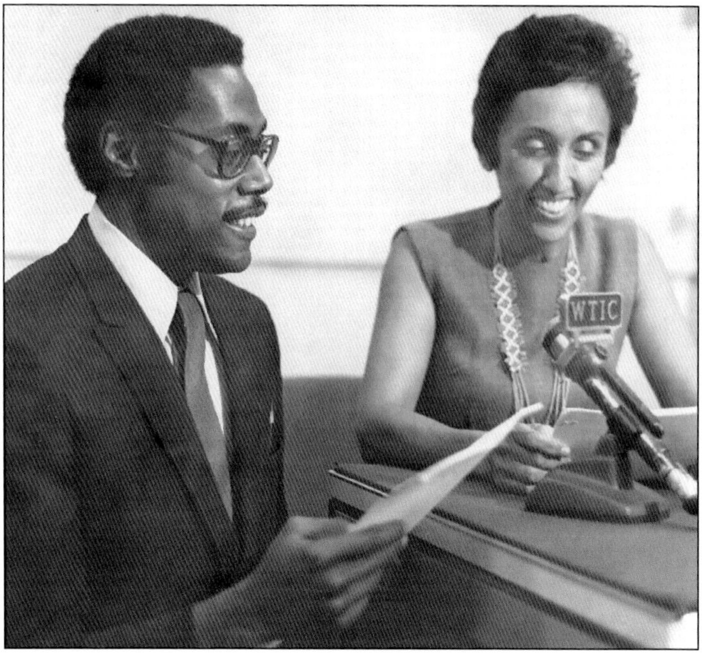


In the summer of 1970, WTIC began a daily news feature for the benefit of Greater Hartford's growing Hispanic community: *WTIC News in Spanish*. The capsule summary of world and local news contained a brief weather forecast. The report was prepared by John Sablon (left) of WTIC News, who also presented some Spanish-English features. The news was translated and delivered by WTIC's community affairs coordinator Reyna Piola (right). (Courtesy of CBS Radio Inc.)

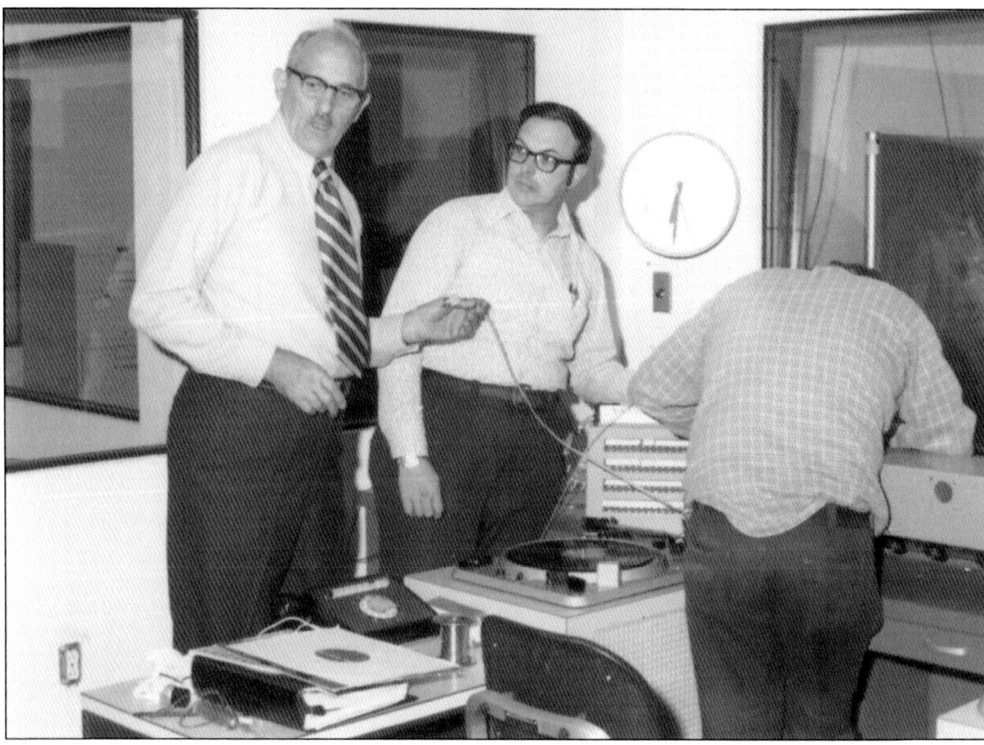

WTIC vice president of engineering Harold Dorschug (left) is pictured with two unidentified engineers during the construction of the new studios in the Gold Building in 1974. As WTIC's engineering director for several decades, Harold was also involved with the construction of many of the Hartford-area noncommercial stations such as WWUH, WJMJ, WFCS, and WQTQ. (Courtesy of Arnold Chase.)

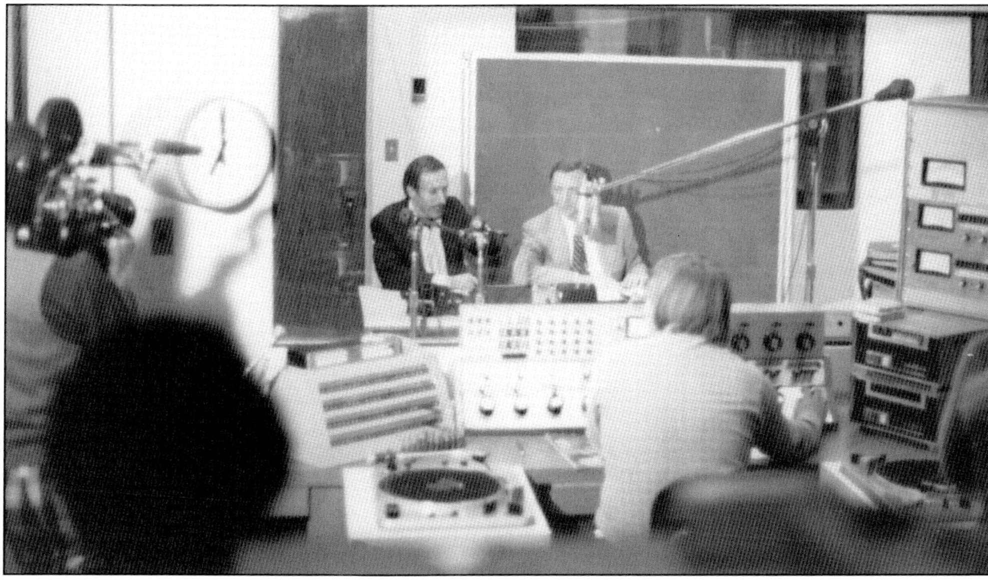

In 1974, WTIC radio moved from Broadcast House on Constitution Plaza to 1 Financial Plaza on Main Street. The first program to air from WTIC's new studio in the Gold Building was Arnold Dean's sports show. In this photograph, camera crews film Dean's opening show from the new facility. (Courtesy of Arnold Chase.)

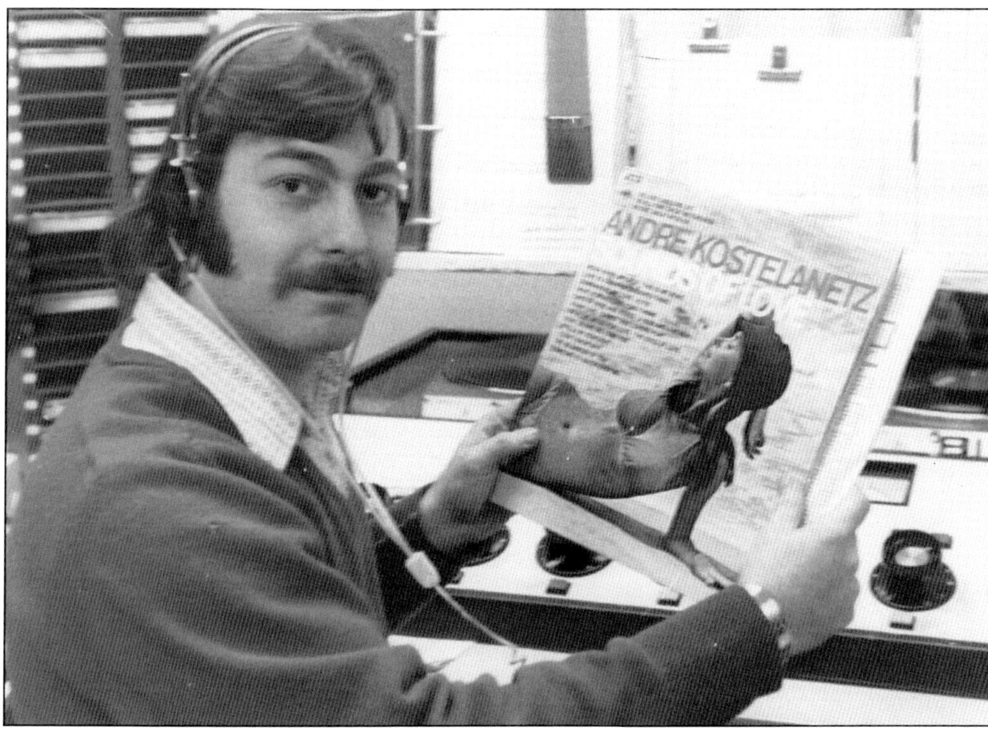


WRCH was a beautiful-music format station for more than two decades. In this photograph, Bob Marx (whose real name was Bart Mazarella) is on the air in the WRCH studio on Birdseye Road in Farmington. Mazarella spent many years at WDRC before moving over to WRCH. (Courtesy of Bart Mazarella.)

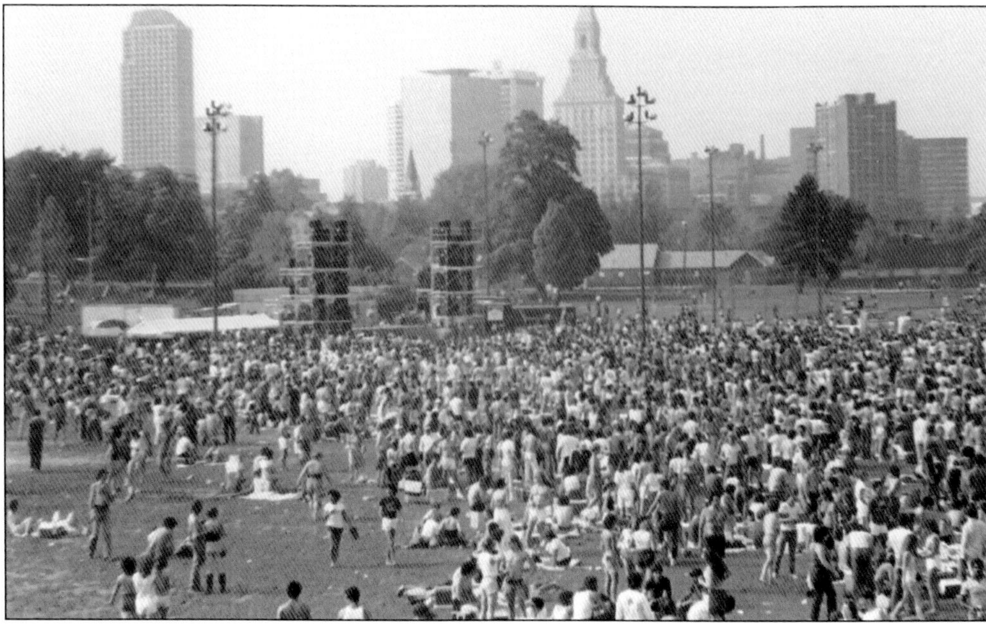

Thousands of fans turned out annually during the 1970s and 1980s for Hartford's New England Fiddle Contest. The event was carried live each year over WWUH 91.3, allowing thousands to listen who could not otherwise attend. This photograph shows the crowds at the only fiddle contest that was held in Colt Park instead of Bushnell Park. (Courtesy of WWUH Radio.)

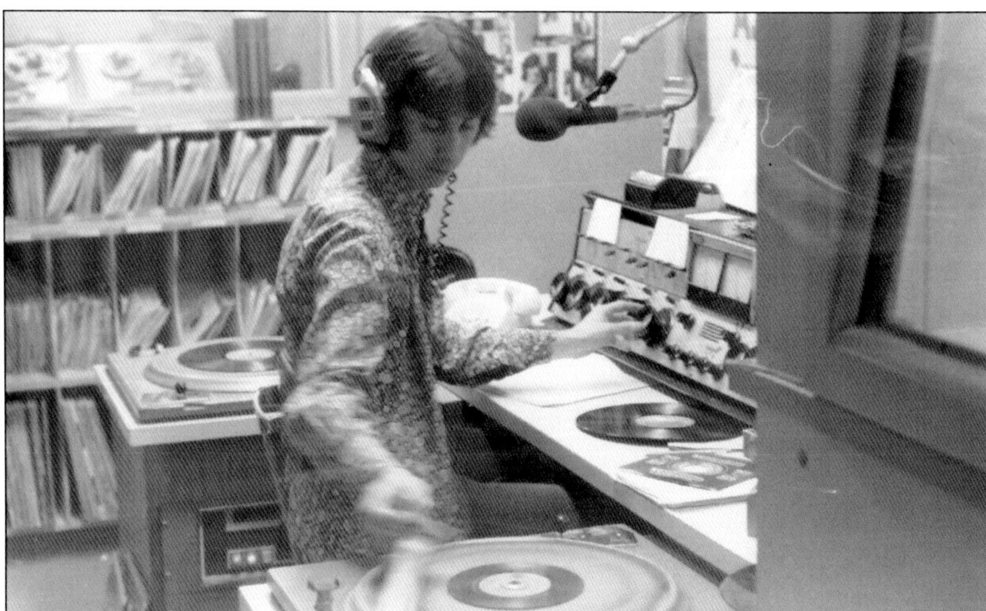

Dan Hayden, who would later become program director of WHCN, is seen at the controls of WCCC-FM's 11 Asylum Street studio in this 1973 photograph. Other notable WCCC jocks of that era include Rusty Potz and Joe Schlosser, who first appeared on WCCC as "Brooklyn Joe" and would later be known as "Sebastian." Dan went by the name "Raccoon Charlie" while on the air at WCCC. (Courtesy of Dan Hayden.)

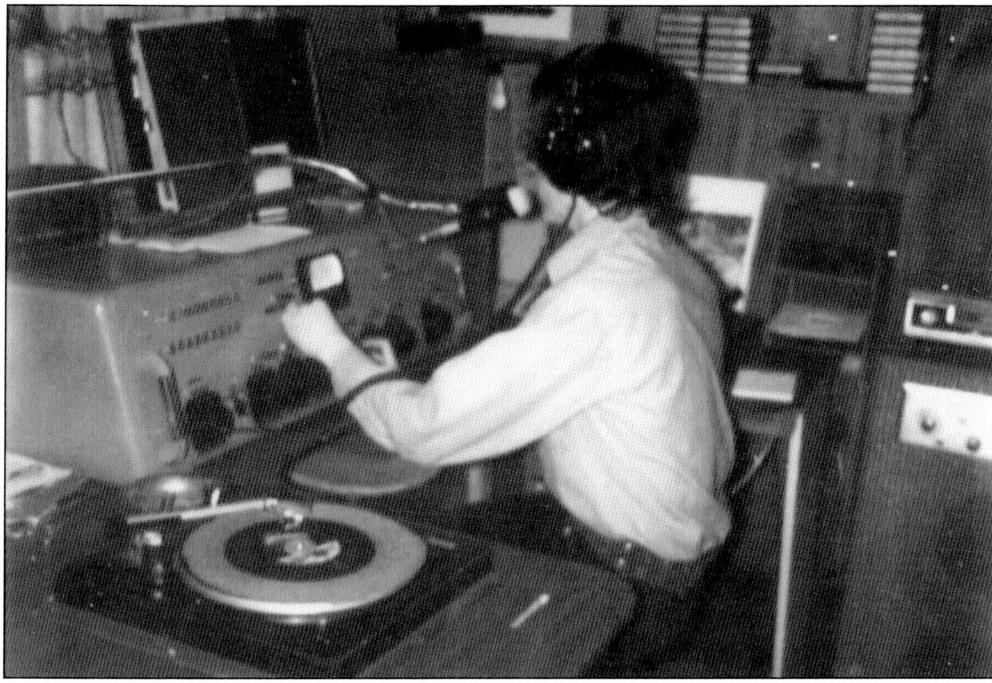

Pirate broadcaster WKOB operated from several locations around New Britain in the 1970s. Its Top 40 sound was very professional, and it attracted quite an audience. A young unidentified DJ is pictured at the controls of the "Mighty 1200" in 1975. (Courtesy of Bob Radil.)

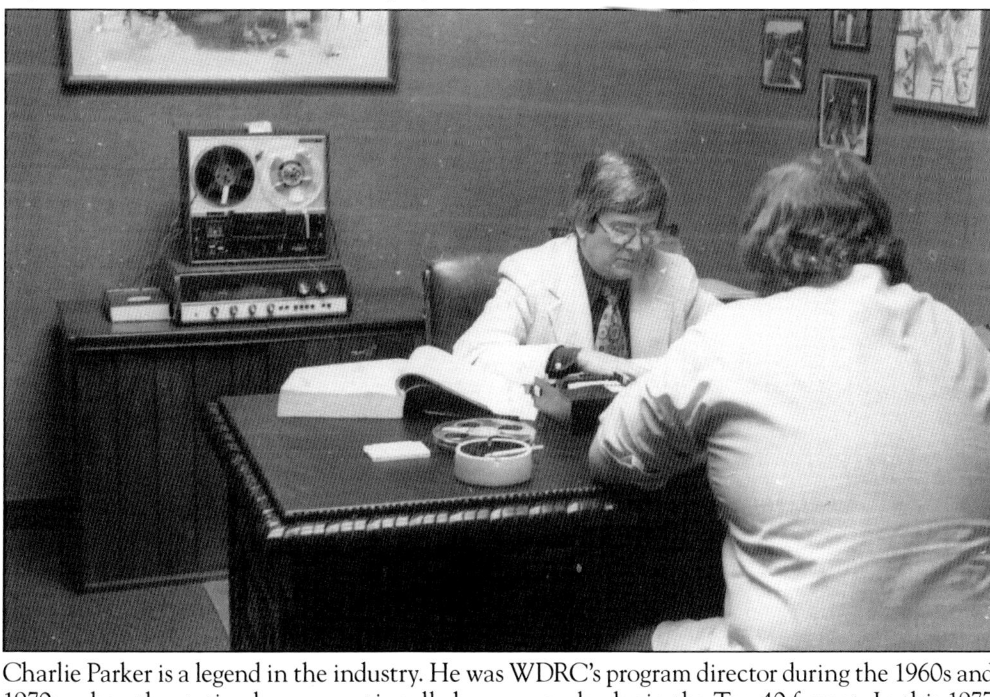

Charlie Parker is a legend in the industry. He was WDRC's program director during the 1960s and 1970s, when the station became nationally known as a leader in the Top 40 format. In this 1977 photograph, Charlie (right) is in his office with "Otis In the Nighttime" (Judd Otis). (Courtesy of Vic Vincz).

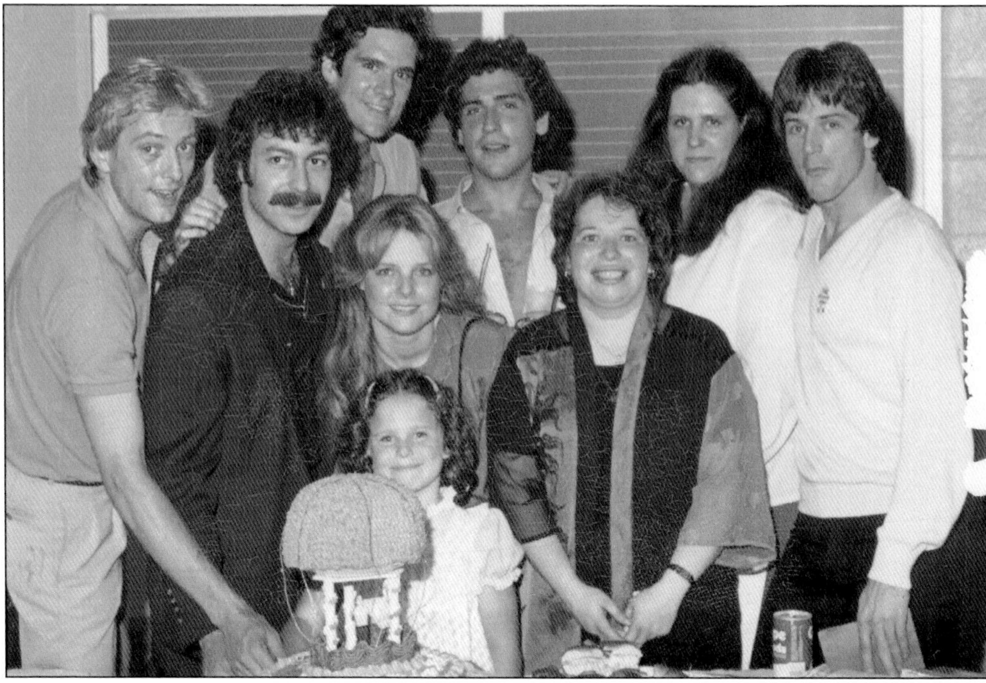

WDRC's Bob Marx (second from left) is pictured with producer David Hasselhoff (third from left) and the casts of the *Guiding Light* and *Another World*. They appeared on WDRC as part of a promotion for the highly rated afternoon soap opera. (Courtesy of Bart Mazzarella.)

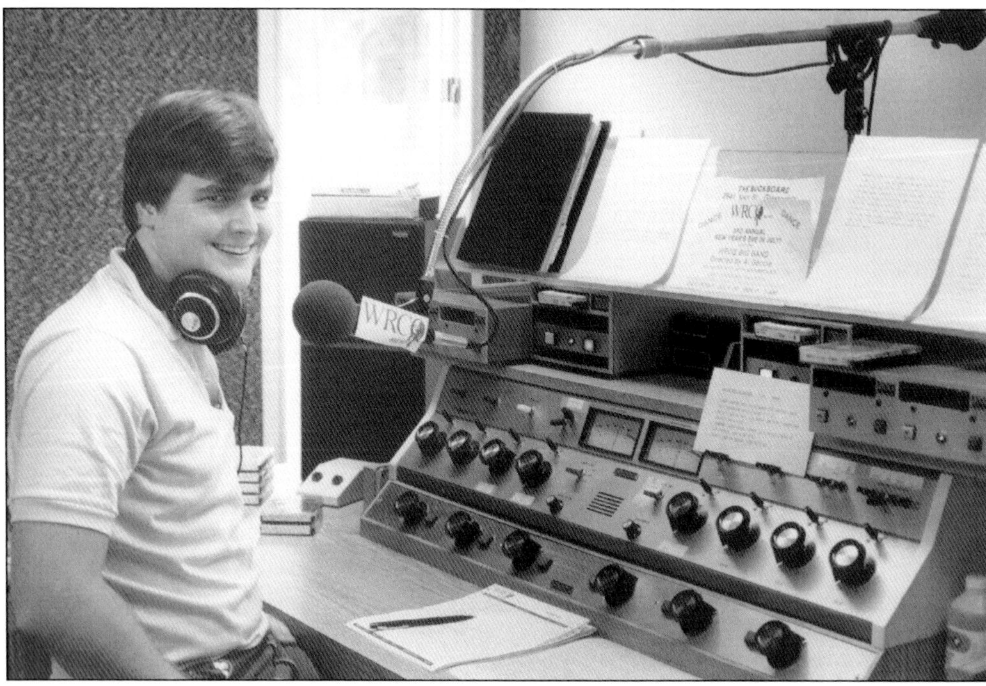

WRCQ in Farmington started out as WHAY and used the call letters WRCH in the 1960s and 1970s. Here, an unidentified announcer is in the WRCQ air studio on Birdseye Road in Farmington around 1979. (Author's collection.)

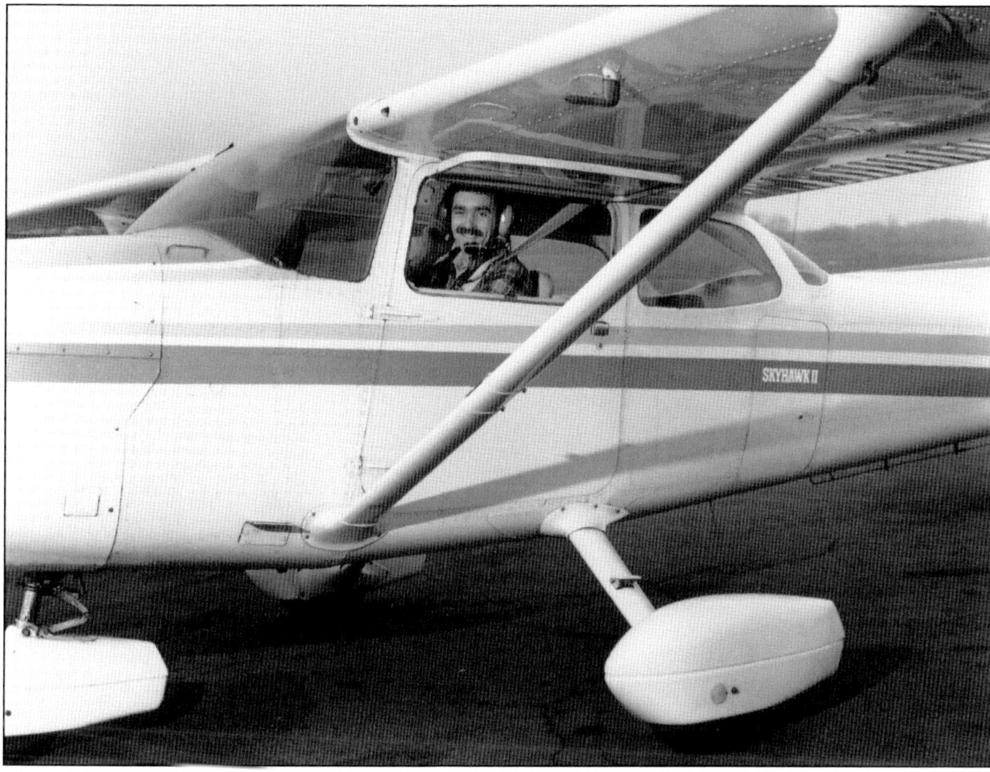


WTIC has been the only station in Hartford to have its own traffic plane that takes flight every morning and afternoon, weather permitting. Mike Allen's airborne traffic reports have helped thousands of commuters over the years. (Courtesy of CBS Radio Inc.)

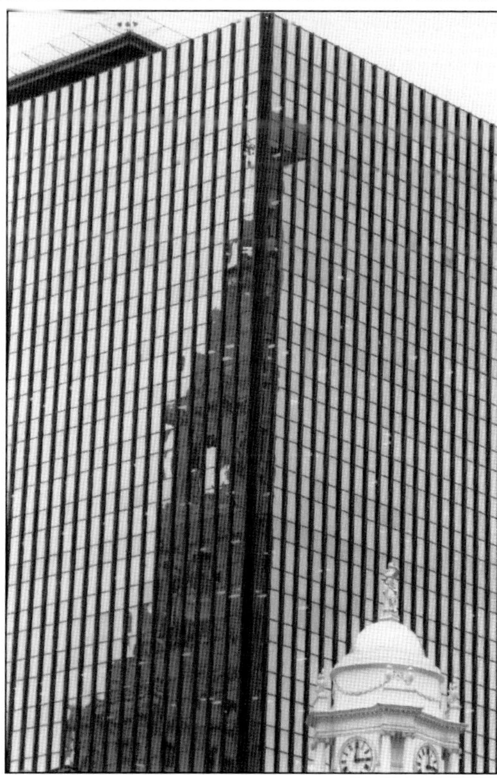

In 1974, when WTIC (AM and FM) split from WFSB Channel 3, the television station stayed behind in Broadcast House at Constitution Plaza while the radio stations moved to 1 Financial Plaza, also known as the Gold Building. WTIC radio occupied the 19th floor of the Gold Building from 1974 to 1999, when it moved to Farmington. (Courtesy of Arnold Chase.)

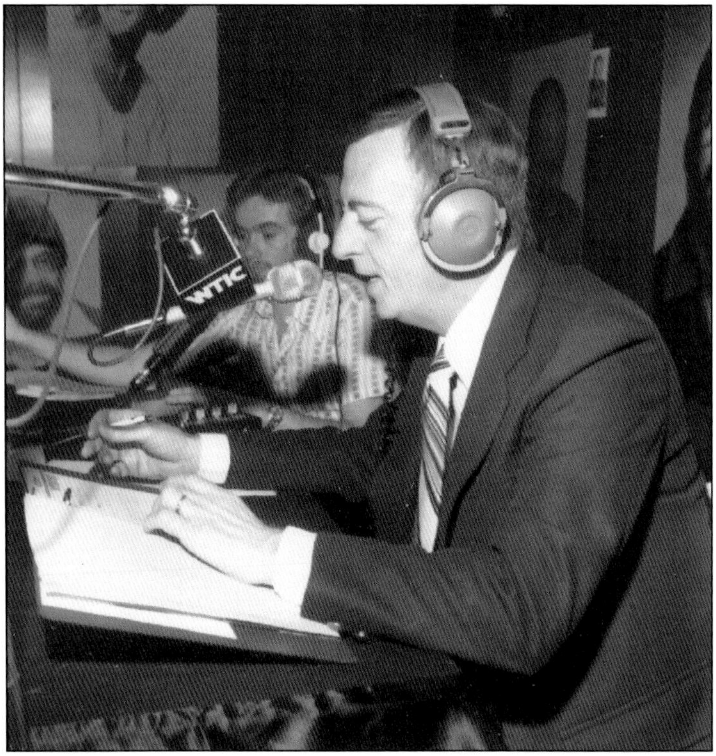


Arnold Dean, pictured here, has distinguished himself in virtually every phase of broadcasting, but his main focus has been on sports. Arnold did color when George Ehrlich was sports director and is best known as the host of WTIC's *SportsTalk*, a program he originated in 1976. He joined the WTIC staff in July 1965, and in July 1998, he celebrated his 50th anniversary in broadcasting. Arnold has been honored as Connecticut's Sportscaster of the Year several times and has won many Associated Press awards. (Courtesy of CBS Radio Inc.)

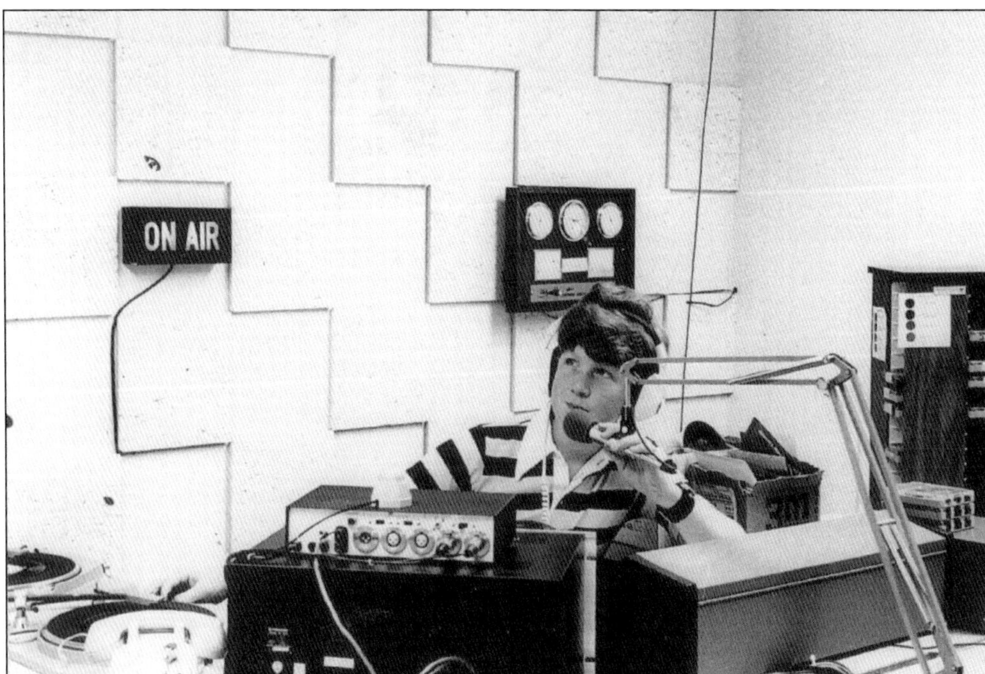


Two Hartford-area high schools, Weaver and Berlin, have stations. These stations are useful in public speaking, public relations, and English. In this image is 16-year-old Dave Lounder on the air on Berlin High School's 10-watt FM station, WERB, in 1979. (Courtesy of Dave Lounder.)

# *Seven*

# The 1980s

One could argue that FM came of age during the 1980s. In the early part of the decade, more Americans were listening to AM than FM. In less than 10 years, that would reverse, with more people preferring FM stations over AM. Why the change? As FM sets became much less expensive and the FM band was included in most factory-installed automobile radios at no extra charge, broadcasters saw the trend and started putting more money into their formats that had migrated from AM to FM in the 1970s. They also started promoting their FM stations with television and newspaper advertising. New formats sprang up on the FM dial as well, attracting even more listeners. The larger listener base caught the attention of advertisers who started to appreciate the power of FM to reach the masses. The migration of listeners from AM to FM made room for the talk radio format, which greatly expanded on the AM band in the late 1980s.

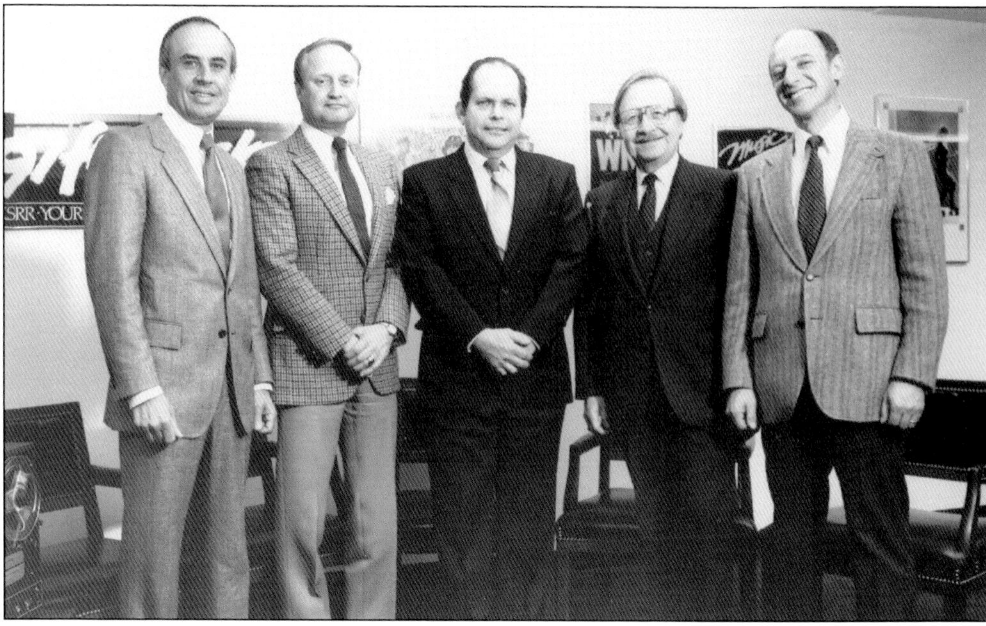

This c. 1984 gathering of Hartford station managers includes, from left to right, Dick Korsen, general manager of WDRC; Bill Ryan, general manager of WFSB; Sy Dresner, owner and general manager of WCCC; Perry Ury, general manager of WTIC; and Enzo DeDominicis, owner and general manager of WRCH. Not shown are Boyd Arnold (WHCN) and Dale Maine (WWUH). (Courtesy of WDRC.)

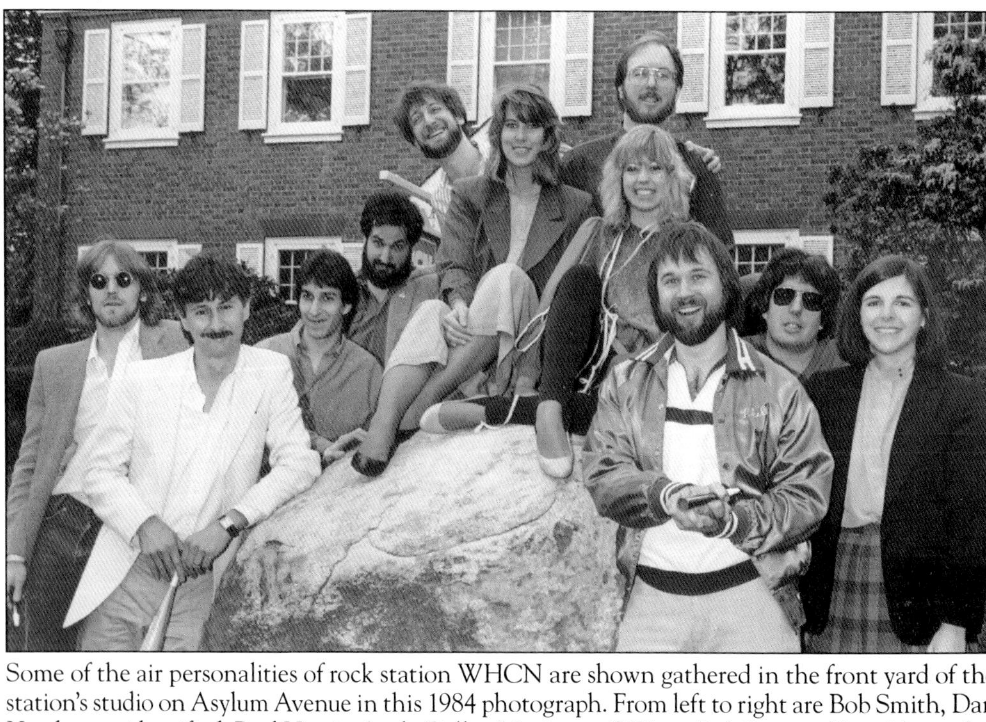

Some of the air personalities of rock station WHCN are shown gathered in the front yard of the station's studio on Asylum Avenue in this 1984 photograph. From left to right are Bob Smith, Dan Hayden, unidentified, Paul Harris, Andy Geller, Marianne O'Hare, Bob Bittens, Kim Alexander, Phil Kirzyk, Bob London, and Phylis Parizek. (Courtesy of Dan Hayden.)

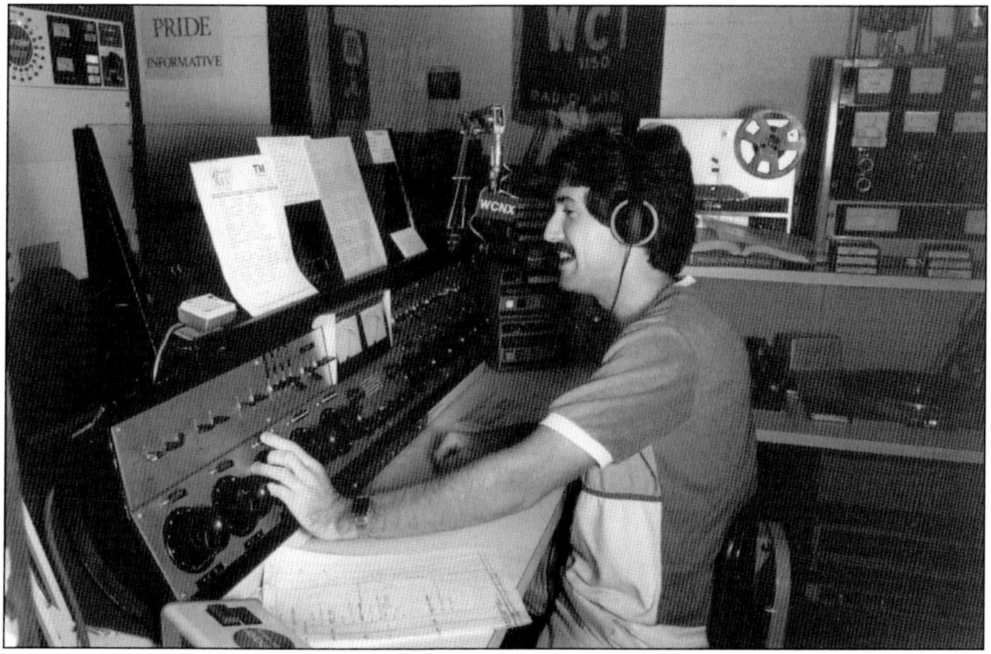


WCNX 1150 Middletown signed on the air for the first time on December 12, 1948, under the ownership of longtime Middletown residents Richard and Bill O'Brien and the local newspaper, the *Middletown Press*. Over the years, it has experienced many formats and is currently on the air as WMRD. In this photograph, Bob Grip is on the air. (Courtesy of Bob Grip.)

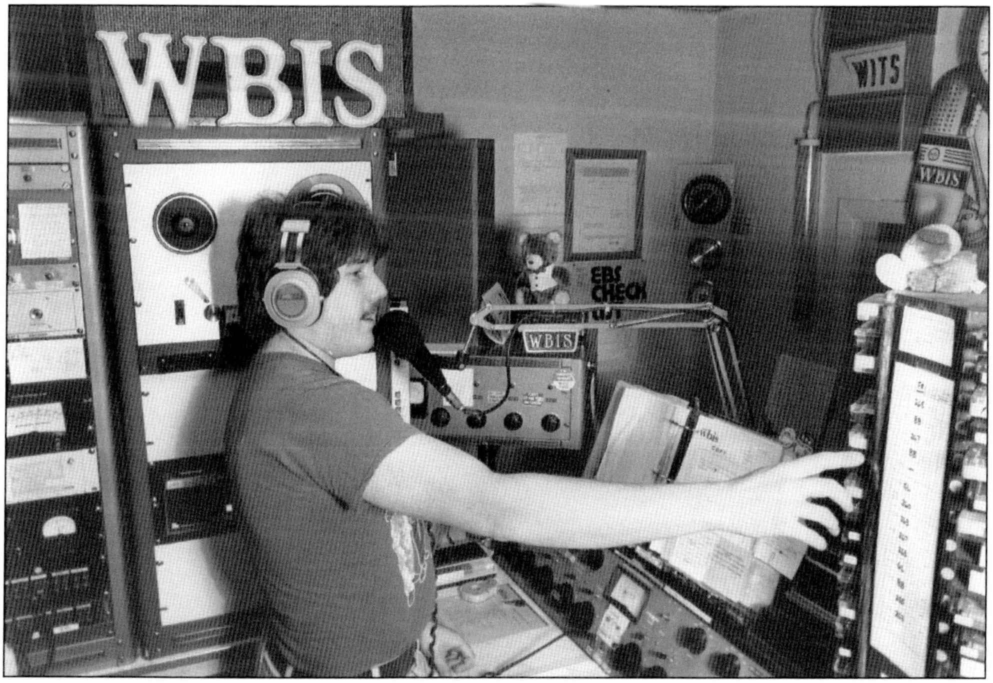


In the late 1940s and 1950s, AM stations sprang up in some of the Hartford suburbs, including Bristol (WBIS), Newington (WKNB), West Hartford (WEXT), and Windsor (WSOR). Here, Bob Grip is on the air at WBIS 1440. (Courtesy of Bob Grip.)

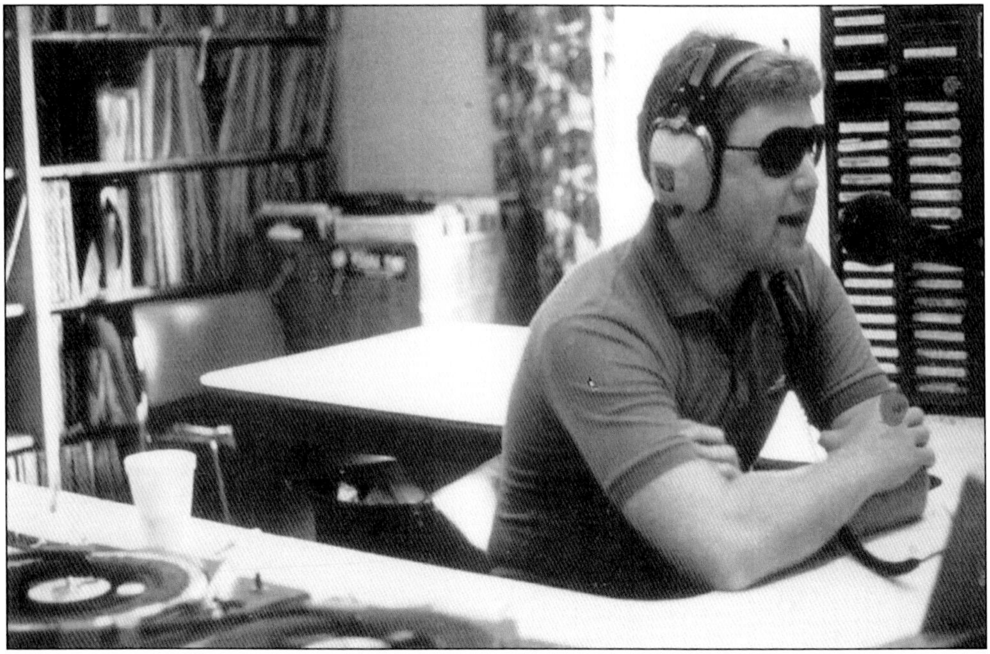

WNTY in Southington came on the air in the late 1960s using a frequency vacated earlier in the decade by WLCR in Torrington, which had gone out of business. WNTY experienced a variety of formats and owners over the years. Dave O'Brian, whose real name is Dave Lounder, is pictured on the air on WNTY around 1983. (Courtesy of Dave Lounder.)

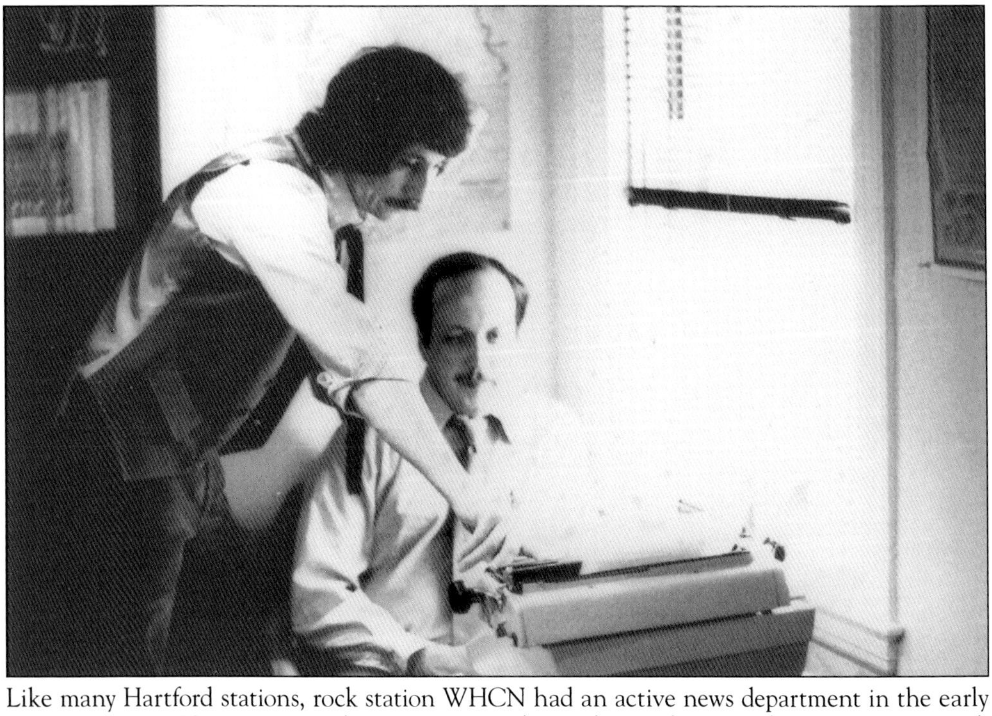

Like many Hartford stations, rock station WHCN had an active news department in the early 1980s. Here, WHCN's program director Dan Hayden and news director Chip Triest are at work in the WHCN production studio on Asylum Avenue in 1981. (Courtesy of Dan Hayden.)

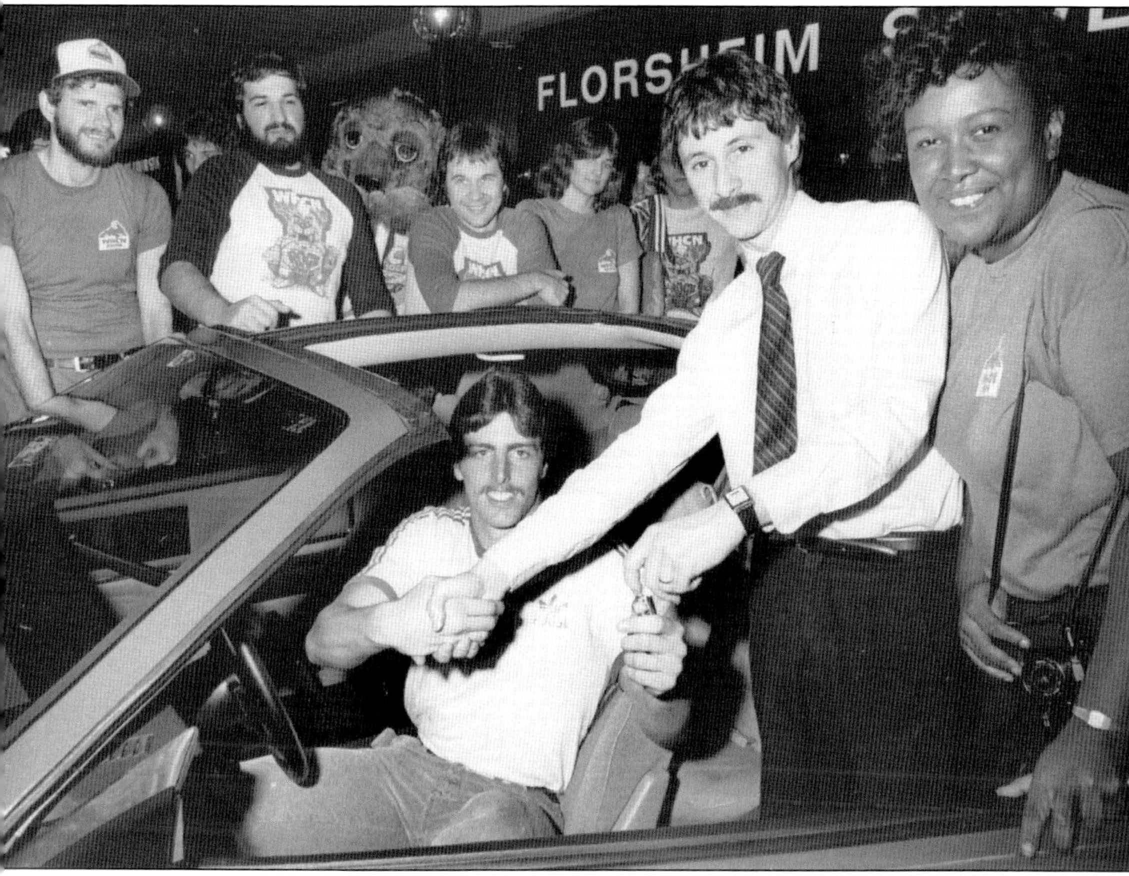

In 1983, WHCN gave away a brand-new Pontiac Trans Am at the Meriden Square Mall. Shown here shaking hands with the winner is program director Dan Hayden, with promotions director Teri Milling at his side. Also pictured are, from left to right, Gary Lee Horn, Paul Harris, George Deangeles (in Walrus costume), Phil Kirzyc, Laurie Gypson, and Bob Smith. (Courtesy of Dan Hayden.)

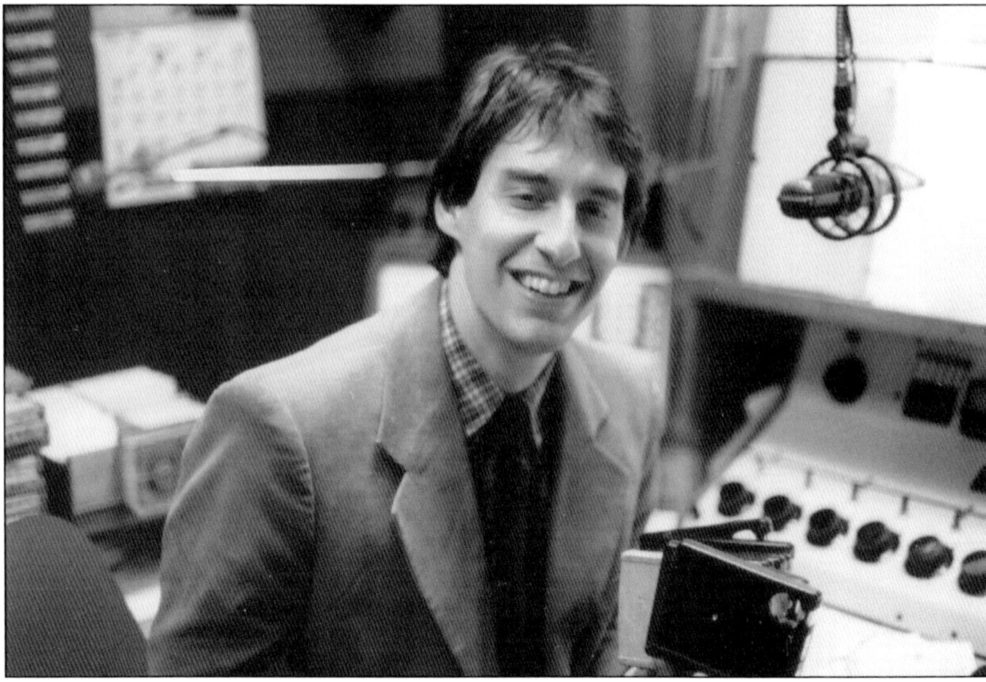

West Hartford native Dean Richards worked just about every shift during his nine years at WDRC-FM before moving to WRCH. He has been the host of the very popular *Pillow Talk* show on WRCH since 1994. Dean is pictured on the air at WDRC-FM in 1984. (Courtesy of Larry Wells.)

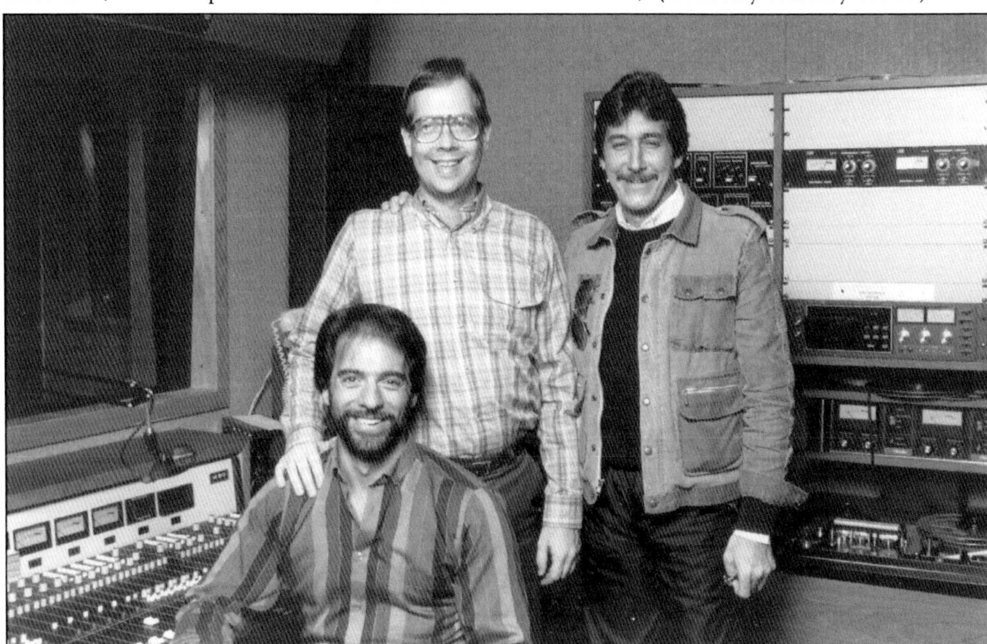

The staff of WTIC-FM's popular morning show *Craig and Company* pose for a group image. Pictured from left to right are Gary Craig, John Elliott, and Roger Stafford. Before joining the WTIC staff, Craig had also worked at Hartford's WKSS and WKSS in Hartford. (Courtesy of CBS Radio Inc.)

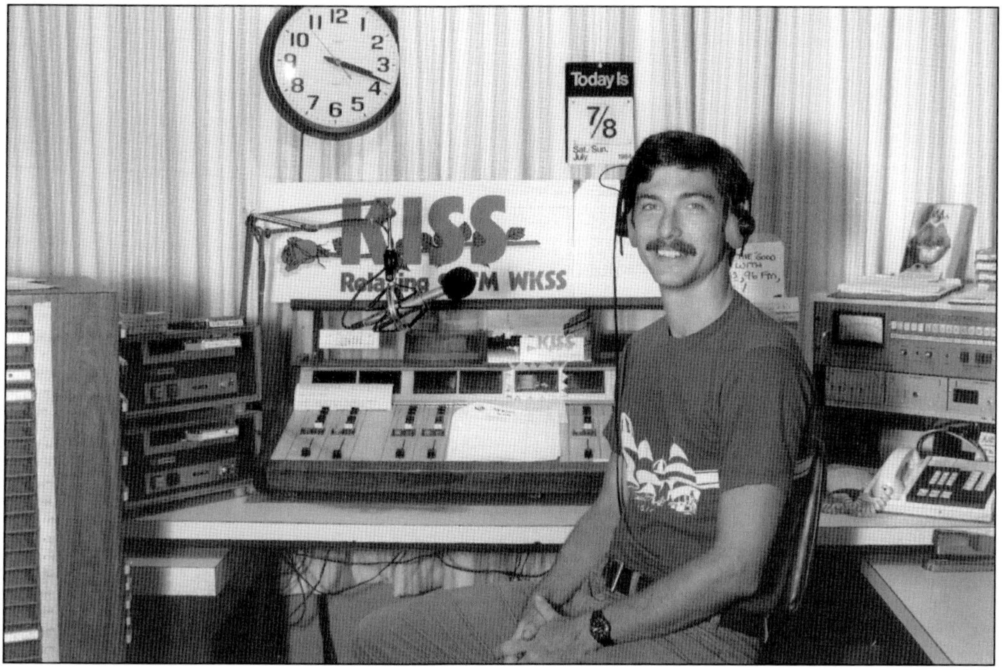


Listeners accustomed to hearing beautiful music on WKSS, a format that had been on the station for close to two decades, were shocked when it suddenly switched to contemporary hit radio in 1984. The WKSS studio is shown shortly before the format switch. (Courtesy of Glenn O'Brien.)

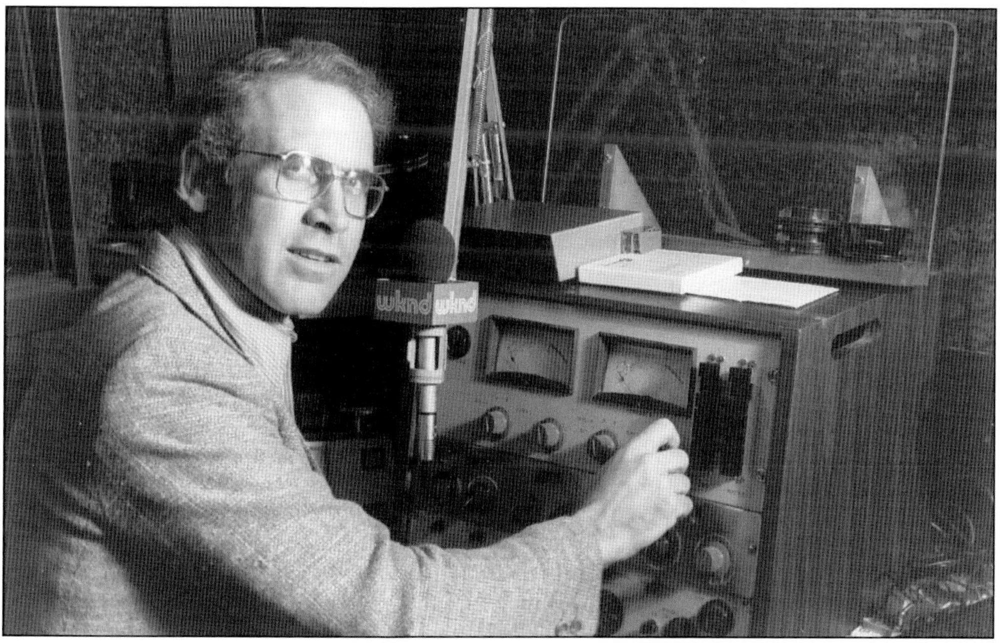


Frank Hastings works in WKND's production studio at the Windsor Parkade. WKND first came on the air in 1961 as WSOR, with studios near 124 Poquonock Avenue in Windsor. The station changed its call letters to WEHW in 1966. In 1969, it adopted a rhythm-and-blues format, which became very popular. WKND's black-urban format was the first in the state, and WKND would later become the first black-owned station in Connecticut. (Courtesy of WDRC.)

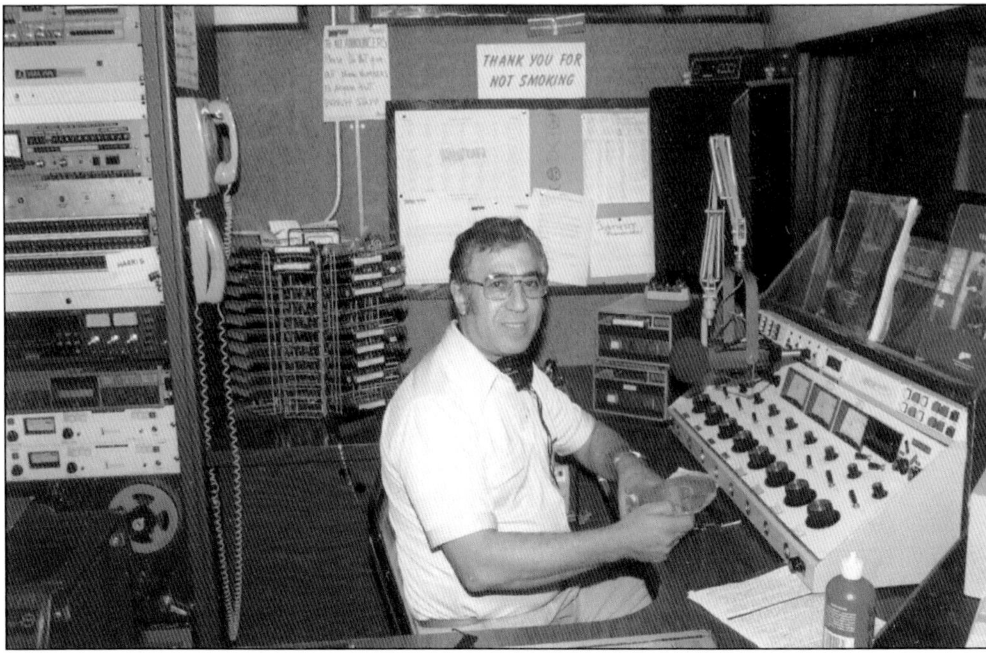


Henrique Ribeiro, shown here in 1988, has been the host of a very popular Portuguese-language program in Hartford for four decades. He started out at West Hartford's WEXT in the 1970s, but for the last 30-plus years, he has hosted his weekly *Cultura e Vida* program on WWUH. (Courtesy of WWUH Radio.)

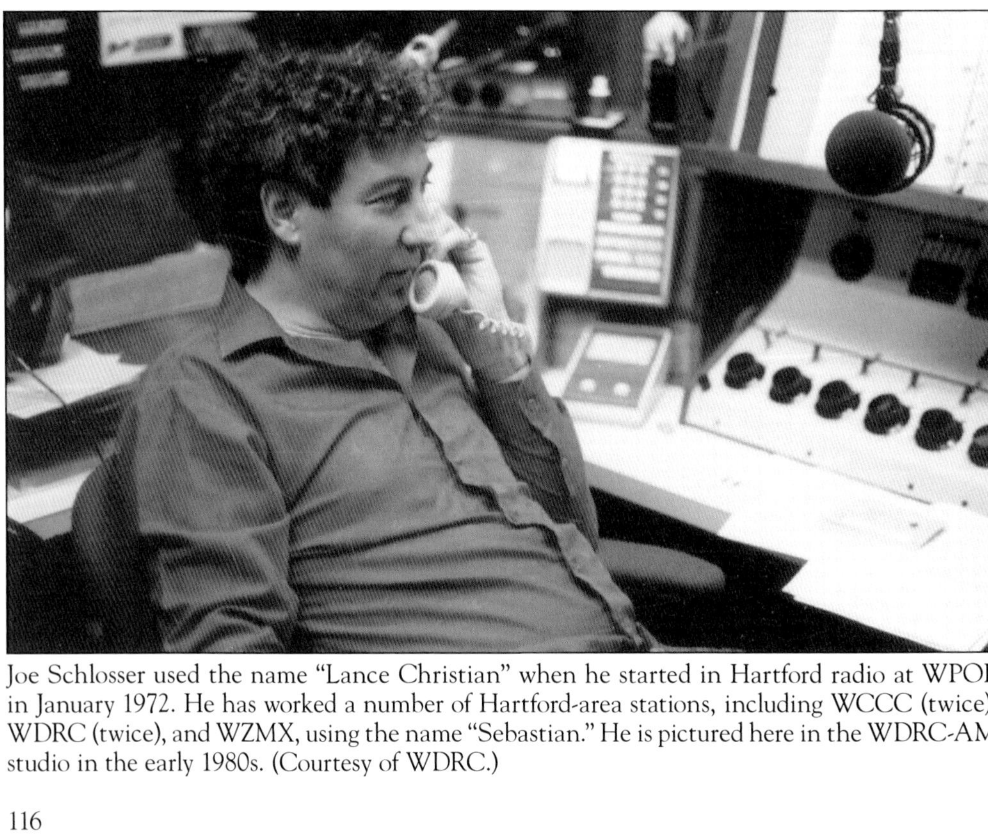

Joe Schlosser used the name "Lance Christian" when he started in Hartford radio at WPOP in January 1972. He has worked a number of Hartford-area stations, including WCCC (twice), WDRC (twice), and WZMX, using the name "Sebastian." He is pictured here in the WDRC-AM studio in the early 1980s. (Courtesy of WDRC.)

# *Eight*

# THE 1990S

As more and more of the most popular music formats moved from AM to FM, talk radio became the dominant AM format. Sports and ethnic programming also took advantage of the void, and by the end of the decade, most major markets had several foreign-language broadcasts on AM. In Hartford, there were no less than four foreign-language stations on the air in 1999.

In an effort to cut costs, station owners invested heavily in program-automation equipment, allowing multiple stations to operate with small staffs. As a result, localism—something most listeners wanted—was often lost in the process.

Group owners also consolidated co-owned stations, creating market clusters with four or more stations in the same building, and laid off redundant employees in the process. In Hartford, Clear Channel Corporation moved five radio stations—WHCN, WKSS, WMRQ, WWYZ, and WPOP—into a new state-of-the-art facility at 10 Columbus Boulevard.

Instead of playing music from CDs, LPs, or tape, more and more stations started using computer hard drives to deliver their music. Many of the smaller stations turned to computer automation to save money.

Talk radio flourished on the AM dial in the 1990s, and many struggling AM stations were saved by conservative talk radio programs, including *The Rush Limbaugh Show.*

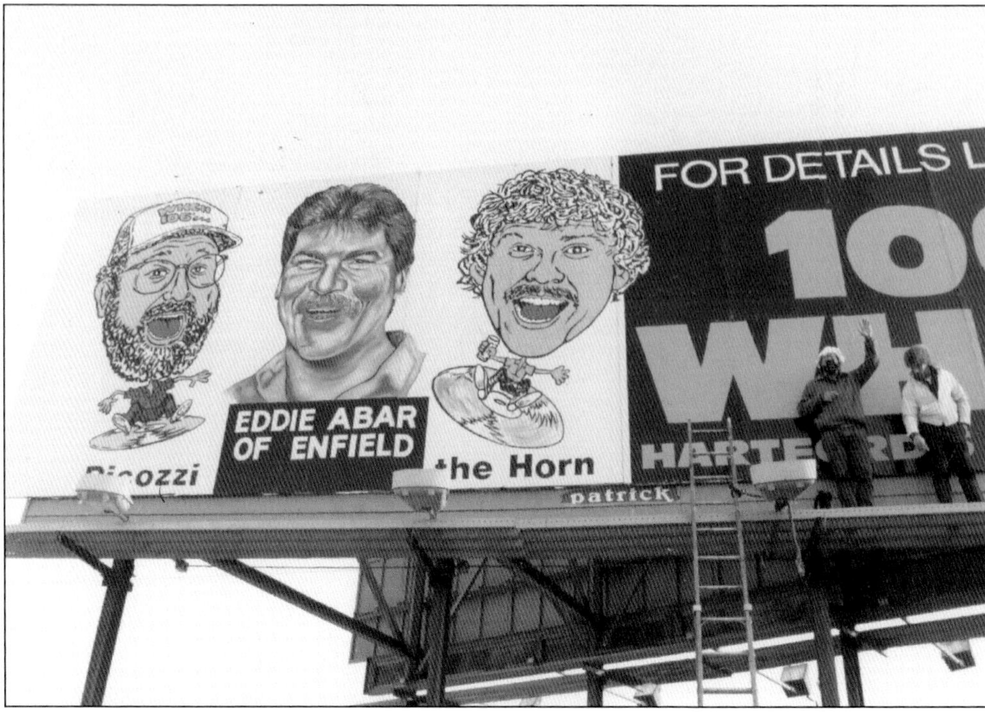


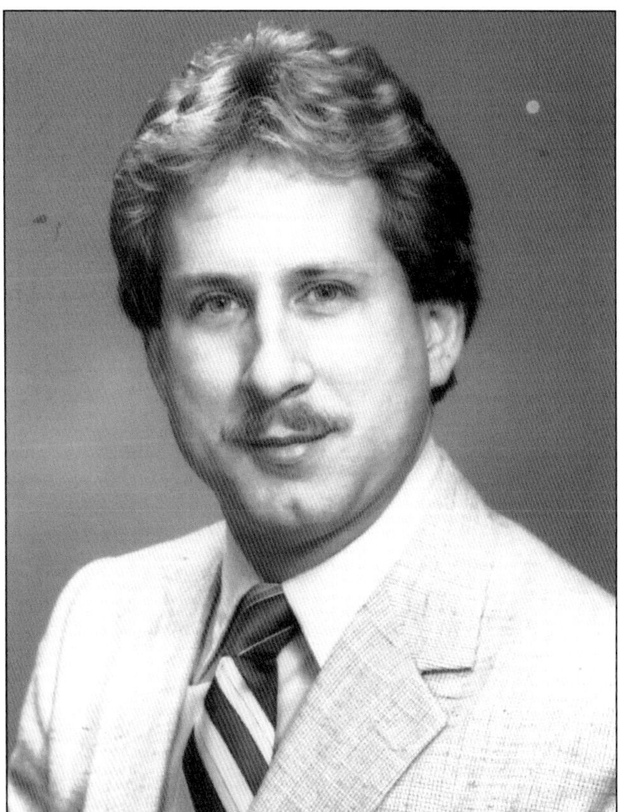

Images of Michael Picozzi, listener Eddie Abar, and Gary Lee Horn appear on a billboard promoting the winner of a contest. The very popular *Picozzi and the Horn* morning show was on WHCN for over 11 years, starting in 1986. Picozzi would later become program director of WCCC. (Courtesy of Gary Lee Horn.)

Jerry Kristafer has been on Hartford radio for more than three decades, having worked at many Hartford area stations, including WKCI, WCCC, and WDRC. He also enjoyed a talk radio stint on New Haven's WELI. Jerry is seen here in a WDRC publicity photograph. (Courtesy of WDRC.)

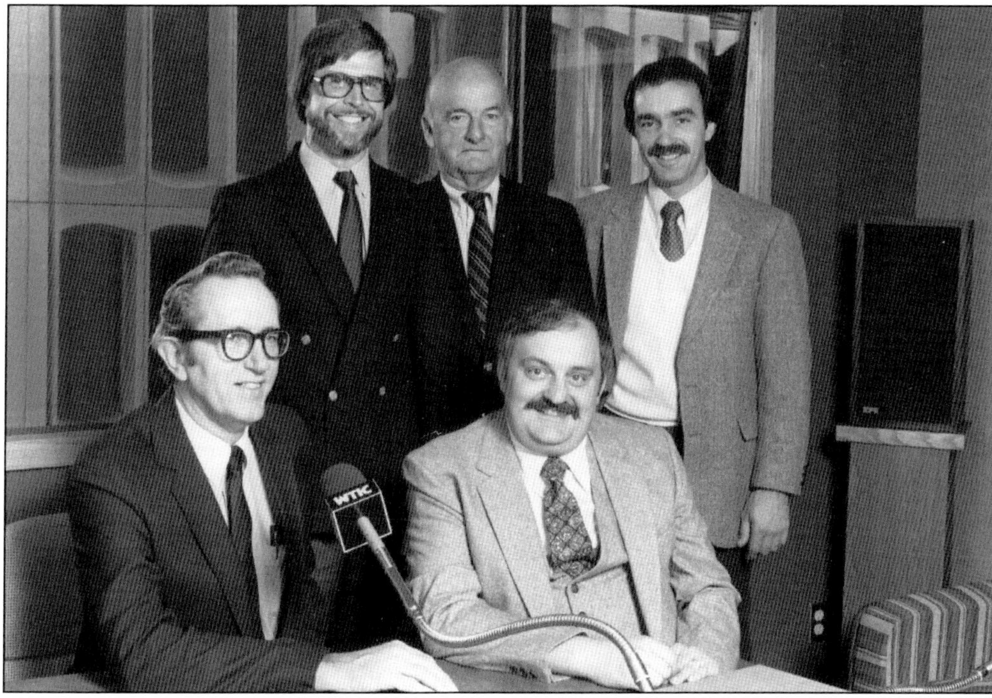

The cast of the Bob Steele's *Morning Watch* program can be seen in this c. 1990 photograph. Pictured from left to right are (first row) Walt Dibble and Bryant Thomas; (second row) Scott Gray, Bob Downes, and Mike Alan. (Courtesy of CBS Radio Inc.)

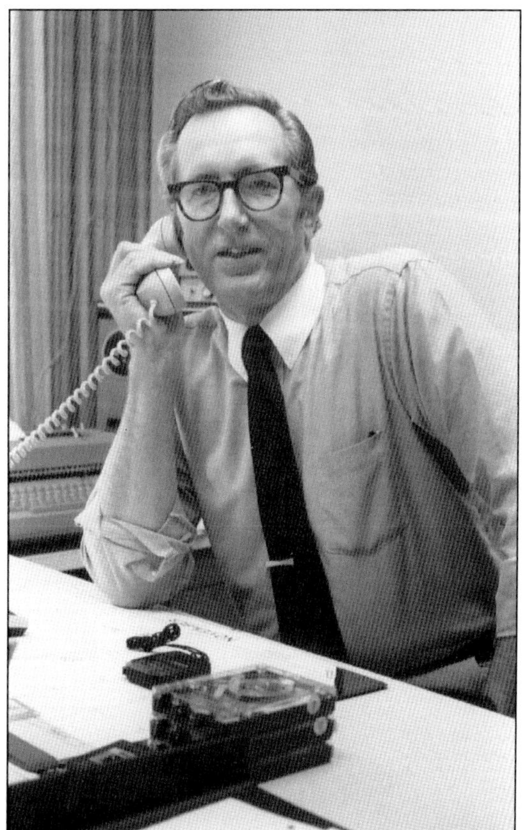

Walt Dibble, pictured around 1990, started out in Hartford in the news department of WDRC in the 1960s. He was the WDRC news director in the early and mid-1970s. In 1977, Dibble left to become news director of WTIC, a position he held for over a decade. (Courtesy of CBS Radio Inc.)

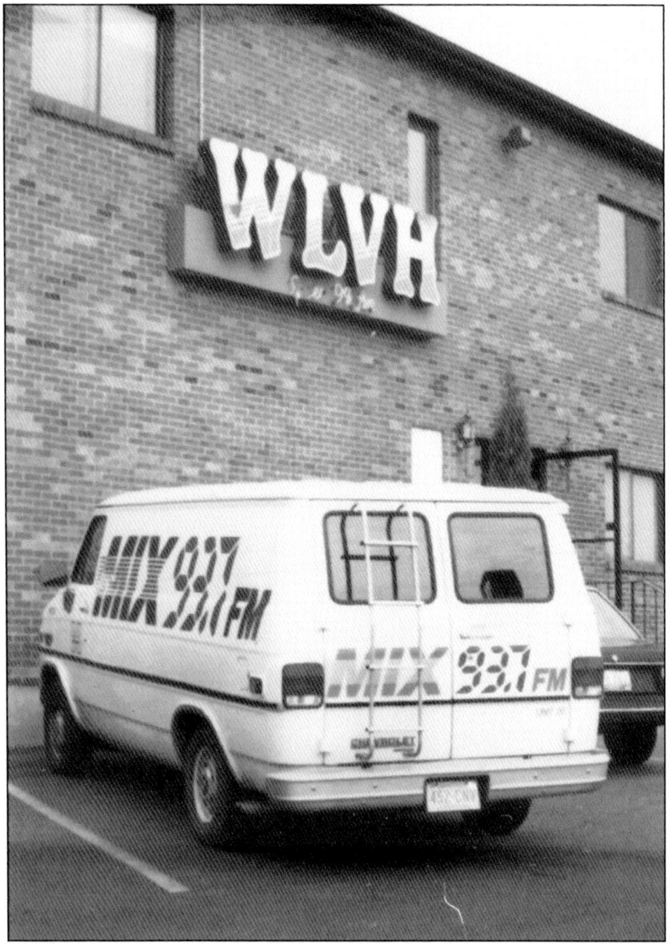


In this photograph are old and new call letters, side by side. In 1969, WLVH became the first minority-owned station in the state with Hispanic ownership and a full-time Spanish-language format that lasted for close to 20 years. The call letters became WZMX around 1990. (Courtesy of Gene Faltus.)

In 1998, Marlin Broadcasting purchased WCCC AM/FM and went on the air from a new facility at 1039 Asylum Avenue. Here, the staff in the WCCC air studio kicks off broadcasting under the new ownership. Pictured from left to right are Jeff Slater, Mike Karolyi, Wendy Brault, Eric Rosenberge, Stephen Wayne, Amy Rocco, Alan Tolz, Anita Brown, Jay Schultz, Gina Gunn, and Woody Tanger. Michael Picozzi is in foreground. (Courtesy of WCCC.)

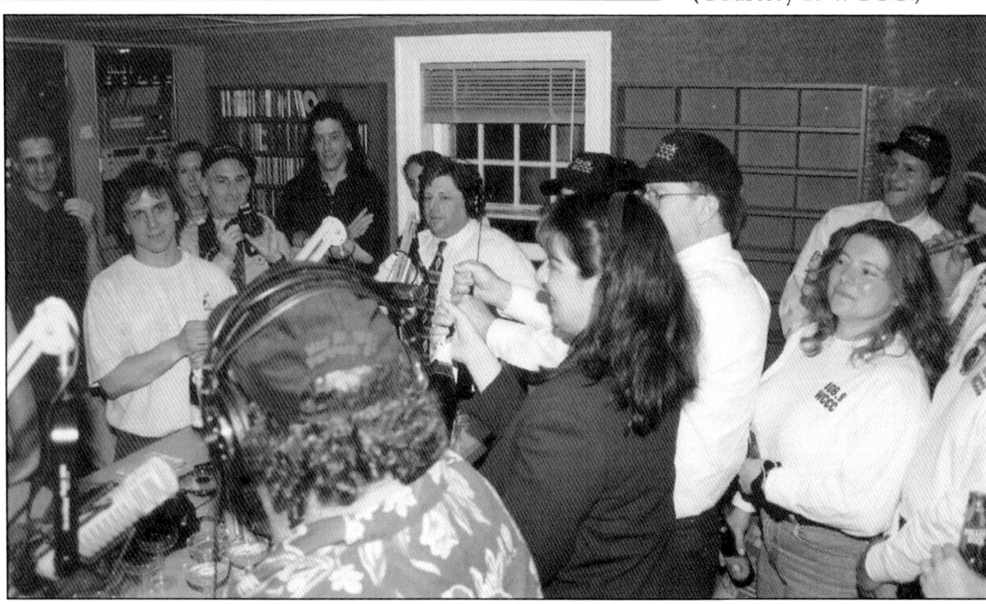

# *Nine*

# 2000 to Present

Foreign-language formats became firmly entrenched during this decade with no less than four Spanish-language stations serving the Hartford market. Ownership consolidation, which started with the deregulation of the telecommunications industry in the late 1990s, continued, with numerous Hartford stations being combined into clusters of commonly owned stations under one roof. Program automation was increasingly used to cut costs, and many of the corporate stations were programmed from their national or regional offices.

During this period, many stations started to take their Web presence seriously, creating webpages that catered to listener participation and feedback. Many stations expanded their streaming to include podcasts and started using the new social media.

The challenge for radio stations during this period (and going forward) is to try to stay relevant in a world where the new media created by the broadband explosion has such a great appeal to young people and others.

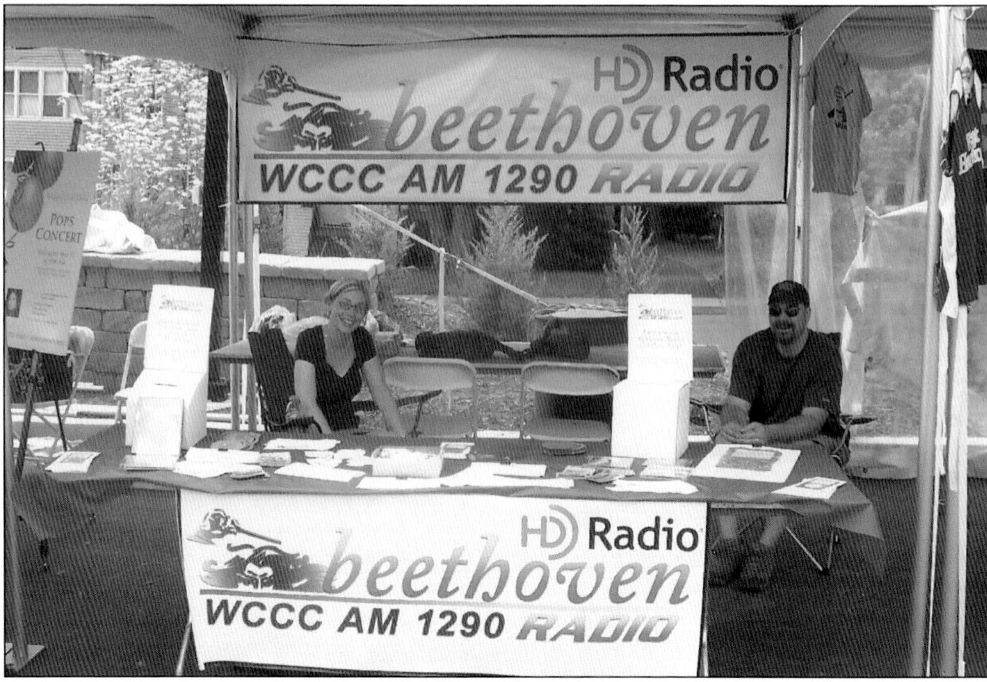


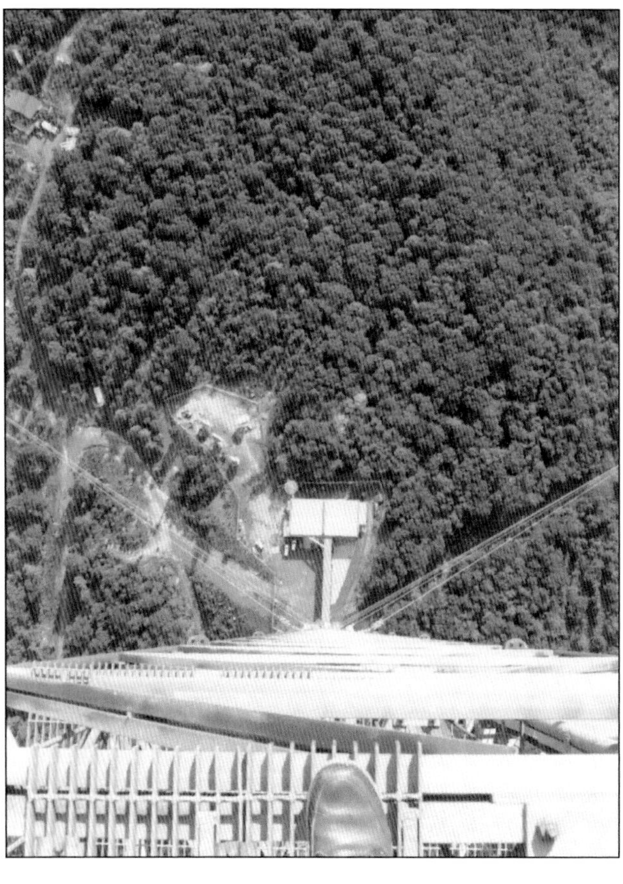

WCCC's 2006 Celebrate West Hartford booth is staffed by announcers Nicole Marie and Scott Birmingham. In 2001, Marlin Broadcasting, owner of WCCC, moved its Beethoven.com webcast station from Miami to Hartford and put the classical format on WCCC-AM 1290. (Courtesy of WCCC.)

This photograph looks down from approximately 1,100 feet in the air atop the WTIC-TV tower constructed on Rattlesnake Mountain in Farmington in 1984. In 1985, the WRCH-FM antenna was moved to this tower from a smaller structure nearby. FM stations require tall towers such as this to reach audiences. (Author's collection.)

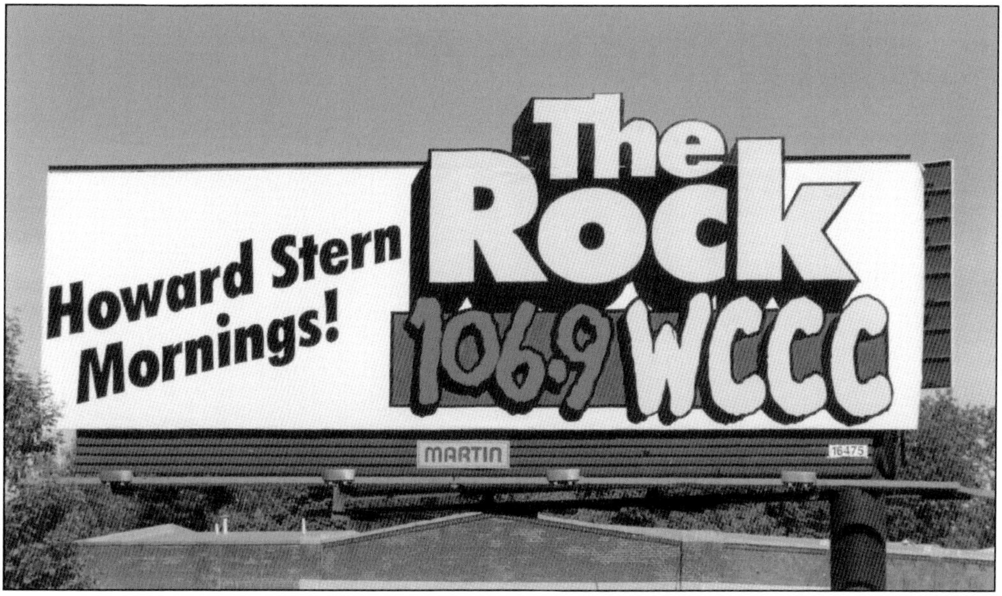


Shock jock Howard Stern and his sidekick Fred Norris worked at WCCC early in their careers in 1979, only to quit over a pay dispute about a year later. After becoming famous, Stern returned to WCCC via his syndicated show in 1997. (Courtesy of WCCC.)

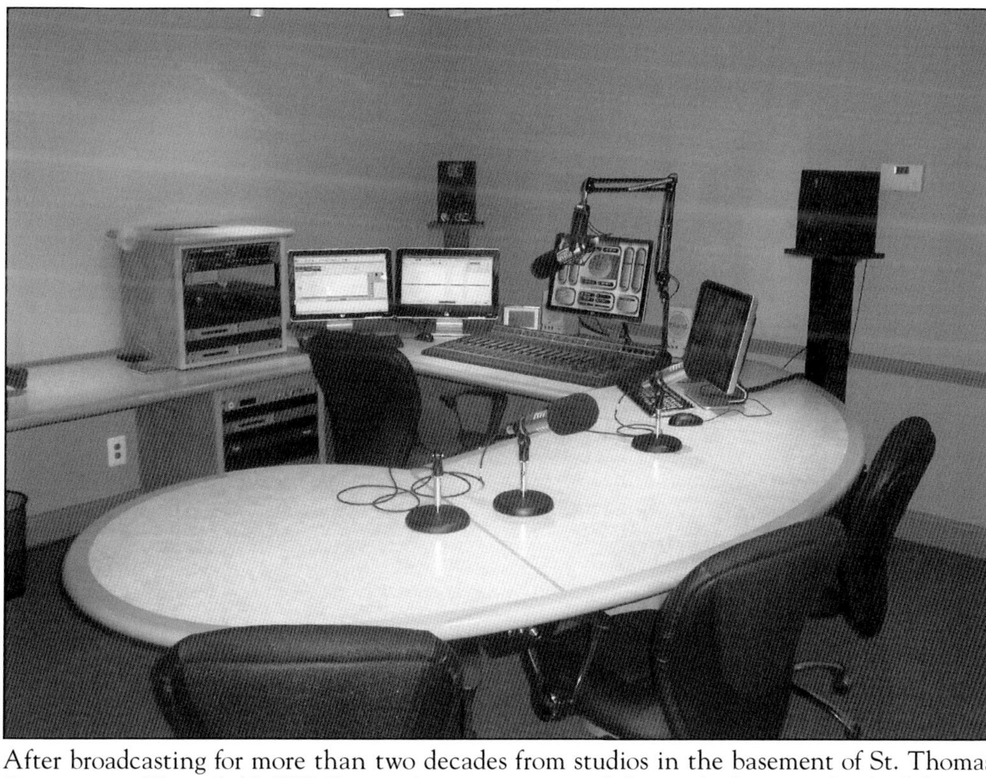

After broadcasting for more than two decades from studios in the basement of St. Thomas Seminary in Bloomfield, WJMJ moved into new state-of-the-art facilities at the Archdiocese Office of Radio and TV in Prospect in 2009. This c. 2010 photograph shows the new air studio. (Author's collection.)

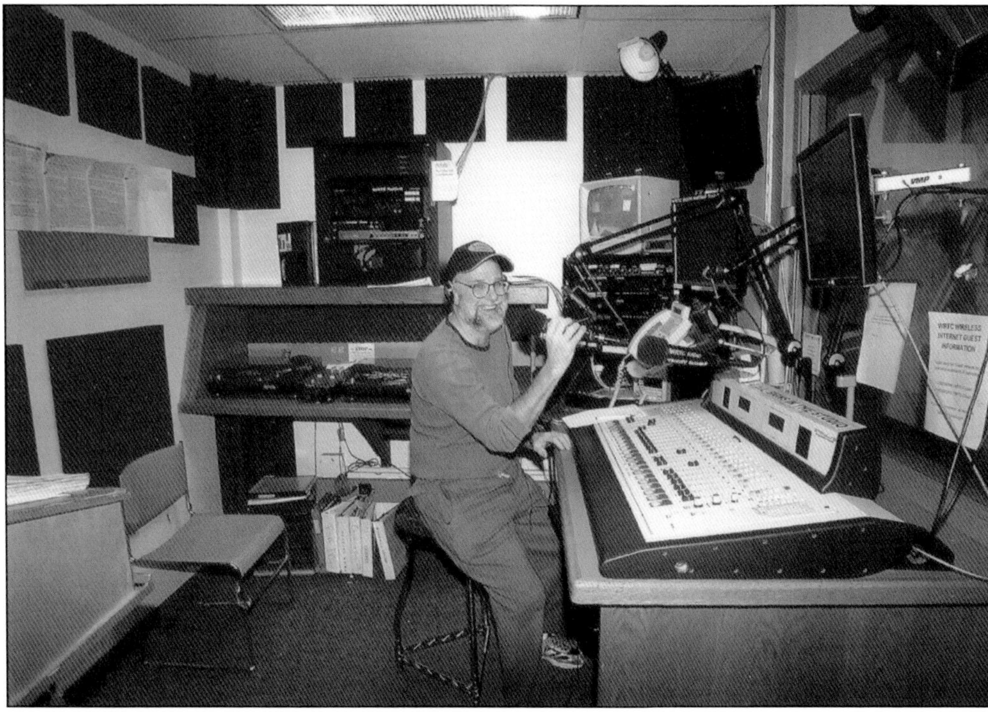

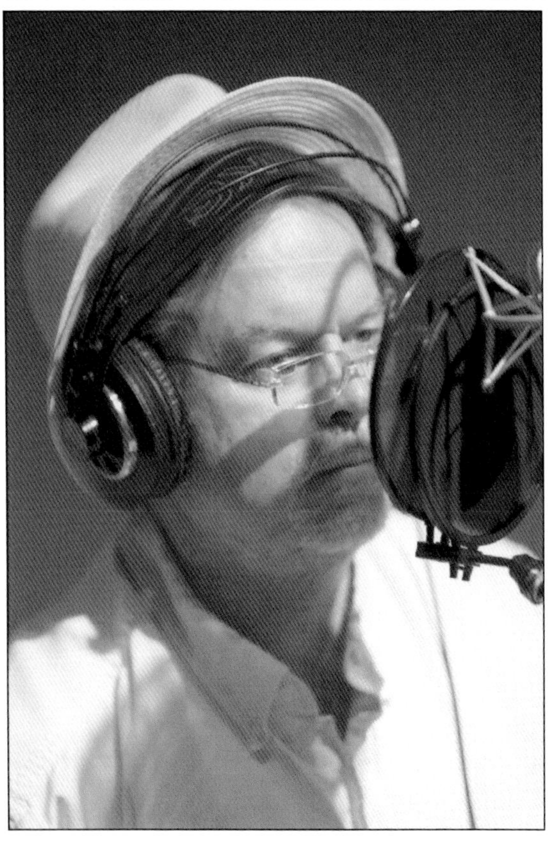

Trinity College's WRTC has a proud tradition of playing an eclectic mix of music and is one of the older college stations in Hartford, with roots going back to the 1940s, when it first came on the air as a campus-only AM station. Here, jazz director Bob Parzych hosts a show in the station's air studio in 2011. (Courtesy of John Schwenk.)

*Hartford Courant* writer and author Colin McEnroe hosted a successful afternoon telephone talk show on WTIC for a number of years before switching over to Connecticut Public Radio. He is seen here in the Hartford studio of flagship station WNPR. (Courtesy of Chion Wolf.)

# Time Line

1922: WPAJ New Haven begins, founded by Franklin Doolittle, later becoming WDRC, Connecticut's oldest radio station.

1922: WCAC Storrs, the Connecticut Agriculture College station, is established as the state's first educational station, known today as WHUS.

1925: WTIC Hartford begins, owned by Travelers Insurance Company.

1930: WDRC moves from New Haven to Hartford and becomes a CBS affiliate.

1939: W1XPW begins broadcasting from West Peak, Meriden, as the state's first FM station, becoming WDRC-FM in 1943 and WHCN in 1956.

1946–1949: Smaller cities around Hartford get their own stations, including Bristol, Meriden, Middletown, and Torrington.

1948: Rural Radio Network, the first full-time FM format for farmers and agricultural interests, begins on WKNB-FM 103.7 New Britain.

1948: Hartford has five FM stations—WMMW-FM 95.7 Meriden (now WKSS), WDRC-FM 93.7 Hartford (now on 102.9), WTIC-FM 96.5 Hartford, WKNB-FM 103.7 New Britain, and WTHT FM 106.1 of the *Hartford Times*.

1953: WDRC 1360 and WDRC-FM 93.7 begins broadcasting certain programs in stereo, with the left channel on AM and right channel on FM.

1954: Low point of FM. Only 5 of the state's original 13 FM stations are on the air and survive; it is this year the inventor of FM, Maj. Edwin Armstrong, took his own life, upset that because of corporate connivance and legal warfare against him, FM was unfairly forced into (at least temporary) financial failure. The Armstrong estate would win his legal cases in 1962, and FM would succeed beyond anyone's wildest dreams in the 1970s and 1980s.

1956: WPOP 1410 Hartford broadcasts *Hound Dog Evenings*, a very early rock-and-roll program in Hartford.

1960: WDRC 1360 ends CBS affiliation and goes rock full-time, shocking Hartford County.

1962: WRYM 840 New Britain becomes the first all–beautiful music station in the state.

1968: University of Hartford's WWUH 91.3 signs on and hosts the state's first daily progressive-rock program, *The Gothic Blimp Works*, every night at midnight—and now entering its sixth decade.

1969: WHCN 105.9 goes progressive rock full-time and is the first album-oriented station in the state of Connecticut.

1969: WLVH 93.7 Hartford (now WZMX) becomes first minority-owned station in the state, with Hispanic ownership and a full-time Spanish format that will last 20 years.

1969: WKND 1480 Windsor is the first in the state to adopt an urban format and later becomes the first black-owned station in Connecticut.

1975: WPOP 1410 Hartford becomes the first all-news station in Connecticut.

1979: Howard Stern joins WCCC 1290 and 106.9 as a local disc jockey early in his career; later, his national show will be carried by his old employer, WCCC.

1996/1997/1998: WDRC 1360 and owner Buckley Broadcasting acquire three AM stations and set up a statewide network of AM stations to provide greater coverage and a wider audience for one of the best-known morning-drive talk hosts, Brad Davis.

2000: WDZK 1550 Hartford (now WSDK) is transferred to Disney Radio and becomes the first children's format radio station in Connecticut.

2002: Bob Steele dies. He joined WTIC radio in 1936 and became the dominant morning host in Connecticut. In the 1970s, Steele earned more listeners than any station in Los Angeles.

2005: WTMI 1290 Hartford (now WCCC), all classical, becomes first HD AM station in the state. These Hartford-area FM stations are broadcasting in HD: WWYZ 92.5, WKSS 95.7, WPKX 97.9, WKCI 101.3, WPHH 104.1, WHCN 105.9, and WCCC 106.

# INDEX

# About the Author

The author has been researching the history of Hartford's radio and television stations for more than a decade. As a broadcast engineer, he has had access to the photograph archives of a number of Hartford stations, and some of those images are included in this book. For more information about the history of Hartford's radio broadcast stations, readers are encouraged to visit the author's website, www.hartfordradiohistory.com. The website was created to help preserve the rich history of broadcasting in Connecticut. The initial focus has been on radio, but the reader will find some information on Hartford's television stations as well. Television coverage will be expanded in the future as time permits.

Several Hartford stations, including WDRC, WPOP, WTIC, and WWUH, are represented on some excellent official or unofficial tribute sites, but the history of many of area's stations has not been well documented previously. The author is always looking for new information, corrections, pictures, memorabilia, and staff recollections. If you can help, please contact the author at admin@hartfordradiohistory.com.

The information in this book is as accurate as possible, but since the material comes from numerous sources, some of which cannot be verified, it should be considered for entertainment purposes only.

Consistent with our mission to preserve history on a local level, this book was printed in South Carolina on American-made paper and manufactured entirely in the United States. Products carrying the accredited Forest Stewardship Council (FSC) label are printed on 100 percent FSC-certified paper.